D1416864

Black American Playwrights, 1800 to the Present:

A Bibliography

by

Esther Spring Arata

and

Nicholas John Rotoli

The Scarecrow Press, Inc.

Metuchen, N.J.   1976

Also by Esther Spring Arata

Black American Writers, Past and Present:
A Biographical and Bibliographical Dictionary, by
Theressa Gunnels Rush, Carol Fairbanks Myers,
and Esther Spring Arata (Scarecrow Press, 2 vols.,
1975).

Library of Congress Cataloging in Publication Data

Arata, Esther Spring.
    Black American playwrights, 1800 to the present.

    Includes index.
    1. American drama--Negro authors--Bibliography.
I. Rotoli, Nicholas John, joint author. II. Title.
Z1229.N39A7   [PS153.N5]   016.812'008   76-2376
ISBN 0-8108-0912-5

DEDICATIONS

To

John, my husband

Dr. William McAvoy
English Department
St. Louis University

My mother

ESA

To

My wife, Bonnie

My daughter, Melinda

My mother, Rita

NJR

CONTENTS

v

ACKNOWLEDGMENTS

The editors wish to acknowledge their indebtedness and appreciation to the following persons:

Carol Fairbanks Myers, for her pioneer research on Black artists and Black writers.

Dr. Kenneth A. Spaulding, English Department.

Mr. Robert Fetvedt, Director of McPhee Library, and his staff; particularly, Mary Alexander, Richard Bell, Eileen Diambra, Eugene Engledinger, Mary Koontz, and Jane Marshall.

Mrs. Lorraine Kearney, Librarian, Eau Claire Technical Institute.

Ruthanne Polk, Carol Lauback, typists.

Sandy Dewitz, Bonnie Rotoli, Louis Tschernack, student assistants.

PREFACE

More than an ethnic fad or a recreational approach to the performing arts, Black Theatre, with its emphasis upon the Black aesthetic, folk-lore, and social protest, contributes a vital force of energy to the Black community. Recognizing the importance of this vitality to life in America, the editors were moved to publish a source book designed to assist those instructors, researchers, readers, and librarians interested in the study of Black playwrights and their works.

This reference work is divided into three sections. Section one comprises an alphabetized listing of Black playwrights and their works, together with criticisms and reviews of the authors and their publications, and awards. Section two offers a selected, general bibliography, and section three is an index of play titles. For purposes of simplicity, abbreviated citations are used in the body of the authors' entries. For example, when an abbreviated citation reads, Childress. Black Scenes. p. 20-25, the reader refers to the General Bibliography for the completed form of the Childress citation.

Although this volume includes 530 Black playwrights and over 1,550 play titles, the editors realize that the possibilities for research in an area such as this is never exhausted. No bibliography of living artists, or of any art form, pretends to be definitive. There is always a need for continued research as old manuscripts are discovered, new plays are published, and critics and reviewers continue to make their evaluations. And furthermore, because the great majority of published materials concerning the Black dramatic arts emanate from the large media centers, many regional writers and theatrical groups produce their works in relative obscurity.

Esther Spring Arata
Nicholas John Rotoli

September 1, 1975.

BLACK AMERICAN PLAYWRIGHTS

ADELL, ILUNGA   (aka William Adell Stevenson III)   (b. Nov.
   27, 1948)
   PLAYS:
      Bugles
      Bulldogs
      Love, Love
      One: The Two of Us
   TELEVISION SCRIPTS:
      Story editor for Sanford and Son

AHMAD, DOROTHY
   PLAY:
      Papa's Daughter
   PLAYS PUBLISHED IN PERIODICALS:
      Papa's Daughter, in Drama Review 12 (Summer 1968):
         39-145

AJAJI, AFOLABI
   PLAYS:
      Akokawe, 1970
      Dream on Monkey Mountain
   REVIFWS OF INDIVIDUAL PLAYS:
      Dream on Monkey Mountain
         New York Times, 15 March 1971, 52:1; April
         1971. II, 3:1

ALDRIDGE, IRA   (1807-1867)
   PLAY:
      The Black Doctor. Adapted for the English Stage.
         Originally written in French by Anicet-Bourgeois
   PLAYS PUBLISHED IN ANTHOLOGIES:
      The Black Doctor, in Hatch and Shine, Black Theater
         USA
   CRITICISMS OF ALDRIDGE:
      Andrews, C. B. "Ira Aldridge." Crisis 42 (Octo-
         ber 1935): 26
      Du Bois, W. F. B. "Can the Negro Serve the

1

Drama?" Theatre Magazine 38 (July 1923): 68
Haddon, Archibald. "Centenary of Negro Drama--Ira
 Aldridge." Crisis 41 (February 1934): 35-36
Johnson, C. S. "Ira Aldridge." Opportunity 3
 (March 1925): 6
Rivers, W. Napoleon, Jr. "Gautier on Aldridge."
 Crisis 39 (January 1932): 459-460
CRITICISMS OF INDIVIDUAL WORKS:
 The Black Doctor
  Hatch and Shine. Black Theater USA. p. 3

ALEXANDER, LEWIS
 PLAY:
 Pierrot At Sea, fantasy in one act

ALLEN, SENA
 MUSICAL:
 Song My Father Me

ALLISON, HUGHES
 PLAYS:
 The Trial of Dr. Beck, 1937
 PLAYS PUBLISHED IN ANTHOLOGIES:
 The Trial of Dr. Beck, in Mantle, Best Plays of
  1937-38
 CRITICISMS OF INDIVIDUAL PLAYS:
 The Trial of Dr. Beck
  Abramson. Negro Playwrights in the American
   Theatre 1925-1959. pp. 63-68, 85
  Hicklin. The American Negro Playwright 1920-
   1964. pp. 227-228
  Taylor, Karen M. People's Theatre in Amerika.
   p. 187

ALONZO, CECIL
 PLAYS:
 Black Voices, poetic revue
 Breakfast Is Served, one act
 Four Hundred Years Overdue, revue in two acts
 O. T. B.
 Somewhere Between Us Two
 Strike One Blow, one act
 FILMSCRIPTS:
 One of Us, science fiction/screen play
 REVIEWS OF INDIVIDUAL PLAYS:
 Black Voices
  Hamilton, Willie L. New York Times, 10 April

1972
Sengali. North Hartford Truth, February 1972
Four Hundred Years Overdue
   Journal and Guide (Norfolk, Va.), 17 June 1972
   New York Amsterdam News, 21 April 1972

AMIS, LOLA (Elizabeth Jones) (b. February 26, 1930)
  PLAYS:
   Helen, in Three Plays. New York: Exposition, 1965
   The Other Side of the Wall, in Three Plays
   The Places of Wrath, in Three Plays

ANDERSON, GARLAND
  PLAYS:
   Appearances, 1925. Also produced in the West End
    of London at the Royalty Theatre, 1930
   Extortion, 1929
  BOOKS:
   From Newsboy and Bellhop to Playwright. San Fran-
    cisco: Author, 1926
  PLAYS PUBLISHED IN ANTHOLOGIES:
   Appearances, in Hatch and Shine, Black Theater USA;
    in New York Public Library, Theatre Collection.
    (Film Reproduction 2-17)
  CRITICISMS BY ANDERSON:
   "How I Became a Playwright." Patterson, Anthology
    of the American Negro in the Theatre, pp. 85-86
  CRITICISMS OF ANDERSON:
   Abramson. Negro Playwrights in the American The-
    ater. pp. 268, 269, 274
   "Actress Quits Play with Negroes in Cast." New York
    Times, 12 September 1925, 22:1
   Archer. Black Images, p. 14
   "Bellhop Sells Second Play to Belasco." (Extortion)
    New York Evening Journal, 7 October 1929
   "Ex-Bellboy's Play Read." New York Times, 7
    April 1925, p. 17: 4
   Mitchell. Black Drama. p. 84
  CRITICISMS OF INDIVIDUAL PLAYS:
   Appearances
    Abramson. Negro Playwrights in the American
     Theatre. pp. 27-32, 39-40, 164
    "Bell Boy's Play to Go On." New York Times,
     22 August 1925, p. 6: 2
    Bigsby. The Black American Writer. p. 117
    Brawley. The Negro Genius. pp. 280-281
    Hatch and Shine. Black Theater USA. pp. 100-

101
Hicklin. The American Negro Playwright 1920-
1964. pp. 159-165
Johnson. Black Manhattan. pp. 202-203
"Negro Playwrights: Young Chicagoan Is First
with All-Negro Play on Broadway." Ebony
14 (April 1959): 100
Rodgers, J. A. "Garland Anderson Invades the
East." The Messenger 7 (June 1925): 233.
[Criticism of reading of play before produced.]
Williams. Stage Left. pp. 15-16, 108
REVIEWS OF INDIVIDUAL PLAYS:
Appearances
"'Appearances' Impressive." New York Times,
15 October 1925, p. 27: 3
"Bell Boy's Play Goes On." New York Times,
22 August 1925, p. 6: 2
"Bell Boy's Play Is Bought." New York Times,
21 June 1925, p. 23: 5
Broun, Heywood. "It Seems to Me." New York
World, 30 October 1925
"The Case of Garland Anderson." Crisis, 31
(January 1926): 112
Mantle. The Best Plays of 1925-26. pp. 473-
474
Mantle. The Best Plays of 1928-29. p. 487
New York Times, 30 March 1930, VIII, p. 2: 6
Wall Street Journal, 27 October 1925

ANDERSON, ODIE (b. October 25, 1943)
PLAY:
Trial of God, a dramatization. New York: Exposi-
tion, 1970

ANDERSON, T. DIANE
PLAYS:
From Distant Rooms
The Unicorn Died At Dawn
REVIEWS OF INDIVIDUAL PLAYS:
From Distant Rooms
Guernsey. The Best Plays of 1966-1967. p. 423

ANDREWS, REGINA
PLAY:
Underground, 1932
CRITICISMS OF ANDREWS:
Mitchell. Black Drama. p. 88

ANGELOU, MAYA (b. April 4, 1928)
   PLAYS:
      Adjou Amissah, 1967
      The Best of These, 1966
      The Clawing Within, 1966-67
   FILM SCRIPT:
      Georgia!! Georgia! [Only black woman to ever do a
         movie screenplay.]
   CRITICISMS OF INDIVIDUAL FILM SCRIPTS:
      Georgia! Georgia!
         Bogle. Toms, Coons, Mulattoes, Mammies, and
            Bucks. p. 198
         Murray, James P. "West Coast Gets the Shaft."
            Black Creation 3 (Summer 1972): 13
   REVIEW OF INDIVIDUAL FILM SCRIPTS:
      Georgia! Georgia!
         "Playboy After Hours: Movies." Playboy 7
         (July 1972): 26
   MEDIA RESOURCES:
      Georgia! Georgia! Cinema Releasing, St. Louis,
         Mo.

ANTHONY, EARL
   PLAYS:
      A Long Way From Here
      The Pearl Maiden
   REVIEWS OF INDIVIDUAL PLAYS:
      The Pearl Maiden
         Mantle and Sherwood. The Best Plays of 1909-
            1919. p. 464

APOLLON, GERALD
   PLAYS:
      Domingo
      Oh, Jesus
      Toussaint L'Ouverture and Son

ARANHA, RAY (b. May 1, 1939)
   PLAYS:
      My Sister, My Sister, 1973
      The Prodigal Sister, 1974
   REVIEWS OF INDIVIDUAL WORKS:
      My Sister, My Sister
         Gussow, M. "Review: 'My Sister, My Sister.'"
            New York Times, 1 October 1973, pp. 46: 1
         "Interview with Seret Scott." New York Times,
            2 July 1974, 28: 1

New Yorker 6 May 1974, p. 4
Peterson, Maurice. "On the Aisle: Theatre and
Film." Essence (September 1974): 24
The Prodigal Sister
New York Times, 16 July 1974, 42: 1; 26 November 1974, 30: 1

ASHBY, WILLIAM MOBILE (b. 1889)
PLAYS:
The Road to Damascus: A Play in Seven Episodes.
Boston: Christopher, 1935

ASHLEY, WILLIAM
PLAYS:
Booker T. Washington, 1939
CRITICISMS OF ASHLEY:
Mitchell. Black Drama. p. 107

ATKINS, RUSSELL (b. February 25, 1926)
PLAYS:
The Nail: A Three Act Play Adapted from Pedro De
Alarcon's Short Story. Cleveland: Free Lance,
1971

AWEUSI, ALLI
PLAYS:
Agent Among the Just. Play Series. New York:
Rannick Amuru, 1973
The Day Pop Threw out the Teevee. Play Series.
New York: Rannick Amuru, 1973

AYBAR, TRUDY
PLAYS:
Morning Train

AYERS, VIVIAN
MUSICAL:
Bow Boly

BAILEY, RIETTA WINN
PLAYS:
Mourners to Glory
Washed in de Blood
PLAYS PUBLISHED IN ANTHOLOGIES:
Mourners to Glory, in Koch, American Folk Plays
PLAYS PUBLISHED IN PERIODICALS:

Washed in de Blood, in Carolina Play-Book, March
1938

BAILEY, ROBERTA
    PLAY:
    New Life

BALDWIN, JAMES (b. August 2, 1924)
    PLAYS:
    Amen Corner. New York: Dial, 1968
    Blues for Mr. Charlie. New York: Dial, 1964;
      New York: Dell, 1965
    Giovanni's Room. Adapted for theatre; performed
      by Actor's Studio Workshop
    One Day When I Was Lost: A Scenario Based on
      "The Autobiography of Malcolm X." New York:
      Dial Press, 1972; London: Joseph, 1972
    PLAYS PUBLISHED IN ANTHOLOGIES:
    Amen Corner, in Hatch and Shine, Black Theater
      USA; Patterson, Black Theatre
    Blues For Mr. Charlie, in Gassner and Barnes,
      Best American Plays, 1963-1967; Oliver and Sills,
      Contemporary Black Drama
    FILM SCRIPTS:
    The Inheritance, 1973
    One Day When I Was Lost
    CRITICISMS BY BALDWIN:
    "Many Thousands Gone." Partisan Review 18 (No-
      vember-December 1951): 665-680
    "Notes for Blues," in Blues for Mr. Charlie. New
      York: Dial, 1964, pp. xiii-xv
    CRITICISMS OF BALDWIN:
    Adams, George R. "Black Militant Drama," Ameri-
      can Imago 28 (Summer 1971): 121-128
    Bigsby, C. W. E. "The Committed Writer: James
      Baldwin as Dramatist." Twentieth Century Litera-
      ture 13 (1967): 39-48
    Brudnoy, David. "Blues for Mr. Baldwin." Nation-
      al Review, 7 July 1972, pp. 750-751
    Clark, Kenneth B. "A Conversation with James
      Baldwin." Freedomways 3 (Summer 1963): 361-
      368
    Cohn, Ruby. "James Baldwin." Dialogue in Ameri-
      can Drama. Indiana University Press, 1971, pp.
      188-192
    Finn, J. "The Identity of James Baldwin." Com-
      monweal 77 (26 October 1962): 113-116

"First Baldwin Play Eliminating Scenery." Wisconsin State Journal, 8 April 1964

Kinnamon, Keneth, ed. James Baldwin: A Collection of Critical Essays. Englewood Cliffs, N.J.: Prentice-Hall, 1974

Lewis. American Plays and Playwrights: Trends of the Decade. pp. 45, 102, 240

Lewis, Allan. American Plays and Playwrights of the Contemporary Theatre. pp. 45, 102, 196, 240

Mitchell, Loften. Black Drama. pp. 200-201, 204

Rubkin. Drama and Commitment. p. 3

Sontag, Susan. Against Interpretation and Other Essays. pp. 151-155

Taylor. Modern American Drama. pp. 12, 146-154

Turpin, Waters E. "The Contemporary American Negro Playwright." CLA Journal 9 (September 1965): 20-21

Tynan, Kenneth. Tynan Right and Left. pp. 144-145

CRITICISMS OF INDIVIDUAL PLAYS:

Amen Corner

Lewis, Emory. Stages: The Fifty Year Childhood of the American Theatre. pp. 157-158

Kennedy. In Search of African Theater. p. 235

Lumley, Frederick. New Trends in 20th Century Drama. p. 339

Meriwether, L. M. "The Amen Corner." Negro Digest 14 (January 1964): 40-47

"Playboy After Hours: Theatre." Playboy 18 (April 1971): 37

Taylor. Modern American Drama. p. 46

Blues for Mr. Charlie

Abramson, Doris E. Negro Playwrights in the American Theatre 1925-1959. pp. 274-275

Adams, George R. "Black Militant Drama." American Imago 28 (Summer 1971): 115-121, passim

Bigsby, C. W. E. Confrontation and Commitment. pp. 122, 129-137, 166

Brustein, Robert. Seasons of Discontent. pp. 161-165

Clurman, Harold. The Naked Image. pp. 37-39

Hernton, Calvin C. "The Masculinization of James Baldwin: or What Killed Blues for Mr. Charlie." Umbra Anthology 1967-68. pp. 19-22

Hicklin. The American Negro Playwright 1930-
1964. Part 2, pp. 424-429
Lewis. American Plays and Playwrights: Trends
of the Decades. pp. 196, 253-255, 257
Lewis, Emory. Stages: The Fifty Year Child-
hood of the American Theatre. p. 158
Lumley, Frederick. New Trends in 20th Century
Drama. pp. 339-340
Phyllis, Louis. The Novelist as Playwright:
Baldwin, McCullers, and Bellow in Modern
American Drama: Essays in Criticism. pp.
146-154
"Playboy After Hours: Theatre." Playboy 11
(August 1964): 14
"Playboy After Hours: Theatre." Playboy 18
(April 1971): 37
Riach, W. A. D. " 'Telling It Like It Is': An
Examination of Black Theatre as Rhetoric."
Quarterly Journal of Speech 46 (April 1970):
184
Taylor. Modern American Drama. pp. 147-152
Tedesco, John L. "Blues for Mr. Charlie: The
Rhetorical Dimension." Players 50 (Fall-Winter
1975): 20-23
Turner, Darwin T. "Negro Playwrights and the Ur-
ban Negro." CLA Journal 12 (September 1968):
24
CRITICISMS OF INDIVIDUAL FILM SCRIPTS:
One Day When I Was Lost (Baldwin's screen adapta-
tion of "The Autobiography of Malcolm X") Com-
monweal, 12 October 1973, pp. 46-47. Reprinted
in Contemporary Literary Criticism vol. 3, De-
troit, Mich.: Gale Research, 1975
REVIEWS OF INDIVIDUAL PLAYS:
Amen Corner
America 112 (8 May 1965): 690
"Baldwin's First Play, 'Amen Corner.'" Jet
(26 March 1964): 60-61
Catholic World 201 (June 1965): 215-216
Commonweal 82 (7 May 1965): 221-222
Guernsey. The Best Plays of 1964-1965. p. 332
Life 58 (14 May 1965): 16
Nation 200 (10 May 1965): 514-515
New York Theatre Critics' Reviews (1965): 349
New York Times, 1865, 5 March, p. 37; 11
April, II: 1; 16 April, 35; 25 April, II: 1; 13
June, 82; 9 August, 19

New Yorker 41 (25 April 1965): 85; 41 (29 May
     1965): 2
Newsweek 65 (26 April 1965): 90
Riley, Clayton. "Theatre Review: 'Amen Cor-
     ner.'" Liberator 5 (May 1965): 26
Saturday Review 48 (1 May 1965): 49
Time 85 (23 April 1965): 59
Vogue 145 (June 1965): 68
Blues for Mr. Charlie
     America 110 (30 May 1964): 776-777
"Baldwin Seeks to Avert Closing." New York
     Times, 27 May 1964, 44: 1
"Baldwin's 'Blues for Mr. Charlie' Folds on
     Broadway." Jet (10 September 1964): 59
"Blues for Mr. Charlie." New York Times, 3
     May 1964, II: 3
Catholic World 199 (July 1964): 263-264
Commonweal 80 (29 May 1964): 299-300
Ebony 19 (June 1964): 188
Ford, Clebert. "Blues for Mr. Charlie."
     Liberator 4 (July 1964): 4
Hewes. The Best Plays of 1963-1964. pp. 335-
     336
Johnson, Roy. "Blues for Mr. Charlie." Libera-
     tor 6 (March 1966): 22
Kerr, Walter. "Blues for Mr. Charlie." New
     York Times, 3 May 1964, II: 3
Nation 198 (11 May 1964): 495-496
National Review 16 (8 September 1964): 780-781
New Republic 150 (16 May 1964): 35-37
New York Theatre Critics' Reviews (1964): 276
New York Times, 19 April 1964, II: 1; 29 June
     1964, 18; 5 May 1965
New Yorker 40 (9 May 1964): 143; 40 (23 May
     1964): 2
Newsweek 63 (4 May 1964): 46
"Playboy After Hours: Theatre." Playboy 11
     (August 1964): 14
Saturday Review 47 (2 May 1964): 27-28
Sontag, Susan. "Going to the Theatre." Partisan
     Review 31 (Summer 1964): 389-399
Taubman, Howard. "Theatre: 'Blues for Mr.
     Charlie.'" New York Times, 24 April 1964,
     24: 1; 3 May 1964, II, 1: 1
Time 83 (1 May 1964): 50; 83 (5 June 1964): 96
Vogue 144 (July 1964): 32
AWARDS:

Foreign Drama Critics Award, 1964

BANKS, B.
  PLAY:
    (with Marc Primus) High John de Conquer, 1969

BARAKA, IMAMU AMIRI (LeRoi Jones) (b. October 7, 1934)
  PLAYS:
    Arm Yourself or Harm Yourself. Newark, N.J.:
      Jihad, 1967
    B. P. Chant, 1968
    Baptism and The Toilet. N.Y.: Grove, 1967
    Bloodrites
    Board of Education, 1968
    Columbia, The Gem of The Ocean, 1972
    Dante, 1962
    Death of Malcolm X
    Dutchman and The Slave: Two Plays. N.Y.: Mor-
      row, 1964
    The Eighth Ditch
    Four Black Revolutionary Plays. Indianapolis:
      Bobbs-Merrill, 1969. (includes Experimental
      Death Unit #2, A Black Mass, Great Goodness of
      Life: A Coon Show, and Madheart)
    A Good Girl is Hard to Find, 1958
    Home on the Range
    Insurrection, 1968
    J-E-L-L-O. Newark, N.J.: Jihad, n.d.; Chicago:
      Third World, 1970
    Junkies Are Full of S-H-H-H
    The Kid Poeta Tragical, 1969
    Police
    A Recent Killing
    The Slave Ship. Newark, N.J.: Jihad Productions,
      1969
  PLAYS PUBLISHED IN ANTHOLOGIES:
    Bloodrites, in King and Milner, Black Drama An-
      thology
    Death of Malcolm X, in Bullins, New Plays from
      the Black Theatre.
    Dutchman, in Barnett, Berman, and Burto, Types of
      Drama: Plays and Essays; Gassner, John and
      Bernard F. Dukore, A Treasury of the Theatre,
      Vol. II; Holmes, Paul C., and Anita J. Lehman,
      Keys to Understanding; Oliver and Sills, Contem-
      porary Black Drama; Patterson, Black Theatre:
      A Treasury of the Theatre, vol. 2; Reinert, Otto,

ed., Drama: An Introductory Anthology; Reinert,
   Classic Through Modern Drama
Great Goodness of Life: A Coon Show, in Caldwell,
   et al., A Black Quartet; Richards, Best Short
   Plays of the World Theatre, 1958-1967
Junkies Are Full of S-H-H-H, in King and Milner,
   Black Drama Anthology
Madheart, in Jones and Neal, Black Fire; Robinson,
   Nommo
The Slave, in Hatch and Shine, Black Theater USA
Slave Ship, in Lahr, John and Jonathan Price, eds,
   The Great American Life Show: 9 Plays from
   the Avant Garde Theatre; Poland and Mailman,
   The Off-Broadway Book: Three Negro Plays
The Toilet, in America's Lost Plays, 1965; Turner,
   Black Drama in America
PLAYS PUBLISHED IN PERIODICALS:
Black Mass, in Liberator 6 (June 1966): 14-16
Home on the Range, in Drama Review 12 (Summer
   1968): 106-111
Police, in Drama Review 12 (Summer 1968): 112-115
Slave Ship, in Negro Digest 16 (April 1967): 62
CRITICISMS BY BARAKA:
"Black (Art) Drama Is the Same as Black Life."
   Ebony 26 (February 1971): 74-76
"Black Power Chant." Black Theatre (April 1970):
   35
"Black Revolutionary Poets Should Also Be Play-
   wrights." Black World 21 (April 1972): 4-7
"Comments on a Recent Killing." New York Times,
   13 March 1973, 30:1
"Communication Project." Drama Review 12 (Sum-
   mer 1968): 53-57
"In the Ring." Nation 198 (29 June 1964): 661-662
"In Search of the Revolutionary Theatre." Negro
   Digest 16 (April 1966): 20-24
"For Maulano and Pharoah Saunders." Black Thea-
   tre 5 (April 1970): 4
"Negro Theatre Pimps Get Big off Nationalism," in
   Jello. Chicago: Third World Press, 1970. pp.
   5-8
"The Revolutionary Theatre." Liberator 5 (July
   1965): 4; also printed in Home, ed. LeRoi Jones.
   New York: Morrow, 1966, pp. 210-215; Black
   Dialogue 1 (Spring 1965): 5-7
Spirit Reach. Newark, N.J.: Jihad Productions,
   1972

"A Symposium on 'We Righteous Bombers.'" Black
  Theatre 4 (April 1970): 15-25
CRITICISMS OF BARAKA:
Abramson. Negro Playwrights in the American
  Theatre 1925-1949. pp. 275-278
Alsop, Seward. "American Sickness." Saturday
  Evening Post 241 (13 July 1968): 6
Baker, John. "LeRoi Jones, Secessionist, and Am-
  biguous Collecting." Yale University Library
  Gazette
Bigsby, C. W. E. "LeRoi Jones," in Confrontation
  and Commitment: A Study of Contemporary
  American Drama 1959-1966. Columbia, Mo.:
  University of Missouri Press, 1967. pp. 138-
  155
Brooks. Reactionary Trends in Recent Black Drama.
  pp. 44-45
Brown, Cecil M. "Apotheosis of a Prodigal Son."
  Kenyon Review 30 (1968): 654-666, 668
_____. "Black Literature and LeRoi Jones."
  Black World 19 (June 1970): 24, 31
Brustein, Robert. "The New American Playwrights,"
  in Phillip Rahv, ed. Modern Occasions. pp. 134-
  135
Burford, Walter W. "LeRoi Jones: from Existen-
  tialism to Apostle of Black Nationalism." Play-
  ers 47 (December-January 1972): 60-64
Clurman, Harold. The Naked Image. pp. 90-91,
  91-93
Cohn, Ruby. "LeRoi Jones." Dialogue in American
  Drama. Bloomington: Indiana University Press,
  1971. pp. 295-302
Coleman, Michael. "What Is Black Theatre? An
  Interview with Imamu Amiri Baraka." Black
  World 20 (April 1971): 32-36
Cox, Kenneth. "LeRoi Jones: Playwright of Pro-
  test," in Educational Theatre Journal 23 (May
  1971): 187, "Doctoral Projects in Theatre Arts,
  1971."
DuKore, Bernard F. "The Noncommercial Theatre
  in New York," in Downer, Alan S., ed. The
  American Theatre Today. pp. 165-166
Fisher, William C. "The Pre-Revolutionary Writings
  of Imamu Amiri Baraka." The Massachusetts
  Review 14 (Spring 1973): 259-305
Gilman, Richard. Common and Uncommon Masks.
  pp. 231-232

Gottfried, Martin. A Theatre Divided: The Postwar American Stage. pp. 78-79

Harrison. The Drama of Nommo. pp. xiii, 38, 57, 60, 66, 86, 142, 159, 174, 182, 196, 197, 203, 212-213

Hudson, Theodore R. From LeRoi Jones to Amiri Baraka: Literary Works. Durham, N.C.: Duke University Press, 1973

Hughes, Langston. "That Boy LeRoi." Chicago Defender, 11 January 1965

Jeffers, Lance. "Bullins, Baraka, and Elder: The Dawn of Grandeur in Black Drama." CLA Journal 16 (September 1972): 32-48

Kaufman, Michael W. "The Delicate World of Reprobation: A Note on the Black Revolutionary Theatre." Educational Theatre Journal 23 (December 1971): 445-460

Lahr, John. Up Against the Fourth Wall. N.Y.: Grove Press, Inc., 1970. pp. 37, 98

Little. Off-Broadway. pp. 225-227

Lumley, Frederick. New Trends in 20th Century Drama. pp. 339-340

Margolies, Edward. "Prospects: LeRoi Jones in Native Sons: A Critical Study of Twentieth Century Negro American Authors. Philadelphia: Lippincott, 1968. pp. 190-200

Miller, Jeanne-Marie A. "The Plays of LeRoi Jones." CLA Journal 14 (March 1971): 331-339

Mitchell. Black Drama. 103, passim

Mootry, Maria K. "Themes and Symbols in Two Plays by LeRoi Jones." Negro Digest 18 (April 1969): 42-47

Neal, L. P. "The Development of LeRoi Jones." Part 1, Liberator 6 (January 1966): 4. Part 2, Liberator 6 (February 1966): 18-19

Pearson, Lou Ann. "LeRoi Jones and a Black Aesthetic." Paunch 35 (1972): 33-36, 51

Phillips, Louis. "LeRoi Jones and Contemporary Black Drama." The Black American Writer. Vol. 2, edited by C. W. E. Bigsby, pp. 203-217

Reed, Daphne S. "LeRoi Jones: High Priest of the Black Arts Movement." Educational Theatre Journal 22 (March 1971): 53-60

Riley, Carolyn, ed. Contemporary Literary Criticism. vol. 3, pp. 35-36

Russell, Charles L. "LeRoi Jones Will Get Us All in Trouble." Liberator 4 (June 1964): 10

Schneck, Stephen. "LeRoi Jones: or Poetics and
Policeman, or Try Heart, Bleeding Heart."
Ramparts (29 June 1968): 14-19
Scott. "The Black Spirit: A Trilogy of Original
Plays, and a Treatise on Dramatic Theory in
Contemporary Black Drama." Ph.D. Disserta-
tion, Bowling Green State University, 1972
Smiley. The Drama of Attack. pp. 20, 72
Taylor. Modern American Drama. pp. 12, 166, 173
Turpin, Waters E. "The Contemporary American
Negro Playwright." College Language Association
Journal 9 (September 1965): 21-22, 24
Watkins, Mel. "Talk with LeRoi." New York Times
Book Review, 27 June 1971, 7: 4
Weales, Gerald. "The Negro Revolution" in The
Jumping Off Place: American Drama in the 1960's.
London: Macmillan, 1969. pp. 134-147
Williams, Shirley Anne. Give Birth to Brightness:
A Thematic Study in Neo-Black Literature. N.Y.:
Dial, 1972. pp. 23-25, 102-104
CRITICISMS OF INDIVIDUAL PLAYS:
Baptism
Hatch, Robert. "The Baptism." The Nation 198
(April 13, 1964): 384
Weales. The Jumping-Off Place. p. 186
Black Masses
Gayle. Black Expression. p. 146
The Dutchman
Adams, George R. "'My Christ' in Dutchman."
CLA Journal 15 (September 1971): 54-58.
_____. "Black Militant Dramas." American
Imago 28 (Summer 1971): 118-119
Barnet, Sylvan, Martin Berman, and William
Burto, eds. Types of Drama: Plays and Es-
says. pp. 245-248
Bermel, Albert. "Dutchman, or the Black Stran-
ger in America." Arts in Society 9 (Fall 1972):
423-433
Bigsby, C. W. E. Confrontation and Commitment.
pp. 122, 142-147, 148, 150-151
Brown, Roscoe C., Jr. "New Themes in Black
Literature." Black Creation 1 (April 1970):
32-33
Clurman, Harold. The Naked Image. pp. 90-91
DuKore, Bernard F. "Off-Broadway and the New
Realism." Modern American Drama: Essays
in Criticism

Eckstein, George. "The New Black Theater."
Dissent 20 (Winter 1973): 111
"Evasive Action" (Dutchman and The Toilet).
Newsweek 64 (December 28, 1964): 56-57
Ferguson, John. "Dutchman and The Slave."
Modern Drama 13 (1971): 398-405
Gaffney, Floyd. "Is Your Door Really Open?"
Drama and Theatre 7 (Fall 1968): 5
Gayle. Black Expression. pp. 116, 137
Gottfried. A Theatre Divided: The Postwar
American Stage. pp. 78-79
Hicklin. The American Negro Playwright 1920-
1964. Part 2. pp. 418-420
Kaufman, Stanley. "LeRoi Jones and the Tradi-
tion of the Fake." Dissent 12 (Spring 1965):
208
Lewis, Allan. American Plays and Playwrights
of the Contemporary Theatre. pp. 233, 253-
254
Lewis, Emory. Stages: The Fifty Year Child-
hood of the American Theatre. pp. 161-165
Lindberg, J. "Dutchman." Black Academy Re-
view 2 (Spring-Summer 1971): 11-17. Re-
printed in Mezu. Modern Black Literature.
Little. Off-Broadway. pp. 225-227
Meyer, J. "Opinion on Negro Aims." Mlle 62
(April 1966): 84, 86, 89
Mitchell. Black Drama. pp. 199, 205, 216
Nelson, Hugh. "LeRoi Jones' Dutchman: A Brief
Ride on a Doomed Ship." Educational Theatre
Journal 20 (February 1968): 53-59
Oliver, Edith. "Over the Edge." New Yorker
(April 4, 1964): 78-79
"Playboy After Hours: Theatre." Playboy 11
(October 1964): 51
Reck, Tom S. "Archetypes in LeRoi Jones'
Dutchman." Studies in Black Literature 1
(Spring 1970): 66-68
Rice, Julian C. "LeRoi Jones' Dutchman: A
Reading." Contemporary Literature 12 (Win-
ter 1971): 42-59
Riley, Carolyn, ed. Contemporary Literary Cri-
ticism. Vol. 1, pp. 35-36
Scott, John S. "Teaching Black Drama." Play-
ers 47 (February-March 1972): 130-131
Sontag, Susan. Against Interpretation and Other
Essays. pp. 152, 155-157

Taylor. Modern American Drama: Essays in
  Criticism. pp. 166, 172-173
Tener, Robert L. "Role Playing as a Dutchman."
  Studies in Black Literature 3 (Autumn 1972):
  17-21
"Three at Cherry Lane." The Nation 198 (April
  13, 1964): 382-384
Turner, Darwin T. "Negro Playwrights and the
  Urban Negro." CLA Journal 12 (September
  1968)
Weales. The Jumping-Off Place. pp. 26, 44,
  125-26, 227
Weisgram, Diane H. "Dutchman: Inter-Racial
  Ritual of Sexual Violence." American Imago
  29 (Fall 1972): 215-232
Witherington, Paul. "Exorcism and Baptism in
  LeRoi Jones' The Toilet." Modern Drama 15
  (September 1972): 159-163
Dutchman [Film]
  Bogle. Toms, Coons, Mulattoes, Mammies, and
    Bucks. pp. 207-208
  Riley, Clayton. "Dutchman." Liberator 7 (April
    1967): 20
Madheart
  Eckstein, George. "The New Black Theater."
    Dissent 20 (Winter 1973): 111
  Peavy, Charles D. "Myth, Magic, and Manhood
    in LeRoi Jones' Madheart." Studies in Black
    Literature 1 (Summer 1970): 12-20
Police, Home on the Range, and Madheart
  Peavy, Charles D. "Satire and Contemporary
    Black Drama." Satire Newsletter 7 (Fall
    1969): 40-49
The Slave
  Bigsby. Confrontation and Commitment. pp. 122,
    140, 147-152, 154-155
  Brustein. Seasons of Discontent. pp. 306-307
    _____. "Three Plays and a Protest." New
    Republic 152 (23 January 1965): 32-33
  Clurman. The Naked Image. pp. 92-93
    _____. "Le Roi Jones, Naughton's Alfie."
    The Nation 200 (January 4, 1965): 383-384
  Dennison, George. "The Demagogy of LeRoi
    Jones." Contemporary Literature 39 (Febru-
    ary 1965): 67-70
  Ferguson, John. "Dutchman and The Slave."
    Modern Drama 13 (February 1971): 398-406

Fuller, Hoyt W. "About The Toilet and The Slave." Negro Digest 14 (July 1965): 49-50

Gayle. Black Expression. pp. 137-138

Gilman, Richard. Common and Uncommon Masks. pp. 231-233

Gottfried, Martin. A Theatre Divided: The Postwar American Stage. pp. 79-80

Kaufman, Stanley. "LeRoi Jones and the Tradition of the Fake." Dissent 12 (Spring 1965): 209-210

Lederer, Richard. "The Language of LeRoi Jones' The Slave." Studies in Black Literature 4 (Spring 1973): 14-16

Turner, Darwin T. "Negro Playwrights and the Urban Negro." CLA Journal 12 (September 1968): 24

Turpin, Waters E. "The Contemporary American Negro Playwright." College Language Association Journal 9 (September 1965): 22-24

Slave Ship

Brecht, Stefan. "LeRoi Jones' Slave Ship." Drama Review 14 (1970): 212-219

Toilet and The Slave

Clurman, Harold. "LeRoi Jones, Naughton's Alfie." The Nation 200 (January 4, 1965): 16-17

————. The Naked Image. pp. 91-93

Costello, Donald P. "LeRoi Jones: Black Man as Victim." Commonweal 88 (June 1968): 436-440

Dennison, George. "The Demogogy of LeRoi Jones." Commentary 39 (February 1965): 67-70

Fuller, Hoyt W. "About The Toilet and The Slave." Negro Digest 14 (July 1965): 49-50

Gayle. Black Expression. p. 137

Hicklin. The American Negro Playwright 1920-1964. Part 2. pp. 420-423

Lewis, Emory. Stages: The Fifty Year Childhood of the American Theatre. pp. 163-164

Little. Off-Broadway. p. 242

Oliver, Edith. "Off Broadway." The New Yorker 40 (December 26, 1964): 50, 52

Pawley, Dr. Thomas D. "The Black Theatre Audience." Players 46 (August-September 1971): 258-259

REVIEWS OF INDIVIDUAL PLAYS:

Dutchman
New York Times, 25 March, 1964, p. 46; 28
June, 1965, p. 34; 17 November, 1965, p. 53
New Yorker 4 April 1964, pp. 78-9; 28 November
1964, p. 4
Newsweek 13 April 1964, p. 60
"Playboy After Hours." Playboy 18 (April 1971):
37
Riley, Clayton. "Dutchman." Liberator 9 (No-
vember 1969): 21
Sontag, Susan. "Going to the Theatre." Partisan
Review 31 (Summer 1964): 389-399
Vogue 144 (July 1964): 32
Experimental Death Unit - #1
New York Times, 20 September 1972, p. 41: 1
Madheart and A Black Mass
Gussow, M. New York Times, 30 September
1972, p. 18: 1
A Recent Killing
Gussow, M. New York Times, 30 January 1973,
p. 25: 1
Novick, J. New York Times, 4 February 1973,
II, p. 3: 5
The Slave
The Nation 4 January 1965, pp. 16-17
National Review 23 March 1965, p. 249
New Republic 23 January 1965, pp. 16-17
New York Times, 17 December 1964, p. 51; 17
November 1965, p. 53, 25 March 1964, p. 46:
2
New Yorker 26 December 1964, p. 50+
Newsweek 28 December 1964, p. 56
Saturday Review 9 January 1965, p. 46
Time 25 December 1964, pp. 62-63
Vogue 1 February 1965, p. 98
The Slave and The Toilet
Neal, Laurence P. "The Slave and the Toilet."
Liberator 5 (February 1964): 22
Slave Ship
Miller. Black Theatre Magazine (April 1970): 5
Riley, Clayton. "Slave Ship." Liberator 9 (De-
cember 1969): 19
Rudin, Seymour. "Arts in Review: The Perform-
ing Arts 1971-1972." The Massachusetts Re-
view 14 (Winter 1973): 209
Walker, Barbara. "Theatre: Bedford-Stuyvesant."
Black Creation 3 (Summer 1972): 22

The Toilet
   Nation 4 January 1964, p. 16
   National Review 23 March 1965, p. 249
   New Republic 23 January 1965, pp. 32-33
   New York Times 17 December 1964, p. 51
   New Yorker 26 December 1964, p. 50
   Newsweek 28 December 1964, p. 56
   Saturday Review 9 January 1965, p. 46
   Time 25 December 1965, p. 62
   Vogue 1 February 1965, p. 98
BIBLIOGRAPHIES OF BARAKA:
   Hudson, Theodore R., comp. An Imamu Amiri
      Baraka (LeRoi Jones) Bibliography, Washington,
      D.C. (1816 Varnum Street, NE), n.d.
   McPherson, James M., et al. Black in America:
      Bibliographic Essays. pp. 249-250, 260-261, 283
   Schatt, Stanley. "LeRoi Jones: A Checklist to Pri-
      mary and Secondary Sources." Bulletin of Bibli-
      ography (April-June 1971): 55-57
AWARDS:
   Obie Award for the Best American Play of the 1963-
   64 season for Dutchman
MEDIA RESOURCES:
   A Black Mass. A phonographic recording of a live
      performance of the play featuring an "All Star
      Cast" and the music of the "Sun-Ra Myth-Science
      Arkestra." Distributed by Jihad Productions,
      Newark, N.J.

BARBOUR, FLOYD
   PLAY:
      The Bird Cage
   PLAYS PUBLISHED IN ANTHOLOGIES:
      The Bird Cage, in Childress, Black Scenes (one
      scene)

BARNES, AUBREY
   PLAY:
      The Superheroes. New York: Rannick Amuru, n.d.

BARRETT, LINDSAY (Eseoghene)
   PLAY:
      Signs of A Slave Dream, one act
   CRITICISMS OF BARRETT:
      "The Fifth Conrad Kent Rivers Memorial Fund
      Award." Black World 2 (August 1971): 61-66

BARRETT, NATHAN (b. May 24, 1933)
   PLAYS:
      The Aunts of Antioch City, 1964
      Engagement in San Dominique, 1964
      Evening of a Black Comedy, 1965
      For Love of Mike, 1967
      Lead Ball, one act, 1962
      Losers: Weepers, one act, 1962
      A Room of Roses, 1964
      S-C-A-R-E-W-E-D, 1960
      Sitting and Chipping, one act, 1965
      While Dames Dine, one act, 1965

BARRY, PHILLIP
   PLAY:
      The Youngest, 3-act comedy, 1933
   CRITICISM OF BARRY:
      Abramson. Negro Playwrights in the American
         Theatre 1925-1959. p. 269

BASS, GEORGE HOUSTON (b. April 23, 1938)
   PLAYS:
      Black Blues, 1968
      Black Masque, 1971
      The Fun House, 1968
      Games, one act, 1967
      The How Long Sweet, 1969
      The Third Party, 1968
      A Trio for Living, 1968
   PLAYS PUBLISHED IN ANTHOLOGIES:
      Games, in Patterson, Introduction to Black Litera-
         ture in America
   FILM SCRIPTS:
      The Game, screen adaptation of the play, 1967
   CRITICISMS OF INDIVIDUAL FILM SCRIPTS:
      The Game
         Turner, Darwin T. "Negro Playwrights and the
         Urban Negro." CLA Journal 12 (September
         1968): 22-23
   AWARDS:
      John Hay Whitney Fellow, 1963-64; American Society
        of Cinematologists' Rosenthal Award, 1964 for the
        most creative film script by a young American
        writer; John Golden Fellow for Playwriting, Yale
        University School of Drama, 1966-1968; Plaque
        of The Lion of St. Marc awarded for The Game,
        1967 at Venice Film Festival, Italy; Artist's Grant

from the Harlem Cultural Council, February
1969.

BASS, KINGSLEY B., JR. (pseudonym attributed to Ed
Bullins)
PLAY:
We Righteous Bombers
PLAYS PUBLISHED IN ANTHOLOGIES:
We Righteous Bombers, in Bullins, New Plays from
the Black Theatre; Turner, Black American Litera-
ture; Turner, Black Drama in America
CRITICISMS OF INDIVIDUAL PLAYS:
We Righteous Bombers
Eckstein, George. "The New Black Theater."
Dissent 20 (Winter 1973): 111
"A Symposium on We Righteous Bombers."
Black Theatre no. 4 (Fall 1969): 14-15
REVIEWS OF INDIVIDUAL PLAYS:
We Righteous Bombers
Orman, Rosco. "The New Lafayette Theatre."
Black Theatre. no. 4 (April 1970): 6

BATTLE, SOL (b. Nov. 20, 1934)
FILM SCRIPTS:
Only 'Til Spring
[With Wale Ogunyemi] The Vow
Underground Man (an adaptation)

BEAL, TITA
PLAY:
A Just Piece, one act
PLAYS PUBLISHED IN PERIODICALS:
A Just Piece, in Liberator 10 (June 1970): 16

BENJAMIN, PAUL
PLAYS:
Memoirs of A Junkie
A Twosome

BENNET, ISADORA
PLAYS:
Coastwise
Deep Dark
God's Own
The Soon Bright Day

BERRY, KELLEY MARIE

PLAYS:
Baku, or How to Save the Whale's Tale, 1970
The Boomp Song, 1973

BIRCHFIELD, RAYMOND
Play:
The Diamond Youth. N.Y.: Amuru, 1973

BLACKWELL, JAMES
PLAY:
The Money Game

BLAKE, EUBIE
PLAYS:
The Blackbirds of 1929
[With Noble Sissle] Chocolate Dandies, 1924
Elsie
Harlem on Parade
[With Flournoy Miller] Lew Leslie's Blackbirds
Musical Melange
The Sepia and Swing Revolution
[With Flournoy Miller, Aubrey Lyles, Noble Sissle]
Shuffle Along, 1921
CRITICISMS OF BLAKE:
Bontemps. The Harlem Renaissance Remembered.
p. 176
Fisher, Rudolph. "The Caucasian Storms Harlem."
American Mercury. 11 (August 1927): 393
Houseman, John. Run-Through. p. 182
Johnson. Black Manhattan. pp. 187, 189, 190, 224
Mitchell. Black Drama. pp. 76-77, 78, 83, 86
CRITICISMS OF INDIVIDUAL PLAYS:
The Blackbirds of 1929
Isaacs, Edith J. R. "The Negro in The American
Theater: The Foreground, 1917-1942." Thea-
tre Arts 26 (August 1942): 501
The Chocolate Dandies
Isaacs, Edith J. R. "The Negro in The American
Theater: The Foreground, 1917-1942." Thea-
ter Arts 26 (August 1942): 501
Harlem on Parade
Isaacs, Edith J. R. "The Negro in The American
Theater: The Foreground, 1917-1942." Thea-
ter Arts 26 (August 1942): 501
The Sepia and Swing Revolution
Isaacs, Edith J. R. "The Negro in The American
Theater: The Foreground, 1917-1942." Thea-

ter Arts 26 (August 1942): 501
Shuffle Along
   Archer. Black Images in The American Theater.
      p. 11
   Isaacs, Edith J. R. "The Negro in The American
      Theater: The Foreground, 1917-1942." Thea-
      ter Arts 26 (August 1942): 498, 501
REVIEWS OF INDIVIDUAL PLAYS:
Chocolate Dandies
   Mantle. The Best Plays of 1924-25. p. 442
   Messenger (October 1924): 323
Elsie
   Mantle. The Best Plays of 1922-23. p. 522
Lew Leslie's Blackbirds
   Mantle. The Best Plays of 1930-31. p. 438
Musical Melange
   Belcher, Fannin S., Jr. "The Negro Theater:
      A Glance Backward." Phylon 11 (Second Quar-
      ter 1950): 123
Shuffle Along
   Mantle. The Best Plays of 1920-21. p. 450
   "Shuffle Along Premiere." The New York Times,
      23 May 1921, p. 16

BLAKELY, NORA
   MUSICAL:
   Future Spirit, 1975

BLOCH, ERNEST
   PLAY:
   Macbeth

BOND, FREDERICK WELDON
   PLAY:
   Family Affair. W. Va.: West Virginia State Col-
      lege Press, 1939
   CRITICISMS BY BOND:
   "The Direct and Indirect Contribution which the
      American Negro Has Made to the Drama and the
      Legitimate Stage, with the Underlying Conditions
      Responsible." Ph.D. Dissertation, New York
      University, 1938
   The Negro and the Drama. College Park, Mary-
      land: McGrath, 1969
   CRITICISMS OF BOND:
   Abramson. Negro Playwrights in the American Thea-
      tre 1925-1959. pp. viii-ix

CRITICISMS OF INDIVIDUAL PLAYS:
Family Affair
Bond. The Negro and the Drama. p. 205

BONNER, MARITA (Marita Bonner Occomy) (b. 1905)
PLAYS:
Exit, An Illusion, 1929
Muddled Dream
The Pot Maker
The Purple Flower, 1928
PLAYS PUBLISHED IN ANTHOLOGIES:
The Purple Flower, in Hatch and Shine, Black Thea-
ter USA
PLAYS PUBLISHED IN PERIODICALS:
Exit, An Illusion, in Crisis 36 (October 1929): 355-
337
The Pot Maker, in Opportunity 5 (February 1927):
43-46
The Purple Flower, in Crisis 35 (January 1928): 9-
11
CRITICISMS OF INDIVIDUAL WORKS:
The Purple Flower, in Hatch and Shine, Black Thea-
ter USA. p. 201
AWARDS:
First Place, Crisis Award, December 1927 for Exit
and The Purple Flower

BONTEMPS, ARNA (October 13, 1902-June 1973)
PLAYS:
Free and Easy, an adaptation of St. Louis Woman
produced in Amsterdam and Brussels, 1959; in
Paris, 1960
MUSICALS:
[With Countee Cullen] The Saint Louis Woman, 1946.
Musical adaptation of God Sends Sunday, 1931.
Revised for Federal Theatre Project by Langston
Hughes
[With Langston Hughes] When Jack Hollers, on micro-
film, 1936, Schomberg Collection
PLAYS PUBLISHED IN ANTHOLOGIES:
The Saint Louis Woman, in Patterson, Black Theatre
CRITICISMS BY ARNA BONTEMPS:
[With Jack Conroy] "Karamu." In Patterson,
Anthology of the American Negro in the Theatre.
pp. 111-115
CRITICISMS OF BONTEMPS:
Van Vechten, Carl. "How the Theater Is Represented

in the Negro Collection at Yale." <u>The Theater</u>
<u>Annual</u> (1943): 34
CRITICISMS OF INDIVIDUAL PLAYS:
<u>When Jack Hollers.</u>
Isaacs, Edith J. R. "The Negroes in The Ameri-
can Theatre: The Hope Ahead." <u>Theatre Arts</u>
26 (August 1942): 541
CRITICISMS OF INDIVIDUAL MUSICALS:
<u>The Saint Louis Woman</u>
Archer. <u>Black Images in the American Theatre.</u>
pp. 83-91
Gilder, Rosamond. "Broadway Bottleneck: the
Season in Review." <u>Theatre Arts</u> 30 (June
1946): 320-323
Hicklin. <u>The American Negro Playwright 1920-</u>
<u>1964.</u> Part 1, pp. 240, 241-244, 290
REVIEWS OF INDIVIDUAL MUSICALS:
<u>The Saint Louis Woman</u>
" '45-46 Season Revived." <u>New York Times,</u> 2
June 1946, II, 1: 2
Jefferson, Miles M. "The Negro on Broadway,
1945-1946." <u>Phylon</u> 7 (Second Quarter 1946):
185, 192-194
_____. "The Negro on Broadway, 1946-1947."
<u>Phylon</u> 8 (Second Quarter 1947): 148
"Lena Horne and 'St. Louis Woman.'" <u>The Pitts-</u>
<u>burgh Courier</u> (16 June 1945): 15
McDermott, William F. "Do You Remember the
Cake-Walk?" <u>Cleveland Plain Dealer</u>, 24 No-
vember 1933, 10: 1
Nichols, Lewis. "The Play." [St. Louis Woman]
<u>New York Times</u>, 1 April 1946, p. 22: 2
Rowe, Billy. "St. Louis Woman." <u>The Pitts-</u>
<u>burgh Courier</u> (15 September 1945): 15
" 'St. Louis Woman' Cast Does Nipups over Stereo-
typed Character." <u>Variety</u> (3 April 1946): 32
Zolotov, Sam. " 'St. Louis Woman' to Close
Saturday." <u>New York Times,</u> 3 July 1946, 20:
1
MEDIA RESOURCES:
Audio-Tape Reel: "Arna Bontemps--Interview: Meet
the Authors." Kankakee, Ill.: 1972. Imperial
International Learning Co., 1972

BRANCH, WILLIAM BLACKWELL (b. September 11, 1927)
PLAYS:
<u>Baccalaureate,</u> 1954

Fifty Steps Toward Freedom; a dramatic presenta-
tion in observance of the Fiftieth Anniversary of
the NAACP, New York, 1959
In Splendid Error,]955. New York Public Library,
Schomburg Collection
Light in the Southern Sky, one act, 1958
A Medal for Willie, 1951. New York Public Li-
brary, Schomburg Collection
To Follow the Phoenix, 1960
A Wreath for Udomo, 1961. (Based on the novel A
Wreath for Udomo by Peter Abrahams)
PLAYS PUBLISHED IN ANTHOLOGIES:
In Splendid Error, in Hatch and Shine, Black Thea-
ter USA; Patterson, Black Theatre
A Medal for Willie, in King and Milner, Black Drama
Anthology
To Follow the Phoenix, scene in Childress, Black
Scenes
CRITICISMS OF BRANCH:
"Negro Playwrights: Young Chicagoan is First with
All-Negro Play on Broadway." Ebony 14 (April
1959): 100
CRITICISMS OF INDIVIDUAL PLAYS:
In Splendid Error
Abramson. Negro Playwrights in the American
Theatre 1925-1959. pp. 179-188, 256-258
Hicklin. The American Negro Playwright 1920-
1964. Part 2, pp. 391-394
Mitchell. Black Drama. pp. 167-168
A Medal for Willie
Abramson. Negro Playwrights in the American
Theatre 1925-1959. pp. 171-179, 255-256
Hicklin. The American Negro Playwright 1920-
1964. Part 2, pp. 388-391
Mitchell. Black Drama. pp. 151-154
Turner, Darwin T. "Negro Playwrights and the
Urban Negro." CLA Journal 12 (September
1968): 23
A Wreath for Udomo
Campbell, Dick. "Is There a Conspiracy Against
Black Playwrights?" Negro Digest 17 (April
1968): 15
Hicklin. The American Negro Playwright 1920-
1964. Part 2, p. 394
Jet 18 (31 March 1960): 60; 19 (2 March 1961): 59
REVIEWS OF INDIVIDUAL PLAYS:
In Splendid Error

Aptheker, Herbert. "The Drama of Douglas and
Brown." Masses and Mainstream, 7 (November 1954): 59
Jefferson, Miles. "The Negro on Broadway,
1954-1955." Phylon 16 (Third Quarter 1955):
308-309
Jewish Life, January 1955, p. 26
New York Post, 22 October 1954
New York Times, 27 October 1954, p. 33-6
A Medal for Willie
Daily Worker, 23 January 1952
Jefferson, Miles M. "The Negro on Broadway,
1951-1952--Another Transparent Season."
Phylon 13 (Third Quarter 1952): 205-206
_____. "The Negro on Broadway, 1953-1954:
A Baffling Season." Phylon 15 (Third Quarter
1954): 260
New York Times, 16 October 1951, 35: 2
Schlechter, Amy. "A Hard-Hitting Play on the
U.S. South." New World Review (December
1951): 63
A Wreath for Udomo
Silverman, Reuben. "A History of the Karamu
Theatre of Karamu House." Ph.D. Dissertation, Ohio State University, Columbus, 1961.
p. 370

BRENNER, ALFRED
PLAY:
The Black Jesus

BROOKS, CHARLOTTE K.
PLAY:
Firm Foundations
PLAYS PUBLISHED IN PERIODICALS:
Firm Foundations, in Negro History Bulletin 17
(March 1954): 23 (April 1960)

BROWN, B. S.
PLAY:
The Snake Chief
PLAYS PUBLISHED IN PERIODICALS:
The Snake Chief, in Negro History Bulletin 34
(March 1971)

BROWN, CECIL M.
PLAYS:

The African Shades: A Comedy in One Act
The Gila Monster
Our Sisters Are Pregnant
PLAYS PUBLISHED IN ANTHOLOGIES:
    The African Shades, in Reed, The Yardbird Reader,
       pp. 17-42
REVIEWS OF INDIVIDUAL PLAYS:
    The Gila Monster
       Miller, Adam David. "News from the San Fran-
       cisco East Bay." Black Theatre No. 4 (April
       1970): 5

BROWN, JAMES
    PLAY:
       King Shotaway, 1823* [may be the first Black drama]

BROWN, JAMES NELSON
    PLAY:
       Tomorrow Was Yesterday. New York: Exposition
       Press, 1966

BROWN, LENNOX JOHN (b. February 7, 1934)
    PLAYS:
       A Ballet Behind the Bridge
       The Captive
       Devil Mas'
       Fire for an Ice Age
       For Drifts in the Spring
       I Have to Call My Father
       The Klinti Train
       The Meeting and Jour Ouvert ("Day Break")
       The Night Class
       Prodigal in Black Stone
       Saturday's Druid
       Snow Dark Sunday
       Song of the Spear
       The Scent of Incense
       The Throne in an Autumn Room
       The Trinity of Four in Caribbean Rhythms: The
         Emerging English Literature of the West Indies,
         James T. Livingston. N.Y.: S & S, 1974
       The Voyage Tonight
       Wine in Winter
    PLAYS PUBLISHED IN ANTHOLOGIES:
       The Captive, in Ottawa Little Theatre. Ranking
         Play Series 2, Catalogue No. 43. Ottawa,
         Canada, September 1965
       Devil Mas', in Harrison, Kuntu Drama

The Klinti Train, in Black American Drama. New
   York: Simon and Schuster. forthcoming
The Meeting and Jour Ouvert, in Ottawa Little Thea-
   tre, Ranking Play Series 2, Catalogue No. 56.
   Ottawa, Canada, October 1966
The Trinity of Four, in Caribbean Rhythms: ...,
   James T. Livingston. N.Y.: S & S, 1974
PLAYS PUBLISHED IN PERIODICALS:
   I Have to Call My Father, in Drama and Theatre
   8 (Winter 1969-70): 118-130
CRITICISMS OF BROWN:
   Chintok, JoJo. "Lennox Brown: A Black Canadian
   Dramatist." black i: a Canadian Journal of Black
   Expression Vol. I, No. 1, pp. 28-29
REVIEWS OF INDIVIDUAL PLAYS:
   A Ballet Behind the Bridge
      The Christian Science Monitor, 19 April 1972,
         p. 4: 1
      New Yorker 18 March 1972, p. 2
AWARDS:
   Canada Council Travel Grant to attend the per-
      formance of prize winning play, 1966
   Canada National One-act Playwrighting Competition
   Yousuf Award
   Birks Medal for The Captive, 1965; Night Sun, 1967;
      Jour Ouvert, 1968
   Dorothy White award for The Meeting, 1966 (Brown
      was the first playwright in history to win four
      prizes in four consecutive years)
   First Prize, Canadian National University Drama
      League Competition for I Have to Call My Father,
      1969
   Runner-Up, Shubert Fellowship, University of Toron-
      to, 1969, for The Night Class
   Eugene O'Neill Memorial Playwriting National Compe-
      tition for Prodigal in Black Stone, 1971

BROWN, OSCAR, JR.
   PLAYS:
      [With Joseph Tuotti] Buck White
      Slave Song
   MUSICALS:
      Joy
      Kicks and Co.
      Sunshine and Shadows
   MUSICALS PUBLISHED IN ANTHOLOGIES:
      Kicks and Co., in Hewes, Best Plays of 1961-1962

CRITICISMS OF BROWN:
"Many Faces of Oscar Brown Jr." Sepia 11 (September 1962): 72-74
Mitchell. Black Drama. pp. 190-192
"Opportunity Please Knock." [Oscar Brown Jr.]
Ebony 22 (August 1967): 104-108
"Oscar Brown Jr.: The Flax That Flipped." Sepia 12 (May 1963): 18-22
"Worlds of Oscar Brown, Jr." The Best Plays of 1964-65. Guernsey, ed.
REVIEWS OF INDIVIDUAL PLAYS:
Buck White
Guernsey. The Best Plays of 1969-1970. p. 307
REVIEWS OF INDIVIDUAL MUSICALS:
Joy
Barnes, C. "Review: Joy." New York Times, 19 July 1970, 50: 1
Goncalves, Joe. "West Coast Drama." Black Theatre No. 4 (April 1970): 27
Guernsey. The Best Plays of 1969-1970. p. 357
New Yorker 13 June 1970, p. 4
Kicks and Co.
Jet 19 (16 March 1961): 61; (23 March 1961): 59; (13 July 1961): 62; (12 October 1961): 58-61; (20 October 1961): 58, 60-61

BROWN, PATRICIA
PLAYS:
Gloria Mundi
REVIEWS OF INDIVIDUAL PLAYS:
Mantle. The Best Plays of 1924-1925. p. 587

BROWN, ROSCOE LEE
PLAY:
A Hand Is on the Gate
REVIEWS OF INDIVIDUAL PLAYS:
A Hand Is on the Gate
Guernsey. The Best Plays of 1966-1967. pp. 353-355
New Yorker 24 September 1966, p. 2

BROWN, WILLIAM WELLS (died November 6, 1884)
PLAYS:
The Escape, or A Leap for Freedom: A Drama in Five Acts. Boston: R. F. Wallcutt, 1858.
Play was written in 1856; the first recorded reading of the play was in Salem, Ohio, 4 Febru-

ary 1847
Experience: Escape: Life at the South. Some-
times listed as Experience: or, How to Give a
Northern Man a Backbone, 1856, or as A South-
side View of Slavery
PLAYS PUBLISHED IN ANTHOLOGIES:
The Escape; or A Leap for Freedom, in Hatch and
Shine, Black Theater USA
CRITICISMS OF BROWN
Abramson. Negro Playwrights in the American
Theatre. pp. 8-14, 18-19
_____. "William Wells Brown: America's First
Negro Playwright." Educational Theatre Journal
20 (October 1968): 370-376
Bigsby. The Black American Writer. vol. 2, pp.
44, 113-114, 133, 203
Bond. The Negro and the Drama. pp. 25-27, 205
Brawley. The Negro Genius. pp. 3, 45, 59-63, 69,
101, 127
Davis and Redding. Cavalcade. pp. 54, 57-64
Farrison, W. Edward. "Brown's First Drama."
CLA Journal 13 (December 1969): 192-197
McPherson, et al. Blacks in America. pp. 51, 94,
104-105, 107
Mitchell. Black Drama. p. 34
Pawley, Dr. Thomas D. "The First Black Play-
wrights." Black World (April 1972): 16-24
Turner. In a Minor Chord. pp. xv, 116
Whitlow. Black American Literature. pp. 24, 39,
42-46, 49, 185
Yellin, Jean. The Intricate Knot. p. 1
CRITICISMS OF INDIVIDUAL PLAYS:
The Escape; or A Leap for Freedom
Abramson. Negro Playwrights in The American
Theater 1925-1959. pp. 8-14, 18-19
Bradley, Gerald. "Goodbye Mr. Bones." Drama
Critique 7 (Spring 1964): 80
Brown. Negro Poetry and Drama. p. 109
Brown, William Wells. The Escape; or A Leap
for Freedom. pp. 4, 10
Hatch and Shine. Black Theater USA. pp. 34-35
Kardiner and Ovesey. The Mark of Oppression.
p. 43
Experience; or How to Give a Northern Man a Back-
bone
Bradley, Gerald. "Goodbye Mr. Bones."
Drama Critique 7 (Spring 1964): 80

REVIEWS OF INDIVIDUAL PLAYS:
    The Escape
        Liberator 1 (August 1856): 124

BROWNE, PATRICIA WILKINS (b. June 6, 1950)
    PLAY:
        In Search of Unity, 1972

BROWNE, THEODORE
    PLAYS:
        A Black Woman Called Moses
        Go Down Moses
        Gravy Train, 1940
        Lysistrata, adaptation
        Minstrel
        Natural Man, formerly titled This Old Hammer
        Swing Gate, Swing
    PLAYS PUBLISHED IN ANTHOLOGIES:
        Natural Man, in Childress, Black Scenes (excerpt);
            Hatch and Shine, Black Theater USA
    CRITICISMS OF BROWNE:
        Abramson. Negro Playwrights in the American
            Theatre. pp. 102-109, 159-160
        Bigsby. The Black American Writer. vol. 2, p. 136
        Brown, John Mason. New York Post, 8 May 1941
        Gayle. Black Expression. p. 155
        Hicklin. The American Negro Playwright 1920-1964.
            Part 1, p. 282
        Mitchell. Black Drama. pp. 113, 114
        Warner, Ralph. Daily Worker, 12 May 1941
        Williams. Stage Left. p. 230
    CRITICISMS OF INDIVIDUAL PLAYS:
        Natural Man
            Abramson. Negro Playwrights in the American
                Theatre. pp. 102-109, 159-160
            Gayle. Black Expression. p. 155
            Hicklin. The American Negro Playwright 1920-
                1964. Part 1, pp. 282-285
            Leonard, Claire. "The American Negro Theatre."
                Theatre Arts 28 (July 1944): 421-423
    REVIEWS OF INDIVIDUAL PLAYS:
        Natural Man
            Atkinson, Brooks. "The Play (Natural Man)."
                New York Times, 8 May 1941, 20: 4

BRUCE, RICHARD
    PLAY:

Sahdji, An African Ballet
PLAYS PUBLISHED IN ANTHOLOGIES:
Sahdji, An African Ballet, in Locke and Montgomery,
Plays of Negro Life

BRUNO, JOANN
PLAYS:
Sister Selena, 1970
Uncle Bud's No Stranger

BRUNSON, DORIS
PLAYS:
[With Roger Thurman] Three Shades of Harlem
CRITICISM OF BRUNSON:
Mitchell. Black Drama. p. 208

BRYANT, FREDERICK JAMES, JR. (b. July 6, 1942)
PLAY:
Lord of the Mummy Wrappings, 1967

BRYANT, HAZEL
MUSICALS:
[With Jimmy Justice] Black Circles 'Round Angela,
1971
[With Hope Clarke and Hank Johnson] Mae's Amis,
1969
[With Gertrude Grenidge and Walter Miles] Makin'
It, 1972
[With Beverly Todd and Hank Johnson] Origins,
1969
[With Jimmy Justice] Sheba, 1972

BULLINS, ED (b. July 2, 1935)
PLAYS:
Clara's Old Man, 1969
The Corner, 1967
Death List, 1971
The Devil Catchers
Dialect Determinism; or The Rally, one act, 1965
Duplex: A Black Love Fable in Four Movements.
New York: Morrow, 1971
The Electronic Nigger
The Fabulous Miss Marie, 1971
[With Shirley Tarbell] The Game of Adam and Eve,
one act, 1966
The Gentleman Caller
Goin' A Buffalo

The Helper, one act, 1966
How Do You Do: A Nonsense Drama, one act.
  Mill Valley, Calif.: Illuminations Press, 1967
The Hungered One
In New England Winter, 1969
In the Wine Time, 1969
It Has No Choice, one act, 1966
Malcolm: '71, or Publishing Blackness, 1975
The Man Who Dug Fish, 1967
A Minor Scene, one act, 1966
The Pig Pen
A Short Play for a Small Theater
A Son, Come Home, 1969
Street Sounds
The Taking of Miss Janie
We Righteous Bombers, written under the pseudonym
  Kingsley B. Bass, Jr.?
You Gonna Let Me Take You Out Tonight, Baby?
PLAYS PUBLISHED IN ANTHOLOGIES:
  Clara's Old Man, in Davis and Redding, Cavalcade;
    Poland and Mailman, The Off-Off Broadway Book;
    Richards, Best Short Plays of 1969
  The Corner, in King and Milner, Black Drama
    Anthology
  Dialectic Determinism; or The Rally, in Owens and
    Feingold, Spontaneous Combustion: Eight New
    American Plays
  The Electronic Nigger, in Hoffman, New American
    Plays. vol. 3; Robinson, Nommo
  The Gentleman Caller, in A Black Quartet; Oliver
    and Sills, Contemporary Black Drama; Richards,
    Best Short Plays of 1970
  Goin' A Buffalo, in Couch, New Black Playwrights;
    Hatch and Shine, Black Theater USA
  How Do You Do: A Nonsense Drama, in Jones and
    Neal, Black Fire
  In the Wine Time, in Lahr and Price, The Great
    American Dream Machine: 9 Plays from the
    Avant Garde Theatre
  A Son, Come Home, in Bain, The Norton Introduc-
    tion to Literature: Drama; Childress, Black
    Scenes; Clayes and Spencer, Contemporary Drama:
    Thirteen Plays; Deer, Selves: Drama in Per-
    spective
  We Righteous Bombers, in Bullins, New Plays from
    The Black Theatre; Turner, Black American Liter-
    ature

You Gonna Let Me Take You Out Tonight, Baby? in
Alhamisi and Wangara, Black Arts
PLAYS PUBLISHED IN PERIODICALS:
Clara's Old Man, in Drama Review 12 (Summer
1968): 159-171
Death List, in Black Theatre 5 (7 October 1971): 38-
43
How Do You Do: A Nonsense Drama, in Black Dia-
logue 1 (July-August 1965): 55-61
Malcolm: '71, or Publishing Blackness, in Black
Scholar 6 (June 1975): 84-86
A Short Play for a Small Theater, in Black World
2 (April 1971): 39
A Son, Come Home, in Negro Digest 17 (April 1968):
54-73
MUSICALS:
House Party
FILM SCRIPTS:
The Box Office
Night of the Beast, 1971
The Ritual Masters, 1972
FILM SCRIPTS PUBLISHED IN PERIODICALS:
The Box Office, in Black Theatre 3 (1970): 17-19
COLLECTIONS:
Five Plays: Goin' A Buffalo; In the Wine Time;
A Son, Come Home; The Electronic Nigger;
Clara's Old Man. Indianapolis: Bobbs-Merrill,
1969
Four Dynamite Plays. New York: Morrow, 1972.
Includes It Bees Dat Way; Death List; Night of
The Beast; The Pig Pen
Four One Act Plays: How Do You Do; A Minor
Scene; Dialect Determinism; It Has No Choice
The Theme is Blackness: The Corner and Other
Plays. New York: Morrow, 1973
CRITICISMS BY BULLINS:
"Black Theater Groups: A Directory." Drama Re-
view 12 (Summer 1968): 172-175
"Black Theater Notes." Black Theatre No. 1 (1968):
4
"Comments on Production of In New England Winter."
New York Times, 20 December 1970, II, 3: 6
[With Clifford Mason and Robert Macbeth] "The
Electronic Nigger Meets the Gold Dust Twins."
Black Theatre 1 (October 1968): 24 ff
"Like It Was: Review of Jones' The Dutchman and
The Toilet." Black Dialogue 1 (Spring 1966): 72-
75

"Short Statement on Street Theater." Drama Review
12 (Summer 1968): 93
"The So-Called Western Avant-Garde Drama."
Liberator (December 1967): 16; reprinted in Gayle,
Black Expression
"Theater of Reality." Negro Digest 15 (April 1966):
60-66
"What Lies Ahead for Blackamericans." Negro Di-
gest 19 (November 1968): 8 (Symposium)
CRITICISMS OF BULLINS:
Abramson. Negro Playwrights in the American Thea-
tre, 1925-1959. pp. 279, 285
Anderson, Jervis. "Profiles: Dramatist." New
Yorker 49 (16 June 1973): 40-79
Archer. Black Images. p. 292
Bermel, Albert. "Ed Bullins." New Leader, 22
April 1968, p. 28
"Black Theater." Negro Digest 18 (April 1969): 9-
16 (Interview by Marvin X.)
Brooks, Mary E. "Reactionary Trends in Recent
Black Drama." Literature and Ideology 10 (1973):
41-48
Cade, Toni. "Review of Four by Ed Bullins."
umbra-blackworks (Summer 1970)
Cameron and Hoffman. A Guide to Theatre Study.
p. 204
Clayborne, Jon L. "Modern Black Drama and the Gay
Image." College English 36 (November 1974):
381-384
Clurman, Harold. "Ed Bullins." Nation 12 May
1969, p. 612
Duberman, Martin. In Partisan Review No. 3 (1969):
489-490
Evans, Don. "The Theater of Confrontation: Ed
Bullins, Up Against the Wall." Black World 23
(April 1974): 14-18
Gaffney, Floyd. "Is Your Door Really Open?"
Drama and Theatre 7 (Fall 1968): 5
Gant, Lisbeth. "New Lafayette Theater." Drama
Review 16 (December 1972): 46-55
Giles, James R. "Tenderness in Brutality: The
Plays of Ed Bullins." Players 48 (October-
November 1972): 32-33
Gussow, Mel. "The New Playwrights." Newsweek
20 May 1968, p. 115
Harrison. The Drama of Nommo. pp. 169, 177-
178, 191, 223-225

Haslam, Gerald W. "Two Traditions in Afro-American Literature." Research Studies 36 (September 1969): 183-193

Hay, Samuel A. "'What Shape Shapes Shapelessness?' Structural Elements in Ed Bullins' Plays." Black World 23 (April 1974): 20-26

Jackman, Kennell, Jr. "Notes on The Works of Ed Bullins and 'The Hungered One.'" CLA Journal 18 (December 1974): 292-299

Jeffers, Lance. "Bullins, Baraka, and Elder: The Dawn of Grandeur in Black Drama." CLA Journal 16 (September 1972): 32-48

Jones, D. A. N. In Listener, 22 August 1968, p. 253

Kroll, Jack. "Black Mood." Newsweek 18 March 1968, p. 110

Kuna, F. M. "Current Literature 1970-II, New Writing: Drama." English Studies 52 (December 1971): 565-573

McPherson, Holland, Banner, Weiss and Bell. Blacks in America. pp. 261, 264, 279-280, 282

Marowitz, Charles. "America's Great Hopes, White and Black?" New York Times, 13 April 1969

Marvin X. "An Interview with Ed Bullins: Black Theatre." Negro Digest 18 (April 1969): 9-11

O'Brien, John. "Interview with Ed Bullins." Negro American Literature Forum 7 (Fall 1973): 108

Riche, James. "The Politics of Black Modernism." Literature and Ideology No. 8 (1971): 85-90

Scott, John Sherman. "The Black Spirit: A Trilogy of Original Plays and A Treatise on Dramatic Theory in Contemporary Black Drama." Ph.D. Dissertation, Bowling Green State University, 1972. p. 32-33, 35

Show Business, 17 October 1970

Smitherman, Geneva. "Ed Bullins/Stage One: Everybody Wants to Know Why I Sing the Blues." Black World 23 (April 1974): 4-13

Trott, Geri. "Black Theater." Harper's Bazaar 101 (August 1968): 150-153

Weales. The Jumping-Off Place. pp. 150, 291

Wesley, Richard. "An Interview with Playwright Ed Bullins." Black Creation 4 (Winter 1973): 8-10

Whitlow. Black American Literature. p. 174

CRITICISMS OF INDIVIDUAL PLAYS:
Clara's Old Man

Lewis. Stages: Fifty Year Childhood of The
American Theatre. p. 158
"Playboy After Hours: Theatre" Playboy 18
(April 1971): 37
Duplex: A Black Love Fable in Four Movements
Archer. Black Images in The American Theatre.
p. 292
Eckstein, George. "The New Black Theater."
Dissent 20 (Winter 1973): 113
Goss, Clay. "Review of The Duplex: A Love
Fable in Four Movements." Black Books Bul-
letin 1 (Spring-Summer 1972): 34-35
The Electronic Nigger
Bailey, Peter. "The Electronic Nigger." Ebony
23 (September 1968): 97-101
Eckstein, George. "The New Black Theater."
Dissent 20 (Winter 1973): 113
Lewis. Stages: Fifty Year Childhood of the
American Theatre. p. 158
"Playboy After Hours: Theatre" Playboy 18
(April 1971): 37
The Fabulous Miss Marie
Eckstein, George. "The New Black Theater."
Dissent 20 (Winter 1973): 113
McElroy, Hilda Njoki. "Books Noted." Black
World 26 (April 1975): 51
Goin' A Buffalo
Eckstein, George. "The New Black Theater."
Dissent 20 (Winter 1973): 113
Orman, Rosco. "The New Lafayette Theatre."
Black Theatre Magazine No. 4 (April 1970): 6
The Hungered One
Riggins, Linda N. "A Review of Ed Bullins' The
Hungered One." Black Scholar 3 (February
1972): 59-60
In the Wine Time
Duberman, Martin. "Theatre 69: Black Theatre."
Partisan Review 36 (1969): 489-490
Eckstein, George. "The New Black Theater."
Dissent 20 (Winter 1973): 113
A Son, Come Home
Eckstein, George. "The New Black Theater."
Dissent 20 (Winter 1973): 113
Lewis. Stages: Fifty Year Childhood of the
American Theatre. p. 158
The Taking of Miss Janie
Kalem, T. E. "Requiem for the 60's" [The

Taking of Miss Janie]. Time 19 May 1975,
p. 80
We Righteous Bombers
Black Theatre No. 4 (8 June 1970): 16
REVIEWS OF INDIVIDUAL PLAYS:
Clara's Old Man
New York Times, 9 March 1968, 23: 2
Duplex: A Black Love Fable in Four Movements
The Christian Science Monitor, 19 April 1972, p.
4: 1
Kroll, Jack. "In Black America." Newsweek
79 (March 20, 1972): 98-99
New York Theater Critics' Reviews (1972): p. 330
The Electronic Nigger
Guernsey. The Best Plays of 1967-1968. pp.
391-392
Miller. Black Theatre Magazine (April 1970): 5
New York Times, 9 March 1968, 23: 2
New Yorker 9 March 1968, p. 4; 13 April 1968,
p. 2
The Fabulous Miss Marie
Gussow, M. "The Fabulous Miss Marie." New
York Times, 12 March 1971, 28: 1
New Yorker 1 May 1971, p. 2
The Gentleman Caller
Guernsey. The Best Plays of 1968-1969. p. 455
New York Times, 13 April 1969, II, 3: 3; 27
April, 92: 1; 4 May, II, 1: 5; 31 July, 28: 1;
3 August, II, 1: 4; 22 September, 36: 1
Goin' A Buffalo
Gussow, M. "Goin' a Buffalo." New York Times,
16 February 1972, 28: 1
Orman, Roscoe: "The New Lafayette Theatre."
Black Theatre Magazine No. 4 (April 1970): 6
House Party
New York Magazine, 12 November 1973, p. 75
New York Theater Critics' Review 34 (26 Novem-
ber 1973): 173-174
New Yorker 5 November 1973, p. 4
Wilson, Edwin. Wall Street Journal, 9 November
1973
How Do You Do
New York Times, 21 May 1968, 42: 1; 13 April
1969, II, 3: 3
In New England Winter
Guernsey. The Best Plays of 1970-1971. p. 341
Gussow, M. "In New England Winter." New York

Times, 27 January 1971, 28: 1
Kerr, W. New York Times, 7 February 1971,
II, 3: 3
New Yorker 30 January 1970, p. 2
Riley, Clayton. New York Times, 7 February
1971, II, 3: 8
_____. "Theatre Reviews: The Pig Pen and
In New England Winter." Liberator 10 (June
1970): 20
In the Wine Time
New York Times, 22 December 1968, II, 7: 2
Orman, Rosco. "The New Lafayette Theatre."
Black Theatre Magazine No. 4 (April 1970): 6
Riley, Clayton. "Theatre Review: In the Wine
Time." Liberator 9 (January 1969): 20
The Pig Pen
Barnes, C. "Review: The Pig Pen." New York
Times, 21 May 1970, 47: 1
Guernsey. The Best Plays of 1969-1970. pp. 341-
342
Kerr, W. "Review: The Pig Pen." New York
Times, 31 May 1970, II, 3: 1
New York Times, 31 May, II, 1: 6
Riley, Clayton. "Theatre Reviews: The Pig Pen
and In New England Winter." Liberator 10
(June 1970): 20
A Son, Come Home
Miller. Black Theatre Magazine No. 4 (April
1970): 5
New York Times, 9 March 1968, 23: 2
Street Sounds
New York Times, 23 October 1970, 32: 1
The Taking of Miss Janie
Hewes, Henry. "The Taking of Miss Janie."
Saturday Review 17 May 1975, p. 52
_____. New Yorker 12 May 1975, p. 4
We Righteous Bombers
Riley, Clayton. "Theatre Review: We Righteous
Bombers." Liberator 9 (June 1969): 21
Who's Got His Own
Orman, Rosco. "The New Lafayette Theatre."
Black Theatre Magazine No. 4 (April 1970): 6
REVIEWS OF COLLECTIONS OF PLAYS:
Four One Act Plays: How Do You Do, A Minor
Scene, Dialect Determinism, It Has No Choice
Barnes, C. New York Times, 5 March 1972,
59: 1

AWARDS:
  Obie Award for The Fabulous Miss Marie; Drama
  Desk-Vernon Rice Award for "Outstanding Achievement in the Off Broadway Theater," 1967-68 season

BURGHARDT, ARTHUR
  PLAY:
  [With Michael Eagan] Frederick Douglass ...
    Through His Own Words

BURRIL, MARY
  PLAYS:
  Aftermath
  They That Sit in Darkness
  PLAYS PUBLISHED IN ANTHOLOGIES:
  They That Sit in Darkness, in Hatch and Shine,
    Black Theater USA
  PLAYS PUBLISHED IN PERIODICALS:
  Aftermath, in Liberator 2 (April 1919)
  They That Sit in Darkness, in Birth Control Review,
    (1919)
  CRITICISMS OF INDIVIDUAL WORKS:
  Aftermath
    Archer. Black Images. p. 141
    "Krigwa Little Theater." [Aftermath] Crisis
      35 (June 1928): 199
  They That Sit in Darkness
    Hatch and Shine. Black Theater USA. p. 178

BURRIS, ANDREW
  PLAY:
  You Mus' Be Bo'n Again, 3 acts, 4 scenes, 1931

BUTCHER, JAMES W., JR.
  PLAY:
  The Seer
  PLAYS PUBLISHED IN ANTHOLOGIES:
  The Seer, in Brown, Davis and Lee, Negro Caravan

BYRD, De REATH IRENE
  PLAY:
  The Yellow Tree, one act

CAIN, BROTHER
  PLAY:

Epitaph to a Triangulated Trinity

CALDWELL, BEN
PLAYS:
All White Caste
Family Portrait, or My Son the Black Militant
The Fanatic (one act), 1968
The First Militant Preacher. Newark, N.J.: Jihad,
1967
Hypnotism, 1966
The Job, 1966
The King of Soul, or The Devil and Otis Redding
Mission Accomplished
Prayer Meeting, or The First Militant Minister
Recognition (one act), 1968
Riot Sale, or Dollar Psyche Fake Out
Run Around
Top Secret, or A Few Million After B.C.
Unpresented (one act), 1967
The Wall (one act), 1967
PLAYS PUBLISHED IN ANTHOLOGIES:
All White Caste, in King and Milner, Black Drama
Anthology
Family Portrait, or My Son the Black Militant, in
Bullins, New Plays from the Black Theatre
Hypnotism, in Afro-Arts Anthology; Simmons and
Hutchinson, Black Culture
The Job, in Kearns, Black Identity; Robinson, Nommo
The King of Soul, or The Devil and Otis Redding, in
Bullins, New Plays from the Black Theatre
Prayer Meeting, or The First Militant Minister, in
Jones and Neal, Black Fire; Caldwell, et al., A
Black Quartet
Riot Sale, or Dollar Psyche Fake Out, in Simmons
and Hutchinson, Black Culture
PLAYS PUBLISHED IN PERIODICALS:
The Job, in Drama Review 12 (Summer 1968)
The King of Soul, or The Devil and Otis Redding, in
Black Theatre No. 3 (1970): 28-33
Mission Accomplished, in Drama Review 12 (Summer
1968)
Riot Sale, or Dollar Psyche Fake Out, in Drama
Review 12 (Summer 1968)
Top Secret or A Few Million After B.C., in Drama
Review 12 (Summer 1968)
CRITICISMS OF CALDWELL:
Bigsby. The Black American Writer. vol. 2., pp.
201-202

Haley, Elsie Galbreath. "The Black Revolutionary
Theatre: LeRoi Jones, Ed Bullins, and Minor
Playwrights." Ph.D. Dissertation, University of
Denver, 1971
Riach, W. A. D. "'Telling It Like It Is': An
Examination of Black Theater as Rhetoric."
Quarterly Journal of Speech 46 (April 1970): 183
CRITICISMS OF INDIVIDUAL PLAYS:
The Job
   Miller, Adam David. "News from the San Fran-
   cisco East Bay." Black Theatre Magazine 4
   (April 1970): 5
The King of Soul
   Eckstein, George. "The New Black Theater."
   Dissent 20 (Winter 1973): 111
   Kaufman, Michael W. "The Delicate World of
   Reprobation: A Note on the Black Revolutionary
   Theatre." Educational Theatre Journal 23 (De-
   cember 1971): 446-460
The First Militant Preacher
   Gayle, Addison, Jr. The Black Aesthetic. pp.
   289-290
Prayer Meeting, or The First Militant Minister.
   Killinger. The Fragile Presence. pp. 144
Riot Sale
   Harrison. The Drama of Nommo. p. 203

CAMPBELL, HERBERT
   PLAYS:
   Goin' Home to Papa
   Middle Class Blacks
   CRITICISMS OF CAMPBELL:
   Walker, Barbara. "Theater: Bedford Stuyvesant
   Theatre." Black Creation 3 (Summer 1972): 22

CAMPBELL, RALPH
   PLAY:
   Nigger. Detroit: Broadside, 1972

CAPEL, SHARON
   PLAY:
   Dreams Are for the Dead

CARROLL, VINNETTE
   PLAYS:
   [With Micki Grant] But Never Jam Today, 1969
   Trumpets of the Lord. (Adapted from J. W. John-

son's "God's Trombones")
MUSICALS:
All the King's Men, an adaptation with music and
lyrics by Malcolm Dodd
[With Micki Grant] Croesus and the Witch, 1972
[With Micki Grant] Don't Bother Me, I Can't Cope,
1972
[With Micki Grant] Step Lively, Boy, 1972
[With Micki Grant] The Ups and Downs of Theophilus
Maitland (Ward), 1975
CRITICISMS OF CARROLL:
Hepburn, D. "Vinnette Carroll, Woman on the Run."
Sepia 10 (October 1961): 57-60
Little. Off-Broadway. p. 131
Mitchell. Black Drama. pp. 191, 205
REVIEWS OF INDIVIDUAL WORKS:
All the King's Men
New Yorker 20 May 1974, p. 2
Croesus and the Witch
New Yorker 4 September 1971, p. 2
Don't Bother Me, I Can't Cope
New Yorker 7 October 1972, p. 2
Trumpets of the Lord
Guernsey. The Best Plays of 1968-69. pp. 413-
414
NBC TV 4, 29 April 1969
New York Daily News, 30 April 1969
New York Post, 30 April 1969
New York Theatre Critics' Reviews 30 (5 May
1969): 301-304
New York Times, 30 April 1969
WABC TV 7, 29 April 1969
WCBS TV 2, 29 April 1969
Wall Street Journal, 1 May 1969
Women's Wear Daily, 30 April 1969
The Ups and Downs of Theophilus Maitland (Ward)
New Yorker 2 December 1974, p. 4

CARTER, JEAN (Emma Loyal Lexa)
PLAY:
Country Gentleman. New York: Exposition, 1950

CARTER, JOHN D.
PLAY:
The Assassin, 1971

CARTER, STEVE

PLAYS:
As You Can See, one act, 1968
One Last Look, 1971
The Terraced Apartment, one act, 1972
PLAYS PUBLISHED IN ANTHOLOGIES:
One Last Look, in Childress, Black Scenes
REVIEWS OF INDIVIDUAL PLAYS:
The Terraced Apartment
New Yorker 1 April 1974, p. 4

CHARLES, MARTA EVANS (Marti Charles)
PLAYS:
Black Cycle, 1972
Jamimma, 1971
Job Security, 1970
Where We At, 1969
PLAYS PUBLISHED IN ANTHOLOGIES:
Black Cycle, in King and Milner, Black Drama
Anthology
Job Security, in Hatch and Shine, Black Theater USA
CRITICISMS OF INDIVIDUAL PLAYS:
Job Security
Hatch and Shine. Black Theater USA. p. 765
REVIEWS OF INDIVIDUAL PLAYS:
Jamimma
New Yorker, 3 June 1972, p. 2

CHILDRESS, ALICE
PLAYS:
The African Garden
Florence: A One-Act Drama
The Freedom Drum
Gold Through The Trees, 1952
[With Alvin Childress] Hell's Alley
Just a Little Simple, 1953; adaptation of Hughes'
Just a Little Simple
A Man Bearing a Pitcher
Mojo: A Black Love Story. New York: Dramatists
Play Service, 1971
String. New York: Dramatists Play Service, 1969
String and Mojo: A Black Love Story. New York:
Dramatists Play Service, 1971
Trouble in Mind (So Early in the Morning), 1955.
Mimeographed copy in possession of Alice
Childress
Wedding Band. New York: Samuel French, 1973
Wine in The Wilderness. New York: Dramatists
Play Service, 1973

The World on a Hill
Young Martin Luther King, Jr., 1969
PLAYS PUBLISHED IN ANTHOLOGIES:
The African Garden, scene in Childress, Black
Scenes
Trouble in Mind, in Patterson, Black Theatre
Wine in The Wilderness, in Hatch and Shine, Black
Theater USA; Major Black Writers (Scholastic
Black Literature Series); Richards, Best Short
Plays of 1972; Sullivan and Hatch, Plays By and
About Women
World on A Hill, in Plays to Remember. New York:
Macmillan, 1968
PLAYS PUBLISHED IN PERIODICALS:
Florence: A One-Act Drama, in Masses and Main-
stream 3 (October 1950): 34-47
Mojo: A Black Love Story, in Black World 20
(April 1971): 54-82
CRITICISMS BY CHILDRESS:
"Black Writer's Views on Literary Lions and Values."
Negro Digest 17 (January 1968): 36
"For a Negro Theatre." Masses and Mainstream 4
(February 1951): 61-64
Harrison. The Drama of Nommo. p. xvii
Hicklin. The American Negro Playwright 1920-1964.
Part 2, pp. 463-464
"Why Talk About That." Negro Digest 14 (April
1967): 17
"A Woman Playwright Speaks Her Mind." Freedom-
ways 6 (Winter 1966): 14-19. Reprinted in Patter-
son, Anthology of the American Negro in the Thea-
tre: A Critical Approach, pp. 75-81
CRITICISMS OF CHILDRESS:
Abramson. The Negro Playwright in the American
Theatre. pp. 258-259, 284
Evans, Donald. "Bring It All Back Home." Black
World 20 (February 1971): 41-45
Hughes and Bontemps. Black Magic. pp. 199, 209,
211, 214, 220, 222, 223
Mitchell. Black Drama. pp. 127, 215, 217, 218
_____. "Three Writers and a Dream." Crisis 72
(April 1965): 219-223
"Negro Playwrights: Young Chicagoan Is First with
All Negro Play on Broadway." Ebony 14 (April
1959): 100
"The Negro Woman in American Literature." Free-
domways 6 (Winter 1966): 45-52

CRITICISMS OF INDIVIDUAL WORKS:
Florence
  Abramson. Negro Playwrights in the American
    Theatre. p. 189
  Hicklin. The American Negro Playwright 1920-
    1964. Part 2, pp. 379-380
  Turner, Darwin T. "Negro Playwrights and the
    Urban Negro." CLA Journal 12 (September
    1968): 24
Gold Through the Trees
  Hicklin. The American Negro Playwright 1920-
    1964. Part 2, pp. 387-388
  Mitchell. Black Drama. p. 154
Just a Little Simple
  Gayle. Black Expression. pp. 156, 250
  Mitchell. Black Drama. pp. 146-147
Trouble in Mind
  Abramson. Negro Playwrights in the American
    Theatre. pp. 189-204
  Campbell, Dick. "Is There a Conspiracy Against
    Black Playwrights?" Negro Digest 17 (April
    1968): 15
  Ewen. Complete Book of the American Musical
    Theatre. p. 26
  Gayle. Black Expression, p. 157
  Hicklin. The American Negro Playwright 1920-
    1964. Part 2, pp. 381-387
  Mitchell. Black Drama. pp. 168-169
  Turner, Darwin T. "Negro Playwrights and the
    Urban Negro." CLA Journal 12 (September
    1968): 23-24
Wedding Band
  Abramson. Negro Playwrights in the American
    Theatre. p. 259
  Rudin, Seymour. "Performing Arts: 1971-1972."
    Massachusetts Review 14 (Winter 1973): 208
Wine in the Wilderness
  Hatch and Shine. Black Theater USA. p. 737
REVIEWS OF INDIVIDUAL PLAYS:
Gold Through the Trees
  Jefferson, Miles M. "The Negro on Broadway,
    1951-1952--Another Transparent Season."
    Phylon 13 (Third Quarter 1952): 205
String
  New York Times, 2 April 1969, p. 37: 1; 13
    April 1969, II, p. 1: 1
Trouble in Mind

New York Times, 5 November 1955, p. 23: 2
Wedding Band
  Gottfried, Martin. Women's Wear Daily, 10
    October 1972
  New York Theatre Critics' Reviews (1972): 163
  New Yorker 4 November 1972, p. 4
  Watt, Douglas. Daily News, 27 November 1972
  Weathers, Diane. Black Creation 4 (Winter 1973):
    60
AWARDS:
  Obie Award for the Best Original Off-Broadway Pro-
    duction: Trouble in Mind, 1956; Grant: The John
    Golden Fund for Playwrights, 1957; Harvard ap-
    pointment to the Radcliffe Institute as scholar-
    writer, 1966-1968

CHILDRESS, ALVIN
  PLAYS:
    [With Alice Childress] Hell's Alley

CHIMBAMUL (Jeri Fowler)
  PLAY:
    How The Spider Became the Hero of Folk Tales
      (children's play), 1971

CHIPHE, LEPPAIGNE
  PLAY:
    [With Chakula cha Jua] A Black Experience

CHISHOLM, EARLE
  PLAYS:
    Black Manhood, 1970
    Two in the Back Room, 1971

CLARK, CHINA DEBRA (b. September 11, 1949)
  PLAYS:
    In Madwoman's Room
    In Sorrow's Room, forthcoming
    Neffie
    Perfection in Black, 1972
    The Sabian
    Why God Hates Rev. Chandler
    The Willow Lottery

CLARKE, SEBASTIAN
  PLAYS:
    Lower Earth

CRITICISMS BY CLARKE:
"Sonia Sanchez and Her Work." Black World 2
(June 1971): 44-46

CLAY, BURIEL II (b. November 11, 1943)
PLAYS:
Buy a Little Tenderness, 1973
San Francisco
X's (Bridges over Troubled Waters), 1973
AWARDS:
Buy a Little Tenderness was chosen to be a part of
the New York Library and Museum of the Per-
forming Arts' Permanent Theatre Collection

CLIMMONS, ARTIE
PLAY:
My Troubled Soul

CODLING, BESS
PLAYS:
The Assassin
Elegy to X, two acts. New York: Amuru, 1973
Mama's Crazy Horse Rockin Again. New York:
Amuru, 1973

COFFMAN, STEVEN
PLAY:
Black Sabbath
PLAYS PUBLISHED IN PERIODICALS:
Black Sabbath, in Negro American Literature Forum
7 (Fall 1973): 91-102

COLE, ROBERT ("Bob") (1869-1911)
PLAYS:
[With Glen MacDonough] Belle of Bridgeport, 1900
Black Patti's Troubadours, 1897
[With John S. McNally] Humpty Dumpty, 1904
[With James Weldon Johnson and John S. McNally]
In Newport, 1904
[With Billy Johnson] A Trip to Coontown, 1896
MUSICALS (OPERETTAS):
[With Rosamund Johnson] Red Moon, 1908
[With Rosamund Johnson] The Shoofly Regiment, 1906
CRITICISMS OF COLE:
Cotton, Lettie Jo. "Negro in The American Thea-
tre." Negro History Bulletin 23 (May 1960): 173
Fisher, Rudolph. "The Caucasian Storms Harlem."

American Mercury 11 (August 1927): 397
Johnson. Black Manhattan. pp. 95, 98, 101-2,
108-9
Mitchell. Black Drama. pp. 41, 46, 47, 84
CRITICISMS OF INDIVIDUAL PLAYS:
Black Patti's Troubadours
Johnson. Black Manhattan. pp. 101-102
Red Moon
Isaacs, Edith J. R. "The Middle Distance:
1800-1917--Heyday of Comedy and Dance."
Theatre Arts 26 (August 1942): 527
Johnson. Black Manhattan. p. 109
Shoofly Regiment
Isaacs, Edith J. R. "The Middle Distance:
1800-1917--Heyday of Comedy and Dance."
Theatre Arts 26 (August 1942): 527
A Trip to Coontown
Abramson. Negro Playwrights in the American
Theatre 1925-1959. p. 19
Cotton, Lettie Jo. "The Negro in The American
Theatre." Negro History Bulletin 23 (May
1960): 173
Isaacs, Edith J. R. "The Middle Distance:
1890-1917--Heyday of Comedy and Dance."
Theatre Arts 26 (August 1942): 527
Johnson. Black Manhattan. p. 102

COLEMAN, RAFT
PLAYS:
The Girl from Back Home, one act
Paradox, one act
PLAYS PUBLISHED IN PERIODICALS:
The Girl from Back Home, in Saturday Evening
Quill, April 1929
Paradox, in Saturday Evening Quill, April 1930

COLEMAN, WANDA
PLAYS:
Black Girl in Search of God
The Girl
[With Lee Williams and Frank Joseph] The Product
TELEVISION SCRIPT:
For "Name of The Game" show, 1970

COLES, EROSTINE
PLAYS:
Festus de Fus', one act

Mimi La Croix, one act, 1934

COLLIE, KELSEY
PLAY:
Randy Dandy's Circus

COLLIER, SIMONE
PLAYS:
In a City
Straw/Baby with Hay Feet

CONWAY, MEL
PLAY:
Best One of 'Em All, 1975

COOK, WILL MARION (1869-1944)
MUSICALS:
[With George Walker] Abyssinia, 1906
[With George Walker] Bandanna Land, 1907
[With Bob Cole and John Isham] Black Patti's
Troubadours
[With Paul Laurence Dunbar] Clorindy--The Origin
of the Cake-Walk, 1898
[With George Walker] In Dahomey, 1902
[With Paul Laurence Dunbar] Jes Lak White Folk:
A Musical Playlet, 1899
[With J. A. Shipp] The Policy Players, 1900
CRITICISMS BY COOK:
"Clorindy, the Origin of the Cake-Walk." Theatre
Arts 31 (September 1947): 61-65. Also in Patter-
son, Anthology of the American Negro in the
Theatre
"Why Has the Aframerican Produced No Creative
Musical Geniuses?" The Messenger 9 (November
1927): 319, 388
CRITICISMS OF INDIVIDUAL MUSICALS:
Abyssinia
Mitchell. Black Drama. pp. 50, 61
Bandanna Land
Johnson. Black Manhattan. p. 107
Mitchell. Black Drama. pp. 51-52
Clorindy--The Origin of the Cake-Walk
Isaacs, Edith. "The Negro in the American Thea-
tre: The Foreground, 1917-1942." Theatre
Arts 26 (August 1942): 517
Johnson. Black Manhattan. pp. 102-103
Mitchell. Black Drama. pp. 47-48

In Dahomey
   Johnson. Black Manhattan. p. 106
   Mitchell. Black Drama. p. 49
Jes Lak White Folk
   Johnson. Black Manhattan. p. 103

COOKSEY, CURTIS
  PLAY:
    Starlight, 1942

COOPER, TED
  PLAY:
    Good Night, Mary Beck

COTTER, JOSEPH SEAMAN (February 2, 1861-1949)
  PLAYS:
    Caleb, The Degenerate. Louisville, Ky.: The
      Bradley and Gilbert Co., 1903; reprint, New
      York: H. Harrison, 1940; New York: AMS
      Press
    Caesar Driftwood and Other One-Act Plays
    On the Fields
  PLAYS PUBLISHED IN ANTHOLOGIES:
    Caleb, The Degenerate, in Hatch and Shine, Black
      Theater USA
  PLAYS PUBLISHED IN PERIODICALS:
    On the Fields of France, in Crisis 20 (June 1920):
      77; Saturday Evening Quill, June 1913
  CRITICISMS BY COTTER:
    "Preface." Caleb, The Degenerate. Louisville,
      Ky.: The Bradley and Gilbert Co., 1903, p. 4
  CRITICISMS OF COTTER:
    Hicklin. The American Negro Playwright 1920-1964.
      Part 1, p. 61
    "Joseph S. Cotter, Sr." Crisis 19 (1920): 126
    Molette, Charlton W., III. "First Afro-American
      Theatre." Negro Digest 19 (April 1970): 4-9
  CRITICISMS OF INDIVIDUAL PLAYS:
    Caleb, The Degenerate
      Abramson. Negro Playwrights in the American
        Theatre. pp. 14-21
      Bradley, Gerald. "Goodbye Mr. Bones." Drama
        Critique 7 (Spring 1964): 81, 84
      Hatch and Shine. Black Theater USA. pp. 61-63
      Hicklin. The American Negro Playwright 1920-
        1964. Part 1, pp. 59-60
      Mitchell. Black Drama. p. 39

COTTON, WALTER
PLAY:
Monday Morning of Homing Brown

COX, JOSEPH MASON ANDREW
PLAY:
Ode to Dr. Martin Luther King, three acts

CREAMER, HENRY S.
MUSICAL:
[With J. Turner Layton] Strut Miss Lizzie, 1922

CULLEN, COUNTEE (May 30, 1903-January 9, 1946)
PLAYS:
Byword for Evil (Medea). Yale University Library
Medea. N.Y.: Harper, 1935
One Way to Heaven. Yale University Library, 1936
[With Owen Dodson] The Third Fourth of July (Com-
missioned by the Drama Division of the New
School for Social Research)
MUSICALS:
[With Arna Bontemps] St. Louis Woman, 1946
PLAYS PUBLISHED IN PERIODICALS:
The Third Fourth of July, in Theatre Magazine 30
(1946): 488-493
MUSICALS PUBLISHED IN ANTHOLOGIES:
St. Louis Woman, in Anthology of the American
Negro in the Theatre. Lindsay Patterson, ed.
Washington, D.C.: Associated, 1967. (Text
only)
CRITICISMS BY CULLEN:
"Review of Earth." Opportunity 5 (April 1927): 118-
119
CRITICISMS OF CULLEN:
Archer. Black Images, pp. 84, 86
Daniel, Walter C. "Countee Cullen as Literary
Critic." CLA Journal 14 (March 1971): 281-290
Dodson, Owen. "Countee Cullen." Phylon 7 (First
Quarter): 19-21
Gayle. Black Expression. pp. 59, 76-79; passim
Kaufman and Henstell. American Film Criticism.
p. 223
McPherson, et al. Blacks in America. pp. 242-
247
Mitchell. Black Drama. pp. 1, 128-129
Smallwood, Will. "A Tribute to Countee Cullen."
Opportunity 24 (Summer 1947): 168-169

Van Vechten, Carl. "How the Theatre Is Repre-
sented in the Negro Collection at Yale." The
Theatre Annual (1943): 34
CRITICISMS OF INDIVIDUAL PLAYS:
Byword for Evil
    Hicklin. The American Negro Playwright 1920-
    1964. Part 1, pp. 231-232
CRITICISMS OF INDIVIDUAL MUSICALS:
St. Louis Woman
    Archer. Black Images. pp. 84-86
    Hicklin. The American Negro Playwright, 1920-
    1964. Part 1, pp. 240, 241-244, 290
    "Lena Horne and 'Saint Louis Woman'." The
    Pittsburgh Courier, 16 June 1945, p. 15
    Mitchell. Black Drama. pp. 128-129
REVIEWS OF INDIVIDUAL PLAYS:
One Way to Heaven
    New York Times, 29 September 1936, 35: 1
REVIEWS OF INDIVIDUAL MUSICALS:
St. Louis Woman
    "Forty-Five, Forty-Six Season Reviewed." New
    York Times, 2 June 1946, II, 1: 2
    Gilder, Rosamond. "Broadway Bottleneck: The
    Season in Review." Theatre Arts 30 (June
    1946): 320-323
    Jefferson, Miles M. "The Negro on Broadway,
    1945-1946." Phylon 7 (Second Quarter 1946):
    140
    _____. "The Negro on Broadway, 1946-1947."
    Phylon 8 (Second Quarter): 148
    McDermott, William F. F. "Do You Remember
    the Cake-Walk?" Cleveland Plain Dealer, 24
    November 1933, 10: 1
    Mantle. The Best Plays of 1945-1946, p. 436
    Nichols, Lewis. "The Play." [St. Louis Woman]
    New York Times, 1 April 1946, 22: 2
    Zolotov, Sam. "'St. Louis Woman' to Close
    Saturday Night." New York Times, 1 April
    1946, 22: 2

CUMMINS, CECIL
    PLAY:
    Young Blood, Young Breed, 1969

CUNEY-HARE, MAUD (1874-1936)
    PLAYS:
    Antar of Araby

PLAYS PUBLISHED IN ANTHOLOGIES:
Antar of Araby, in Richardson, Plays and Pageants
from the Life of the Negro
CRITICISMS BY CUNEY-HARE:
"Musical Comedy." Negro Musicians and Their
Music. Washington, D.C.: Associated Publish-
ers, 1936. Also in Patterson, Anthology of the
American Negro in the Theatre, pp. 36-49
CRITICISMS OF INDIVIDUAL PLAYS:
Antar of Araby
Hicklin. The American Negro Playwright 1920-
1964. Part I, pp. 138-139.

DAFORA, ASADATA
PLAY:
Kykunkor, 1934

DANIEL, GLORIA
PLAY:
The Male Bag

DAVIDSON, NORBERT R., JR. (b. 1940)
PLAYS:
El Haji Malik, 1968
Falling Scarlet, 1971
The Further Emasculation of ..., 1970
Jammer, 1970
Short Fun, 1970
Window, 1970
PLAYS PUBLISHED IN ANTHOLOGIES:
El Haji Malik, in Bullins, New Plays from the Black
Theatre
CRITICISMS OF INDIVIDUAL WORKS:
El Haji Malik
Killinger. The Fragile Presence: Transcendence
in Modern Literature. p. 128
REVIEWS OF INDIVIDUAL WORKS:
El Haji Malik
New Yorker 4 December 1971, p. 2

DAVIDSON, WILLIAM P.
PLAY:
Learn, Baby Learn, 1969

DAVIS, A. I.
PLAYS:
Better Make Do, 1971

Cirema The Beautiful
The Cock Crows, 1971
Man, I Really Am, 1969
A Man Talking, 1971
RADIO SCRIPT:
  P.B.A. for WHA/Earplay. University of Wisconsin,
    Madison
AWARD:
  1972 Grant, New York Council on the Arts

DAVIS, AL
  PLAY:
    Black Sunlight
  REVIEWS OF INDIVIDUAL PLAYS:
    Black Sunlight
      New Yorker 25 March 1974, p. 4

DAVIS, JERI TURNER
  PLAY:
    A Cat Called Jesus, one act

DAVIS, MILBURN
  PLAYS:
    Nightmare
    The 100,000 Nigger, 1969
    Sometimes a Switchblade Helps, 1969

DAVIS, NOLAN (b. July 23, 1942)
  TELEVISION:
    Senior writer and producer, KNXT-TV (CBS), 1970
    Writer and producer of The Stellar Story, Stellar
      Industries Corp., 1970
    Story writer, Grave Undertaking, for Tandom Pro-
      ductions (Sanford and Son, NBC), 1970

DAVIS, OSSIE (December 18, 1917)
  PLAYS:
    Alexis Is Fallen, 1974
    Alice in Wonder, one act, 1953
    The Big Deal, 1953; an expansion of Alice in Wonder
    Clay's Rebellion, 1951
    Curtain Call Mr. Aldrich Sir, one act, 1963
    The Mayor of Harlem, 1949
    Point Blank, 1949
    Purlie Victorious: A Comedy in Three Acts. New
      York: French, 1961
    What Can You Say to Mississippi?, one act, 1955

PLAYS PUBLISHED IN ANTHOLOGIES:
    Curtain Call Mr. Aldrich Sir, in Reardon and Paw-
       ley, The Black Teacher and the Dramatic Arts
    Purlie Victorious: A Comedy in Three Acts, in
       Adams, Conn and Slepian, Afro-American Litera-
       ture: Drama; Brasmer and Consolo, Black
       Drama; Childress, Black Scenes (excerpts);
       Davis and Redding, Cavalcade; Faderman and
       Bradshaw, Speaking for Ourselves; Oliver and
       Sills, Contemporary Black Drama; Patterson,
       Black Theatre; Turner, Black Drama in America:
       An Anthology
MUSICALS:
    Purlie, a musical based on the play, Purlie Vic-
       torious, with lyrics by Peter Udell, music by
       Gary Geld; book by Davis, Rose and Udell. New
       York: Samuel French, 1971
FILM SCRIPTS:
    An Adaptation of Malcolm X's Autobiography
    Cotton Comes to Harlem, 1969
    Countdown at Kusini
    Gone Are the Days (new title from the play, Purlie),
       1963
TELEVISION SCRIPTS:
    Schoolteacher, 1963
CRITICISMS BY DAVIS:
    Hurd, Laura. "Director Ossie Davis Talks About
       Black Girl." Black Creation 4 (Winter 1973): 38
    "Purlie Told Me." In Patterson. Anthology of the
       American Negro in the Theatre, pp. 165-168
    "Tell It Like It Is." Newsweek 64 (August 1964): 84
CRITICISMS OF DAVIS:
    Funk, Lewis. "The Curtain Rises: The Story of
       Ossie Davis." [Purlie Victorious] New York:
       Grosset and Dunlap, 1971
    Little. Off-Broadway. pp. 125-243
    "Playboy After Hours: Movies." Playboy 17 (Au-
       gust 1970): 30-31
    "Purlie Told Me." Freedomways 2 (Spring 1962):
       155-160
    Russell, Charles L. "The Wide World of Ossie
       Davis: Exclusive Interview." Liberator 3
       (December 1963): 11-12
    "The Task of the Negro Writer as Artist." Negro
       Digest 14 (April 1965): 54-83
CRITICISMS OF INDIVIDUAL PLAYS:
    Alice in Wonder (the Big Deal)

Gayle. Black Expression. pp. 156-157
Hicklin. The American Negro Playwright 1920-
1964. Part 2, pp. 404-405
Mitchell. Black Drama. pp. 155-156
Pollock, Arthur. "Theatre Time." The Daily
Compass, 29 September 1952
Big Deal
Hicklin. The American Negro Playwright 1920-
1964. Part 2, p. 405
Purlie Victorious
Atkinson. Broadway. pp. 500
Campbell, Dick. "Is There a Conspiracy Against
Black Playwrights?" Negro Digest 17 (April
1968): 15
Davis. "The Wonderful World of Law and Order."
In Hill, Anger and Beyond. pp. 154-180
Gaffney, Floyd. "Is Your Door Really Open?"
Drama and Theater 7 (Fall 1968): 5
Gayle. Black Expression. p. 158
Hatch, Robert. "Theatre." [Purlie Victorious]
Nation 194 (14 October 1961): 254-255
Hewes, Henry. "Tenth Play? On Selecting the
Ten Best." Saturday Review of Literature 45
(12 May 1962): 51
Hicklin. The American Negro Playwright 1920-
1964. Part 2, pp. 405-408
Lewis. American Plays and Playwrights of the
Contemporary Theatre. pp. 52
Lewis, Emory. Stages: The Fifty Year Child-
hood of the American Theater. p. 159
Luce, Phillip A. "Purlie Victorious." Main-
stream 15 (February 1962): 62
Mitchell. Black Drama. pp. 188-190
"Offstage: Actor's Revenge." Theatre Arts 45
(October 1961): 67
Turner, Darwin T. "Negro Playwrights and the
Urban Negro." CLA Journal 12 (September
1968): 24
Turpin, Waters E. "The Contemporary American
Negro Playwright." CLA Journal 9 (Septem-
ber 1965): 19-20
REVIEWS OF INDIVIDUAL PLAYS:
Alice in Wonder (The Big Deal)
New York Times, 7 March 1953, p. 13: 6
Purlie Victorious
Black, Susan. "Play Reviews." Theatre Arts
45 (December 1961): 12

Guernsey. The Best Plays of 1968-1969. p. 455
Leaks, Sylvester. "Purlie Emerges Victorious."
    Freedomways 1 (Fall 1961): 347
New York Theatre Critics' Reviews, (1961): 256
New York Times, 29 September 1961, 29: 1; 8
    October, II, p. 1: 1; 29 April 1962, II, p. 1:
    1; 22 March 1970, II, p. 3: 1
New Yorker 24 February 1962, p. 2
"Playboy After Hours: Theater." Playboy 17
    (July 1970): 34
REVIEWS OF INDIVIDUAL MUSICALS:
  Purlie
    America 106 (9 December 1961): 376
    Ebony 17 (March 1962): 55-56
    Nation 193 (14 October 1961): 254-255
    New Republic 145 (6 November 1961): 22
    New York Daily News, 16 March 1970
    New York Post, 16 March 1970
    New York Sunday Times, 22 March 1970
    New York Theatre Critics' Reviews (1961): 256
    New York Times, 24 September 1961, II: 1; 29
        September 1961: 29; 8 October 1961: 1; 16
        March 1970: 53: 1
    New Yorker 37 (7 October 1961): 130; 46 (14
        November 1970): 4; 48 (23 December 1972): 2
    Reporter 25 (26 October 1961): 52
    Riley, Clayton. "Theatre Review: Purlie."
        Liberator 10 (April 1970): 21
    Saturday Review 44 (14 October 1961): 78
    Theatre Arts 45 (December 1961): 12
    Time 78 (6 October 1961): 88
    Wall Street Journal, 19 March 1970
    Women's Wear Daily, 16 March 1970

DE ANDA, PETER
  PLAYS:
    Ladies in Waiting
  PLAYS PUBLISHED IN ANTHOLOGIES:
    Ladies in Waiting, in King and Milner, Black Drama
        Anthology
  REVIEWS OF INDIVIDUAL WORKS:
    Ladies in Waiting
        Gussow, M. "Ladies in Waiting." New York
            Times, 16 October 1973, p. 53: 1
        Riley, Clayton. "Ladies in Waiting." Liberator
            8 (August 1968): 21

DE COY, ROBERT H. (b. Oct. 11, 1920)
PLAYS:
  The Castration, 1970
FILM SCRIPTS:
  The Black Prodigal and The Priest, 1971

De RAMUS, BETTY
PLAY:
  That's Just What I Said, 1971

DE WINDT, HAL
PLAY:
  Us Versus Nobody, 1972

DEAN, PHILIP HAYES
PLAYS:
  Every Night When the Sun Goes Down, 1969
  Freeman, 1971. Complete Catalogue of Plays
    1973-74. New York: Dramatists Play Service,
    Inc., 1973
  The Owl Killer
  Sty of The Blind Pig and An American Night Cry:
    A Trilogy. New York: Bobbs, 1972 (An Ameri-
    can Night Cry includes The Minstrel Boy and The
    Thunder in the Index); cited by Time, 1971 as one
    of the best 10 plays. Has been performed in
    Europe
  This Bird of Dawning Singeth All Night Long. New
    York: Dramatists, 1971; also part of a trilogy
    entitled American Night Cry; Complete Catalogue
    of Plays 1973-74. New York: Dramatists Play
    Service, Inc., 1973
PLAYS PUBLISHED IN ANTHOLOGIES:
  The Owl Killer, in King and Milner, Black Drama
    Anthology; Richards, Best Short Plays of 1974
  Sty in the Blind Pig, in Harrison, Kuntu Drama
TELEVISION SCRIPTS:
  Johnny Ghost, 1969
CRITICISMS OF DEAN:
  Reische. The Performing Arts in America. pp.
    69, 72
REVIEWS OF INDIVIDUAL WORKS:
  Freeman
    Cue, 24 February 1973, p. 19
  Sty of The Blind Pig
    Barnes, C. New York Times, 24 November
    1971, 21: 1

Gant, Liz. "Sty of The Blind Pig." Black
World 21 (April 1972): 81-82
Kalem, T. E. Time 6 December 1971
Kerr, W. New York Times, 5 December 1971,
II, 3: 4
Kroll, Jack. Newsweek 6 December 1971
New York Theatre Critics' Reviews (1971): 157
New Yorker 1 January 1972, p. 2
Rudin, Seymour. "Performing Arts: 1971-1972."
Massachusetts Review 14 (Winter 1973): 215
This Bird of Dawning Singeth All Night Long
New York Times, 31 December 1968, 19: 1; 12
January 1969, II, 1: 1

DEDEAUX, RICHARD A. (b. Sept. 24, 1940)
PLAYS:
And Baby Makes Three
The Decision
[With Otis Smith and Kiiln Hamilton] The Rising
Sons--Wisdom and Knowledge. Los Angeles: The
Watts Prophets, 1973
FILMSCRIPTS:
The Rip Off
TELEVISION SCRIPTS:
A Duel With Destiny
[With the Watts Prophets] Victory Will Be My
Moon, documentary
AWARDS:
Emmy Award nomination for television documentary,
Victory Will Be My Moon

DELANY, CLARISSA SCOTT (1901-1927)
PLAY:
Dixie to Broadway, 1924

DENT, THOMAS C. (Kush)
PLAYS:
Feathers and Stuff, 1970
Inner Black Blues: A Poem/Play for Black Bros.
and Sisters
Negro Study #34A, one act, 1969
Riot Duty, one act, 1969
Ritual Murder, one act, 1967
Snapshot, one act, 1969
[With Val Ferdinand] Song of Survival, one act,
1969
PLAYS PUBLISHED IN PERIODICALS:

Inner Black Blues, in Nkombo 8 (August 1972): 28-
43
EDITOR:
[With Richard Schechner and Gilbert Moses] The
Free Southern Theatre by the Free Southern Thea-
tre. Indianapolis: Bobbs-Merrill, 1969
CRITICISMS BY DENT:
"Beyond Rhetoric Toward a Black Southern Theatre."
Black World 2 (April 1971): 14-24
"The Free Southern Theatre, an Evaluation."
Freedomways 6 (Winter 1966): 26; reprinted in
Patterson, Anthology of the American Negro in
the Theatre
"The Free Southern Theatre." Negro Digest 14
(April 1967): 40
"Report on Black Theatre." Negro Digest 18 (April
1969): 24-26

DICKERSON, GLENDA
PLAYS:
Jesus Christ--Lawd Today, 1971
The Torture of Mothers, 1973

DIXON, MELVIN
PLAYS:
Confrontation, 1969
Kingdom, or The Last Promise, 1972
Ritual: For Malcolm, 1970

DODSON, OWEN (b. November 28, 1914)
PLAYS:
Americus, manuscript
Amistad, 1931. Commissioned by and performed
at Talledaga College in 1939
The Ballad of Dorie Miller, 1942
Bayou Legend, 1946
Black Mother Praying
Boomsdale Tale, 1941
The Christmas Miracle, one act, 1955, a libretto
Climbing to the Soul
Divine Comedy, 1938. New York: Harper and
Row (forthcoming)
Don't Give up the Ship
Everybody Join Hands
Freedom the Banner, 1942
Gargoyles in Florida, one act, 1936
Heroes on Parade, No. 3: Climb to the Soul

Including Laughter, 1936
Jonathan's Song
Lord Nelson, Naval Hero
Media in Africa, 1964
New World A-Coming, A pageant in seven scenes
performed at Madison Square Garden during World
War II to help the Blacks gain equality in the
Armed Forces.
Old Ironsides
Someday We're Gonna Tear Them Pillars Down
The Southern Star, 1941
[With Countee Cullen] The Third Fourth of July.
(Commissioned by the Drama Division of the New
School for Social Research)
Tropical Table
PLAYS PUBLISHED IN ANTHOLOGIES:
Bayou Legend, in Turner, Black Drama in America
Divine Comedy, in Brown, Davis and Lee, Negro
Caravan (excerpt); Hatch and Shine, Black Theater
USA
PLAYS PUBLISHED IN PERIODICALS:
Dorie Miller, in Theatre Arts 28 (1942)
Everybody Join Hands, in Theatre Arts 28 (1942)
Someday We're Gonna Tear Them Pillars Down, in
Negro Quarterly 1 (Summer 1942): 161-166
The Third Fourth of July, in Theatre Arts 30 (Au-
gust 1946): 488-490
MUSICALS:
[With Mark Fay] Till Victory Is Won, opera, 1967
With This Darkness, 1939 (Music by Shirley Graham).
This title was changed to Garden of Time, 1945
CRITICISMS BY DODSON:
"Countee Cullen (1903-1946)." Phylon 7 (First
Quarter 1946): 19-21; also in Hatch and Shine.
Black Theater USA
"World Seemed Wide and Open." Theatre Arts, 34
(March 1950): 55
CRITICISMS OF DODSON:
Abramson. Negro Playwrights in the American
Theatre 1925-1959. p. 92
Archer. Black Images. p. 17
Bigsby. The Black American Writer. vol. 2, p. 136
Gayle. Black Expression. pp. 85, 94, 110
Greene, Marjorie. "Young Man of the Theatre and
His Left Hand." Opportunity 24 (Fall 1946): 200
Mitchell. Black Drama. pp. 8-9, 105, 113, 114,
123

Peck, Seymour. "Owen Dodson, New Writer." PM
(March 7, 1945)

Van Vechten, Carl. "How the Theater Is Represented in the Negro Collection at Yale." The
Theatre Annual (1943): 33-34

CRITICISMS OF INDIVIDUAL PLAYS:

The Amistad
   Hicklin. The American Negro Playwright 1920-
   1964. Part 1, p. 279

The Ballad of Dorie Miller
   Hicklin. The American Negro Playwright 1920-
   1964. Part 2, pp. 327-328

Bayou Legend
   "Negro Playwrights: Young Chicagoan Is First
   with All Negro Play on Broadway." Ebony 14
   (April 1959): 100

A Christmas Miracle
   Hume, Paul. "New Opera, A Christmas Miracle,
   Has Premiere." Washington Post and Times
   Herald, 7 March 1958

Divine Comedy
   Hicklin. The American Negro Playwright 1920-
   1964. Part 1, pp. 280-282

Everybody Join Hands
   Hicklin. The American Negro Playwright 1920-
   1964. Part 2, p. 326

Freedom the Banner
   Hicklin. The American Negro Playwright 1920-
   1964. Part 2, p. 327

New World A-Coming
   Hicklin. The American Negro Playwright 1920-
   1964. Part 2, p. 328

Someday We're Gonna Tear Them Pillars Down
   Hicklin. The American Negro Playwright 1920-
   1964. Part 2, p. 325

CRITICISMS OF INDIVIDUAL MUSICALS:

With This Darkness
   Hicklin. The American Negro Playwright 1920-
   1964. Part 1, pp. 277-279

REVIEWS OF INDIVIDUAL MUSICALS:

The Garden of Time
   New York Times, 10 March 1945, 13: 7

AWARDS:

Gargoyles in Florida won first prize, contest, 1941--
   Department of Drama of the School of Education at
   Tuskegee Institute, Alabama; Rosenwald and Gen-
   eral Education Board Fellowship; Guggenheim Fel-

lowship, 1953; Rockefeller Grant, 1968

DOLAN, HARRY
    PLAYS:
        The Iron Hand of Nat Turner, 1970
        Losers Weepers, one act
    PLAYS PUBLISHED IN ANTHOLOGIES:
        Losers Weepers, in Schulberg, From the Ashes
    TELEVISION SCRIPTS:
        Losers Weepers, 1966 (NBC television production
           under the title, "Love Song for a Delinquent")
    CRITICISMS BY DOLAN:
        "On Black Theater in America: A Report." Negro
           Digest 19 (April 1970): 31-34
    CRITICISMS OF DOLAN:
        Wilkerson, Margaret. "Black Theater in California."
           Drama Review (December 1972): 35-38

DONOGHUE, DENNIS
    PLAYS:
        The Black Messiah, 1939
        Legal Murder
    CRITICISMS OF INDIVIDUAL PLAYS:
        Legal Murder
           Bond. The Negro and the Drama. pp. 113-114

DOUGLAS, RODNEY K.
    PLAYS:
        The Marijuana Trap
        The Voice of the Ghetto, 1968

DOUGLASS, FREDERICK (February 1817-1895)
    PLAYS:
        My Bondage and My Freedom
    CRITICISMS OF INDIVIDUAL PLAYS:
        Rowell, Charles H. "Sterling A. Brown and the
           Afro-American Folk Tradition." Studies in the
           Literary Imagination 7 (Fall 1974): 143

DOWNING, HENRY FRANCES (b. 1851)
    PLAYS:
        The Arabian Lovers; or, The Sacred Jar, an Eastern
           Tale in Four Acts. London: F. Griffiths, 1913
        Human Nature; or, The Traduced Wife, an original
           English domestic drama in four acts. London;
           F. Griffiths, 1913
        Incentives: A Drama in Four Acts, 1914, 98 pp.

Lord Eldred's Other Daughter. London: F. Griffiths, 1913
A New Coon in Town, a farcical comedy made in England, 1914, 80 pp.
Placing Paul's Play. London. F. Griffiths, 1913
The Shuttlecock; or, Israel in Russia. London: F. Griffiths, 1913
Voodoo. London: F. Griffiths, 1914

DRAYTON, RONALD
 PLAYS:
  Black Chaos, 1966
  The Conquest of Africa, 1968
  Nocturne on the Rhine
  Notes from a Savage God
 PLAYS PUBLISHED IN ANTHOLOGIES:
  Nocturne on the Rhine, in Jones and Neal. Black Fire
  Notes from a Savage God, in Jones and Neal. Black Fire

DREER, HERMAN (b. September 12, 1889)
 PLAY:
  The Man of God, one act
 PLAYS PUBLISHED IN PERIODICALS:
  The Man of God, in Oracle Magazine (September 1936)
 BOOKS:
  Literature by Negro Authors: An Anthology. N.Y.: Macmillan, 1950

DU BOIS, SHIRLEY GRAHAM (Shirley Lola Graham) (b. Nov. 11, 1907)
 PLAYS:
  Coal Dust
  Dust to Earth. Princeton: Yale Drama School, 1941
  Elijah's Ravens, 1941
  I Gotta Home, 1942
  It's Morning
  Track Thirteen. Boston: Expression Co., 1941
 MUSICAL:
  Tom-Tom. Cleveland: n.p., 1932
 CRITICISMS BY DU BOIS:
  "Towards an American Theatre." The Arts Quarterly 1 (October-December 1937): 18-20
 CRITICISMS OF DU BOIS:

Chrisman, Robert. "The Black Scholar Hosts
Shirley Graham Du Bois." Black Scholar 2 (De-
cember 1970): 50-52
"Conversation: Ida Lewis and Shirley Graham Du
Bois." Essence 1 (January 1971): 22-27
CRITICISMS OF INDIVIDUAL MUSICALS:
Tom-Tom
Hicklin. The American Negro Playwright 1920-
1964. Part 2, pp. 314-315
AWARDS:
Julius Rosenwald Fellowship for Playwriting, 1938

DU BOIS, WILLIAM EDWARD BURGHARDT (February 23,
1868-August 27, 1963)
PLAYS:
The Christ of the Andes
George Washington and Black Folk: A Pageant for
the Centenary, 1732-1932
Haiti
The Star of Ethiopia, 1911; a four-page leaflet is-
sued in November 1915, and again in 1925 in
program form: The Star of Ethiopia: A Pageant.
Hollywood Bowl, 15 and 18 June 1925
PLAYS PUBLISHED IN PERIODICALS:
The Christ of the Andes, in Horizon 4 (November-
December 1908): 1-14. (two scenes)
George Washington and Black Folk, in Crisis 39
(1932): 121-124
CRITICISMS BY DU BOIS:
"Can the Negro Serve the Drama?" Theatre Maga-
zine 38 (July 1923): 12, 68
"The Colored Audience." The Crisis 12 (September
1916): 217
"The Criteria of Negro Art." Crisis 32 (October
1926): 290
"Drama Among Black Folk." Crisis 12 (August
1916): 169-173
"The Ethiopia Art Theatre." Crisis 26 (July 1923):
103-104
"The Krikwa Little Theatre." Crisis 32 (July 1926):
134
"The Negro Theatre." Crisis 15 (February 1918): 165
[With Walter White] "Paul Robeson: Right or
Wrong." Negro Digest 8 (March 1950): 8-18
CRITICISMS OF DU BOIS:
Abramson. Negro Playwrights in the American
Theatre 1925-1959. pp. 20, 26, 70

Archer. Black Images. pp. 15, 117-118, 120, 132
Mitchell. Black Drama. pp. 13, 88
CRITICISMS OF INDIVIDUAL PLAYS:
   Haiti
      Atkinson. Broadway. p. 308
      Bond. The Negro and The Drama. pp. 171-72
      Isaacs, Edith J. R. "The Negro in the American
         Theatre: The Foreground, 1917-1942." Thea-
         tre Arts 26 (August 1942): 519
      Mitchell. Black Drama. pp. 102-3
      Rabkin. Drama and Commitment. pp. 111-112
      Smith. Stage Left. pp. 230, 235
   Star of Ethiopia
      Archer. Black Images. pp. 108-112
REVIEWS OF INDIVIDUAL PLAYS:
   Haiti
      Isaacs, Edith. "Revival and Survival: Broadway
        in Review." Theatre Arts Monthly 22 (May
        1938): 333

DUDLEY, S. H.
   PLAYS:
      [With Henry Troy] Dr. Beans from Boston, 1911
      The Smart Set, 1896

DUKE, BILL
   PLAY:
      An Adaptation: Dream, 1972

DUMAS, AARON
   PLAY:
      Poor Willie, 1970

DUNBAR, PAUL LAURENCE (June 27, 1872-February 9,
   1906)
   PLAYS:
      Herrick, 1902 (?)
      The Quibbler's Wife, fragment
      The Stolen Calf, 1901 (?)
      Winter Roses, undiscovered manuscript
   MUSICALS:
      [With Will Marion Cook] Clorindy, or The Origin
        of the Cakewalk, 1898
      Dream Lovers, an operatic romance, 1898
      [With Alex Rogers and J. A. Shipp] In Dahomey,
        1902
      [With Will Marion Cook] Jes Lak White Folk, 1900

On the Island of Tanawana
Uncle Eph's Christmas, one-act vaudeville sketch,
  1900
CRITICISMS OF DUNBAR:
  Brawley, The Negro Genius. pp. 176-177
  Pawley, Thomas. "Dunbar as Playwright." Black
    World 26 (April 1975): 70-88
  Turner, Darwin T. "Paul Laurence Dunbar: The
    Rejected Symbol." Journal of Negro History 52
    (January 1967): 1-14
CRITICISMS OF INDIVIDUAL PLAYS:
  Clorindy, or The Origin of the Cakewalk
    Bigsby. The Black American Writer. Vol. II,
      p. 133
    Brawley. The Negro Genius. p. 177
    Gayle. The Black Aesthetic. pp. 297-298
      _____. Black Expression. p. 151
    Johnson. Black Manhattan. pp. 102-103
    Mitchell. Black Drama. pp. 47-48
  Dream Lovers
    Pawley, Thomas. "Dunbar as Playwright."
      Black World 26 (April 1975): 79
  Herrick
    Pawley, Thomas. "Dunbar as Playwright."
      Black World 26 (April 1975): 74-77
  In Dahomey
    Mitchell. Black Drama. p. 49
  Jes Lak White Folk
    Johnson. Black Manhattan. p. 103
  On the Island of Tanawana
    Pawley, Thomas. "Dunbar as Playwright."
      Black World 26 (April 1975): 71-73
  The Quibbler's Wife
    Pawley, Thomas. "Dunbar as Playwright."
      Black World 26 (April 1975): 73
  The Stolen Calf
    Pawley, Thomas. "Dunbar as Playwright."
      Black World 26 (April 1975): 71
  Uncle Eph's Christmas
    Pawley, Thomas. "Dunbar as Playwright."
      Black World 26 (April 1975): 77
  Winter Roses
    Pawley, Thomas. "Dunbar as Playwright."
      Black World 26 (April 1975): 77

DUNBAR-NELSON, ALICE MOORE (July 19, 1875-1935)
  PLAY:

Mine Eyes Have Seen, one act
PLAYS PUBLISHED IN ANTHOLOGIES:
Mine Eyes Have Seen, in Hatch and Shine. Black
Theater USA
PLAYS PUBLISHED IN PERIODICALS:
Mine Eyes Have Seen, in Crisis 15 (1918): 271

DUNCAN, THELMA
PLAYS:
Black Magic
Sacrifice
PLAYS PUBLISHED IN ANTHOLOGIES:
Black Magic, in Yearbook of Short Plays, 1st Series.
Evanston, Ill.: Row Peterson and Co., 1931
Sacrifice, in Richardson, Plays and Pageants
MUSICALS:
The Death Dance, musical score by Victor Kerney,
one act, 1923
MUSICALS PUBLISHED IN ANTHOLOGIES:
The Death Dance, in Locke and Gregory, Plays of
Negro Life
CRITICISMS OF INDIVIDUAL PLAYS:
Sacrifice
Hicklin. The American Negro Playwright 1920-
1964. Part I, p. 138
CRITICISMS OF INDIVIDUAL MUSICALS:
The Death Dance
Hicklin. The American Negro Playwright 1920-
1964. Part I, pp. 136-138

DUNSTER, MARK
PLAY:
Sojourner

DURRAH, JIM
PLAY:
The Ho-Hum Revolution

EASTON, SIDNEY
PLAY:
Miss Trudie Fair, 1953
FILM SCRIPTS:
Go Back Where You Stayed Last Night
Lifeboat
CRITICISMS OF EASTON:
Mitchell. Black Drama. pp. 44-45, 46, 93

CRITICISMS OF INDIVIDUAL PLAYS:
Miss Trudie Fair
  Mitchell. Black Drama. pp. 159-160
CRITICISMS OF INDIVIDUAL FILM SCRIPTS:
Go Back Where You Stayed Last Night
  Mitchell. Black Drama. p. 160
Lifeboat
  Mitchell. Black Drama. pp. 160-161

EASTON, WILLIAM E.
  PLAY:
    Christo-phe. Los Angeles: Grafton Publishing Co.,
    1911

ECHOLS, ANN J.
  PLAY:
    Black Hands Play Noisy Music

EDMONDS, HENRIETTE
  PLAY:
    Mushy Mouth

EDMONDS, RANDOLPH (b. 1900)
  PLAYS:
    Badman
    Bleeding Hearts
    The Breeders
    The Call of Jubah
    Christmas Gift, one act, 1923
    Denmark Vesey, one act, 1929
    The Devil's Price, 1930
    Doom, one act, 1924
    Drama Enters the Curriculum: A Purpose Play,
      one act, 1930
    Earth and Stars, 1946; revised 1961
    Everyman's Land
    For Fatherland, one act, 1934
    Gangsters over Harlem
    G.I. Rhapsody, 1943
    Hewers of the Wood
    The Highwayman, one act, 1934
    Illicit Love, 1927
    Job Hunting, one act, 1922
    The Land of Cotton, 1942
    The Man of God, 1931
    Meek Mose, one act
    A Merchant of Dixie, one act, 1923

Nat Turner
The New Window
Old Man Pete
One Side of Harlem, 1928
The Outer Room, one act, 1935
Peter Stith, one act, 1923
The Phantom Treasure
Prometheus and The Atom, 1955
Rocky Roads, 1926
Shades and Shadows
The Shadow Across the Path, one act, 1943
The Shape of Wars to Come, one act, 1943
Silas Brown
Simon in Cyrene, 1939
Sirlock Bones, one act, 1928
Takazee: A Pageant of Ethiopia, 1928
The Trial and Banishment of Uncle Tom, one act,
    1945
The Tribal Chief
The Virginia Politician, one act, 1927
Whatever the Battle Be: A Symphonic Drama, 1950
Wives and Blues, 1938
Yellow Death
PLAYS PUBLISHED IN ANTHOLOGIES:
Bad Man, in Brown, Davis and Lee, Negro Caravan;
    Edmonds, Six Plays for a Negro Theatre; Hatch
    and Shine, Black Theater USA
Bleeding Hearts, in Edmonds, Six Plays for a Negro
    Theatre
The Breeders, in Edmonds, Six Plays for a Negro
    Theatre
The Call of Jubah, in Edmonds, Shades and Shadows
The Devil's Price, in Edmonds, Shades and Shadows
Earth and Stars, in Turner, Black Drama in America
Everyman's Land, in Edmonds, Shades and Shadows
Gangsters Over Harlem, in Edmonds, The Land of
    Cotton and Other Plays
Hewers of The Wood, in Edmonds, Shades and
    Shadows
The High Court of Historia, in Edmonds, The Land
    of Cotton and Other Plays
The Land of Cotton, in Edmonds, The Land of Cotton
    and Other Plays
Meek Mose, in Shay, Fifty More Contemporary One-
    Act Plays
Nat Turner, in Edmonds, Six Plays for a Negro
    Theatre; Richardson and Miller, Negro History in

Thirteen Plays

The New Window, in Edmonds, Six Plays for a Negro
Theatre

Old Man Pete, in Edmonds, Six Plays for a Negro
Theatre

The Phantom Treasure, in Edmonds, Shades and
Shadows

Shades and Shadows, in Edmonds, Shades and Shadows

Silas Brown, in Edmonds, The Land of Cotton and
Other Plays

The Tribal Chief, in Edmonds, Shades and Shadows

Yellow Death, in Edmonds, The Land of Cotton and
Other Plays

MUSICAL:

Stock Exchange, 1927

CRITICISMS BY EDMONDS:

"Negro Drama in the South." The Carolina Play
Book (June 1940): 73-78

"Some Reflections on The American Negro in The
American Drama." Opportunity 8 (October 1930):
303-305

CRITICISMS OF EDMONDS:

Bond. The Negro's God. pp. 123-128, 136

Hicklin. The American Negro Playwright, 1920-
1964. Part 1, p. 266

Mitchell. Black Drama. p. 9

CRITICISMS OF INDIVIDUAL WORKS:

Bad Man

Bond. The Negro and the Drama. p. 125

Brawley. Negro Genius. p. 286

Hicklin. The American Negro Playwright 1920-
1964. Part 1, pp. 266-269

Kock, Frederick H. "The Negro Theatre Advancing." The Carolina Play-Book (December
1933): 102

Bleeding Hearts

Bond. The Negro and the Drama. p. 126

Hicklin. The American Negro Playwright 1920-
1964. Part 1, p. 271

The Breeders

Bond. The Negro and the Drama. p. 126

Brawley. Negro Genius. p. 284

Hicklin. The American Negro Playwright 1920-
1964. Part 1, pp. 270-271

Gangsters Over Harlem

Hicklin. The American Negro Playwright 1920-

1964. Part 2, p. 272
High Court of Historia
　Hicklin. The American Negro Playwright 1920-
　　1964. Part 1, p. 225
Nat Turner
　Bond. The Negro and the Drama. pp. 126, 128
　Hicklin. The American Negro Playwright 1920-
　　1964. Part 1, p. 270
The New Window
　Bond. The Negro and the Drama. p. 127
　Hicklin. The American Negro Playwright 1920-
　　1964. Part 1, pp. 271-272
Old Man Pete
　Bond. The Negro and the Drama. p. 125
　Hicklin. The American Negro Playwright 1920-
　　1964. Part 1, pp. 269-270
Yellow Death
　Hicklin. The American Negro Playwright 1920-
　　1964. Part 1, pp. 224-225
REVIEWS OF INDIVIDUAL WORKS:
　Meek Mose
　　New York Times, 7 February 1928, 30: 1
AWARDS:
　Honorable Mention, Crisis Contests, October 1926
　　for Illicit Love, and Peter Stith; June 1927 for
　　Bleeding Hearts

EDWARDS, H. T. V.
　PLAY:
　　Job Hunters, one act
　PLAYS PUBLISHED IN PERIODICALS:
　　Job Hunters, in Crisis 38 (December 1931): 417

EDWARDS, JUNIUS
　PLAY:
　　If We Must Die. N.Y.: Doubleday, 1963

EKULONA, ADEMOLA (Ronald Floyd)
　PLAYS:
　　Last Hot Summer
　　Mother of the House
　　Three Black Comedies

EL, LEATRICE
　PLAY:
　　Black Magic, Anyone?, 1972

ELDER, LONNE III
  PLAYS:
    Ceremonies in Dark Old Men. New York: Farrar,
      Straus, and Giroux, 1969; New York: Samuel
      French, n.d.
    Charades on East Fourth Street
    A Hysterical Turtle in a Rabbit Race, 1961
    Kissin' Rattlesnakes Can Be Fun, one act, 1966
    Seven Comes Up Seven Comes Down, one act, 1966
    The Terrible Veil, 1963
  PLAYS PUBLISHED IN ANTHOLOGIES:
    Ceremonies in Dark Old Men, in Patterson, Black
      Theatre; Hatlen, Drama: Principles and Plays
    Charades on East Fourth Street, in King and Milner,
      Black Drama
  FILM SCRIPT:
    Wrote the script for Sounder, 1971; Melinda, 1972
    Staff writer for N.Y.P.D., TV series, 1968; for
      McCloud series, 1970-1971
  TELEPLAY:
    Deadly Circle of Violence
  CRITICISMS OF ELDER:
    Bigsby. The Black Writer in America. vol. 2,
      pp. 219-226
    Gant, Liz. "An Interview with Lonne Elder III."
      Black World 22 (April 1973): 28-48
    Harrison. The Drama of Nommo. p. 27
    "Interview." New York Times, 8 February 1969,
      p. 22: 1
    Jeffers, Lance. "Bullins, Baraka and Elder: The
      Dawn of Grandeur in Black Drama." CLA Jour-
      nal 16 (September 1972): 32-48
    Little. Off-Broadway. p. 252
    Mitchell. Black Drama. pp. 215, 216
    Pawley, Dr. Thomas D. "The Black Theatre Audi-
      ence." Players 46 (August-September 1971): 257-
      259
    Rosenberg, Harold. "The Artist as Perceiver of
      Social Realities: The Post-Art Artist." Arts in
      Society 8 (Summer 1971): 509-510
  CRITICISMS OF INDIVIDUAL PLAYS:
    Ceremonies in Dark Old Men
      Duberman, Martin. "Theater 69: Black Thea-
        ter." Partisan Review 36 (1969): 488-489
      Eckstein, George. "The New Black Theater."
        Dissent 20 (Winter 1973): 112
      Killinger. The Fragile Presence: Transcendence

in Modern Literature. p. 127

Reardon, Tom R. "'Ceremonies in Dark Old Men': A Remarkable Achievement in Black Drama." in Drama Principles and Plays, 2nd ed. Theodore W. Hatlen, ed. University of California, Santa Barbara, 1975

Rudin, Seymour. "Theatre Chronicle: Winter-Spring 1969." The Massachusetts Review 10 (Summer 1969): 583-593

REVIEWS OF INDIVIDUAL PLAYS:

Ceremonies in Dark Old Men

Gussow, M. New York Times, 15 February 1971, p. 17: 1

New York Daily News, 6 February 1969

New York Post, 6 February 1969

New York Sunday Times, 23 February 1969

New York Theatre Critics' Reviews 30 (16 June 1969): 272-275

New York Times, 6 February 1969

New York Times, 27 May 1972, 18: 1

New Yorker 26 April 1969, p. 2

"Playboy After Hours: Theatre." Playboy 16 (July 1969): 37

Riley, Clayton. "Ceremonies in Dark Old Men." Liberator 9 (March 1969): 21

Walker, Barbara. "Theatre." Black Creation 3 (Summer 1972): 22

Wall Street Journal, 19 February 1969

Women's Wear Daily, 6 February 1969

AWARDS:

Ceremonies in Dark Old Men: Drama Desk Award, 1969

ELLINGTON, DUKE
PLAY:
Beggar's Holiday

EMERUWA, LEATRICE
PLAY:
Black Magic Anyone?, 1971
CRITICISMS BY EMERUWA:
"Reports on Black Theatre: Cleveland, Ohio." Black World 22 (April 1973): 19-26

ENGEL, LEHMAN
MUSICAL:
[With Joanna Roos] Golden Ladder

CRITICISMS OF INDIVIDUAL MUSICALS:
Golden Ladder
Tobin, Terrence. "Karamu Theater: Its Distinguished Past and Present Achievement."
Drama Critique 7 (Spring 1964): 86-91

ERROL, JOHN
PLAYS:
Moon on a Rainbow Shawl. London: Faber and Faber, 1958; New York: Grove, 1962; New York: Samuel French, n.d.
CRITICISMS OF INDIVIDUAL PLAYS:
Moon on a Rainbow Shawl
Hewes, Henry. "Tenth Play?: On Selecting the Ten Best." Saturday Review of Literature 45 (12 May 1962): 51

EVANS, DON
PLAYS:
Orrin, one act, 1973
Nothin But the Blues
Sugar Mom Don't Dance No More
PLAYS PUBLISHED IN PERIODICALS:
Sugar Mom Don't Dance No More, in Black World 22 (April 1973): 54-77
CRITICISMS BY EVANS:
"Bring It All Back Home: Black Playwrights of the Fifties." Black World 20 (February 1971): 41-45
"Segregated Drama in Integrated Schools." English Journal 60 (Fall 1971): 260-263
"The Theatre of Confrontation: Ed Bullins, Up Against the Wall." Black World 23 (April 1974): 14-18
AWARDS:
"Best Director" award, Rider College Drama Festivals, 1966 and 1968

EVERETT, RON
PLAYS:
The Babbler, 1970. Includes three one-act plays: The Babbler, A Cup of Time, Wash Your Back

EZILIE
PLAY:
Have You Seen Sunshine?

FABIO, SARAH WEBSTER (b. January 20, 1928)
    PLAY:
        M. L. King Pageant, 1967
    CRITICISMS BY FABIO:
        "Black Writers' Views on Literary Lions and Values."
           Negro Digest 17 (January 1968): 39

FAIR, RONALD L. (b. October 27, 1932)
    PLAY:
        Sails and Sinkers, 1969

FANN, AL
    PLAY:
        King Heroin, 1970

FANN, ERNIE
    PLAY:
        Colors, 1972

FELTON, HALEEMON SHAIK
    PLAYS:
        Backstage
        Drifting Souls
        House of Eternal Darkness
    CRITICISMS OF FELTON:
        Hicklin. The American Negro Playwright 1920-
           1964, Part 2, pp. 309-310

FERDINAND, VAL see Salaam, Kalamu Ya

FIELDS, LOUISA MAY
    PLAY:
        Twelve Years a Slave. Indianapolis: n.p., 1897.
           Also in the Rare Book Collection, Library of
           Congress

FIGGS, CARRIE LAW MORGAN
    PLAYS:
        Select Plays: Santa Claus Land, Jepthah's Daughter,
           The Prince of Peace, Bachelors' Convention.
           Chicago: By the Author, 1923

FISHER, JOHN (b. September 14, 1926)
    PLAY:
        Beyond the Closet

FISHER, RUDOLPH (May 9, 1897-1934)

PLAYS:
The Conjure Man Dies, 1936. In Schomburg Collection; mimeographed
CRITICISMS BY FISHER:
"The Caucasian Storms Harlem." American Mercury 11 (August 1927): 393-398
CRITICISMS OF INDIVIDUAL PLAYS:
The Conjure Man Dies
Abramson. Negro Playwrights in the American Theatre. pp. 59-63, 86-87
Bond. The Negro and the Drama. pp. 118-119
Hicklin. The American Negro Playwright 1920-1964. Part 1, p. 227
REVIEWS OF INDIVIDUAL PLAYS:
The Conjure Man Dies
Crisis 39 (1932): 293
Davis, Arthur P. Opportunity 10 (October 1932): 320

FLAGG, ANN
PLAY:
Great Gittin' Up Mornin', one act, New York: Samuel French, 1964. NYP.
CRITICISMS OF FLAGG:
Tabbot, William. "Every Negro in His Place." Drama Critique 7 (Spring 1964): 95
AWARDS:
1963--Annual National Collegiate Playwrighting Contest

FOLANI, FEMI
PLAY:
A Play for Zubena, 1972

FOSTER, ALEX
PLAY:
Community Kitchen

FRANKLIN, CLARENCE (b. 1932)
PLAY:
Copper Pig

FRANKLIN, J. E.
PLAYS:
Black Girl. Complete Catalogue of Plays--1973-1974. New York: Dramatists Play Service, Inc., 1973

Cut Out the Lights and Call the Law, 1972
First Step to Freedom, 1964
Four Women
The In-Crowd, 1967
Mau-Mau Room
[With Micki Grant] The Prodigal Sister
Two Flowers
FILM SCRIPTS:
Black Girl
CRITICISMS OF FRANKLIN:
"The Adventures of the Black Girl in Her Search
for God." Jet 36 (May 1969): 60-61
Beauford, Fred. "A Conversation with Black Girl's
J. E. Franklin." Black Creation 3 (Fall 1971):
38-40
Ebony 28 (April 1973): 108
"Interview." New York Times, 13 July 1971, 9: 1
CRITICISMS OF INDIVIDUAL FILM SCRIPTS:
Black Girl
Hurd, Laura. "Director Ossie Davis Talks about
Black Girl." Black Creation 4 (Winter 1973):
38
REVIEWS OF INDIVIDUAL PLAYS:
Black Girl
Barnes, C. New York Times, 17 June 1971, 49:
1
Kalen, T. E. Time 28 June 1971
Kerr, W. New York Times, 4 July 1971, II, 3:
3
Lester, E. New York Times, 11 July 1971, II,
5: 1
Murray, James P. Black Creation 4 (Winter
1973): 67
The National Observer 16 December 1972, p. 23
(review of movie)
New York Theatre Critics' Reviews (1971): 219
New Yorker 1 January 1972, p. 2
The Prodigal Sister
Christian Science Monitor 29 November 1974,
pp. 12-14
New York Times, 16 July 1974, 42: 1; 26 Novem-
ber 1974, 30: 1
New Yorker 2 December 1974, p. 2

FRAZIER, LEVI, JR.
PLAY:
A Tribute to Richard Wright, 1972

FREEMAN, CAROL S. (b. 1941)
> PLAY:
>   The Suicide
> PLAYS PUBLISHED IN ANTHOLOGIES:
>   The Suicide, in Jones and Neal, Black Fire

FREEMAN, H. LAWRENCE (b. October 9, 1875)
> OPERAS:
>   Athalia, 3 acts, December 1915
>   The Flapper, 4 acts, December 25, 1929
>   Kelschina, 1925
>   The Martyr, 2 acts, July 1893
>   Nada
>   Octoroon, 4 acts, 1904
>   Plantation, 1915
>   Prophecy, 1 act, May 1911
>   The Slave, 1925
>   Tryst, 1 act, 1909
>   Uzziaha
>   Valdo, 1 act, 1915
>   Vendetta, 3 acts, 1923
>   Voodoo, 3 acts, 1924
> CRITICISMS OF FREEMAN:
>   Brawley, Benjamin. "A Composer of Fourteen
>   Operas." Southern Workman 62 (September 1933):
>   311-315
> REVIEWS:
>   New York World, September 1928
> BROADCASTS: (REVIEWS)
>   WGBS, 20 May 1928
> AWARDS:
>   Harmon Award in Music, 1930

FULLER, CHARLES (b. March 5, 1939)
> PLAYS:
>   Ain't Nobody, Sarah, But Me, 1969
>   Cabin, 1969
>   Candidate!
>   In My Many Names and Days
>   In the Deepest Part of Sleep
>   Indian Givers, 1969
>   JJ'S Game, 1969
>   Love Song for Robert Lee, 1967
>   The Perfect Party, or The Village, a Party, 1969
>   The Rise
>   Three Plays: "Sunflower," "Untitled Play," and
>   "First Love," 1971

Two Plays: "The Layout" and "Emma," 1970
PLAYS PUBLISHED IN ANTHOLOGIES:
The Rise, in Bullins, New Plays from the Black
Theatre
TELEVISION SCRIPTS:
Black America, 1970-71, WKYW-TV 3 Philadelphia
Mitchell, 1968, WCAU-TV 12 Philadelphia
Roots, Resistance and Renaissance, 1967, WHYY-TV
10 Philadelphia
RADIO SCRIPTS:
The Black Experience, 1970-71, WIP Radio, Phila-
delphia
CRITICISMS OF INDIVIDUAL PLAYS:
The Perfect Party
Archer. Black Images. p. 188
Jet 36 (17 April 1969): 58
The Rise
Kaufman, Michael W. "The Delicate World of
Reprobation: A Note on the Black Revolution-
ary Theatre." Educational Theatre Journal
23 (December 1971): 446-460
REVIEWS OF INDIVIDUAL WORKS:
Candidate!
New Yorker 25 March 1974, p. 2
In My Many Names and Days
New Yorker 17 June 1972, p. 2
In the Deepest Part of Sleep
The Christian Science Monitor 26 June 1974, p. 6:
2
The Perfect Party
New York Times, 21 March 1969, 42: 1
The Village: A Party
New York Times, 13 November 1968, 39: 1
AWARDS:
Rockefeller Grant for Playwriting

FURMAN, ROGER
PLAYS:
Fool's Paradise, one act, 1952
The Gimmick, 1970
The Long Black Block, 1972
The Quiet Laughter, one act, 1952
To Kill a Devil
[With Doris Brunson] Three Shades of Harlem,
1964?
PLAYS PUBLISHED IN ANTHOLOGIES:
To Kill a Devil, in Childress, Black Scenes (excerpt)

CRITICISMS OF FURMAN:
Mitchell. Black Drama. pp. 154-155, 207-208, 221
REVIEWS OF INDIVIDUAL PLAYS:
The Long Black Block
Gussow, M. "Long Black Block." New York
Times, 17 November 1973, 28: 3

GABUGAH, O. O. (b. December 2, 1945)
PLAYS:
Go All the Way Down and Come Up Shakin'
Transistor Willie and Latrine Lil

GAINES, J. E.
PLAYS:
Don't Let It Go to Your Head, 1970
Heaven and Hell's Agreement
It's Colored, It's Negro, It's Black Man?, 1970
Sometimes a Hard Head Makes a Soft Behind, 1972
What If It Had Turned Up Heads?, 1970
PLAYS PUBLISHED IN ANTHOLOGIES:
What If It Had Turned Up Heads?, in Bullins, The
New Lafayette Theatre Presents
CRITICISMS OF INDIVIDUAL PLAYS:
What If It Had Turned Up Heads?
McElroy, Hilda Njoki. "Books Noted." Black
World 26 (April 1975): 51-52
REVIEWS OF INDIVIDUAL PLAYS:
Don't Let It Go to Your Head
Gussow, M. "Don't Let It Go to Your Head."
New York Times, 22 January 1972, 35: 1
New Yorker 29 January 1972, p. 2
Heaven and Hell's Agreement
New Yorker 8 April 1974, p. 4
Sometimes a Hard Head Makes a Soft Behind
Bailey, P. "Sometimes a Hard Head Makes a
Soft Behind." New York Times, 13 August
1972, II, 2: 4
New Yorker 19 August 1972
What If It Had Turned Up Heads?
Gussow, M. "What If It Had Turned Up Heads?"
New York Times, 7 November 1972, 25: 1
New Yorker 14 October 1972, p. 4
Walker, Barbara. Black Creation 4 (Winter
1973): 68

GAINES-SHELTON, RUTH

PLAY:
The Church Fight
PLAYS PUBLISHED IN ANTHOLOGIES:
The Church Fight, in Hatch and Shine, Black Thea-
ter USA
PLAYS PUBLISHED IN PERIODICALS:
The Church Fight, in Crisis 31-32 (May 1926): 17+
CRITICISMS OF INDIVIDUAL WORKS:
The Church Fight
Hatch and Shine. Black Theater USA, p. 188
Hicklin. The American Negro Playwright 1920-
1964. Part 1, pp. 133-134
AWARDS:
Second Prize, Crisis Contest 1925, for The Church
Fight

GARRETT, JIMMY
PLAY:
And We Own the Night
PLAYS PUBLISHED IN ANTHOLOGIES:
And We Own the Night, in Chambers and Moon,
Right On!; Jones and Neal, Black Fire; Simmons
and Hutchinson, Black Culture; Singh and Fel-
lowes, Black Literature in America: A Casebook
PLAYS PUBLISHED IN PERIODICALS:
And We Own the Night, in The Drama Review 12
(Summer 1968): 62-69
CRITICISMS OF INDIVIDUAL PLAYS:
And We Own the Night
Bigsby. The Black American Writer. Vol. 2,
pp. 200-201
Gayle. The Black Aesthetic. pp. 189, 287-289
Harrison. The Drama of Nommo. pp. 7, 203
Kaufman, Michael W. "The Delicate World of
Reprobation: A Note on the Black Revolution-
ary Theatre." Educational Theatre Journal
23 (December 1971): 446-460
Killinger. The Fragile Presence: Transcendence
in Modern Literature. p. 142
Riach, W. A. D. "'Telling It Like It Is:' An
Examination of Black Theater as Rhetoric."
Quarterly Journal of Speech 46 (April 1970):
182
Scott, John. "Teaching Black Drama." Players
47 (February-March 1972): 131
Whitlow. Black American Literature. p. 175

GARVEY, MRS. AMY ASHWOOD
    MUSICAL:
    Hey! Hey!
    CRITICISMS OF INDIVIDUAL MUSICALS:
    Hey! Hey!
        Lewis, Theophilus. "Sweet and Low Comedy."
        The Messenger 8 (December 1926): 362

GARVIN, LARRY
    PLAY:
    [With James V. Hatch and Aida Morales] Con-
        spiracy, 1970

GATEWOOD, L. A.
    PLAY:
    Ghetto: A Place, 1970

GIBSON, POWELL WILLARD (b. 1875)
    PLAY:
    Jake Among the Indians: A Serio-Comic Play De-
        picting the Trials of an Indian Maid With Her
        Father. Winchester, Va.: W. P. Gibson, 1931

GILBERT, MERCEDES (?-March 1, 1952)
    PLAYS:
    Environment, one act
    In Greener Pastures
    Ma Johnson's Harlem Rooming House, serial, 1938
    PLAYS PUBLISHED IN ANTHOLOGIES:
    Environment, in Gilbert, Selected Gems of Poetry,
        Comedy and Drama. Boston: Christopher Publ.
        Co., 1931
    EDITOR:
    Selected Gems of Poetry, Comedy and Drama.
        Boston: Christopher Publ. Co., 1931

GLADDEN, FRANK A.
    PLAY:
    The Distant Brother, 1972

GORDON, CHARLES see Oyamo

GORDON, KEN
    PLAY:
    Black Fog Poem

GORDONE, CHARLES (b. October 12, 1925)

PLAYS:
Gordone Is a Muthah
No Place to Be Somebody. Indianapolis: Bobbs-
    Merrill, 1969
Out of Site (one act)
The Thieves
Worl's Champeen Lip Dansuh an' Wahtah Mellon
    Jooglah, 1969
PLAYS PUBLISHED IN ANTHOLOGIES:
Gordone Is a Muthah, in Richards, Stanley, ed.,
    The Best Short Plays of 1973, pp. 193-208
No Place to Be Somebody, in Oliver and Sills, Con-
    temporary Black Drama; Patterson, Black Thea-
    tre; Weiss, Samuel A. Drama in the Modern
    World. pp. 571-665
PLAYS PUBLISHED IN PERIODICALS:
Out of Site, in Black Theatre 4 (8 June 1970)
CRITICISMS BY GORDONE:
"From the Muthah Lode." Newsweek 25 May 1970,
    p. 95
"Interview: No Place to Be Somebody." New York
    Times, 17 May 1970; II, 1: 5
"On No Place to Be Somebody." New York Times,
    25 January 1970; II, 1: 3
"Quiet Talk with Myself." Esquire 73 (January
    1970)
"Yes, I Am a Black Playwright, But..." New York
    Times, 25 January 1970; 27: 1
CRITICISMS OF GORDONE:
Archer. Black Images. p. 287
"Beyond the Pulitzer: An Interview with Charles
    Gordoné." Sepia 2 (February 1971): 14-17
"Black Pulitzer Prize Awardees." Crisis 77 (May
    1970): 186-188
Clayborne, Jon L. "Modern Black Drama and the
    Gay Image." College English 36 (November 1974):
    381-384
Hughes, Caroline. Plays, Politics, and Polemics.
    pp. 53-59
Simon, John. "Underwriting, Overreaching." New
    Yorker June 1969, p. 56
Walcott, Ronald. "Ellison, Gordone, and Tolson:
    Some Notes on the Blues." Black World 22 (De-
    cember 1972): 4-29
Wetzsteon, Ross. "Theatre Journal." The Village
    Voice, 22 May 1969
CRITICISMS OF INDIVIDUAL PLAYS:

Gordone Is a Muthah
Richards, Stanley, ed. The Best Short Plays of
1973. pp. 191-192
No Place to Be Somebody
Atkinson. Broadway. pp. 488, 496, 502
Bosworth, Patricia. "From Nowhere to 'No
Place'." New York Times, June 1969; II, 1: 1
Eckstein, George. "The New Black Theater."
Dissent 20 (Winter 1973): 112
Kraus, Ted M. "Theatre East." Players 47
(February-March 1972): 132
Lewis, Allan. The Contemporary Theatre. pp.
358-359
Little. Off-Broadway. pp. 125, 282
Murray, James P. "West Coast Gets the 'Shaft'."
Black Creation 3 (Summer 1972): 13
"Playboy After Hours: Theatre." Playboy 16 (Au-
gust 1969): 34-35
Scott, John. "Teaching Black Drama." Players
47 (February-March 1972): 131
REVIEWS OF INDIVIDUAL PLAYS:
No Place to Be Somebody
America 121 (6 September 1969): 145
Gill, Brendan. New Yorker 10 January 1970, p.
64
Gussow, Mel. New York Times, 31 December
1969, 17: 1
Kerr, Walter. "Not Since Edward Albee." New
York Times, 18 May 1969
N.B.C. TV, 4 May 1969
Nation 208 (19 May 1969): 644
New York Daily News, 5 May 1969
New York Theatre Critics' Reviews (1969): 256-
268
New York Post, 7 June 1969
New York Sunday Times, 18 May 1969
New York Times, 5 May 1969, p. 53: 3; II, 8
June 1969, p. 1; II, 25 January 1970, p. 1;
II, 17 May 1970, p. 1
New Yorker 45 (17 May 1969): 112+; 45 (10 Janu-
ary 1970): 64; (25 September 1971): 2
Newsweek 73 (2 June 1969): 101
Riley, Clayton. New York Times, 18 May 1969,
II, 1: 1; 22: 1
Rudin, Seymour. "Theatre Chronicle: Winter-
Spring 1969." The Massachusetts Review 10
(Summer 1969): 583-593

Saturday Review 52 (31 May 1969): 18
Time 93 (16 May 1969): 85-86
Variety, 26 August 1970
Wall Street Journal, 6 May 1969
Women's Wear Daily, 5 May 1969
AWARDS:
No Place to Be Somebody: Pulitzer Prize, 1969,
and Drama Desk Award for The Most Promising
Playwright, 1969

GOSS, CLAY (b. May 26, 1946)
PLAYS:
Andrew, one act, 1972
Homecookin, one act, 1972
Homecookin: Ten Plays. Washington, D.C.:
Howard University Press, 1975
Mars
(on) Of Being Hit, 1970
Ornette
Oursides, one act
Space in Time
PLAYS PUBLISHED IN ANTHOLOGIES:
(on) Of Being Hit, in Bullins, The New Lafayette
Theatre Presents
CRITICISMS OF INDIVIDUAL PLAYS:
(on) Of Being Hit
Bullins. The New Lafayette Theatre Presents.
pp. 115-116
McElroy, Hilda Njoki. "Books Noted." Black
World 26 (April 1975): 52
REVIEWS OF INDIVIDUAL PLAYS:
Andrew
New Yorker 24 May 1972, p. 2

GRAHAM, ARTHUR
PLAY:
The Last Shine, 1969

GRAHAM, OTTIE
PLAY:
Holiday, one act, 1923
PLAYS PUBLISHED IN PERIODICALS:
Holiday, in Crisis 26 (May 1923)

GRAHAM, SHIRLEY see Du Bois, Shirley Graham

GRAINER, PORTER

PLAYS:
[With Leigh Whipper] De Board Meetin, 1925
[With Freddie Johnson] Lucky Sambo, 1925
MUSICALS:
[With Leigh Whipper] We's Risin: A Story of the
    Simple Life in the Souls of Black Folk, a musical
    comedy in two acts and ten scenes, 1927

GRANT, CLAUDE D. (b. December 20, 1944)
PLAY:
Where Is the Sky, 1972

GRANT, MICKI
MUSICALS:
[With Vinnette Carroll] Croesus and the Witch, 1972
[With Vinnette Carroll] Don't Bother Me, I Can't
    Cope, 1972
[With J. E. Franklin] Prodigal Sister
[With Vinnette Carroll] Step Lively, Boy, 1972
[With Vinnette Carroll] The Ups and Downs of
    Theophilus Maitland Ward (A West Indian Musical)
    1975
CRITICISMS OF GRANT:
Archer. Black Images. p. 293
Reische. The Performing Arts in America. p. 73
CRITICISMS OF INDIVIDUAL MUSICALS:
Don't Bother Me, I Can't Cope
    Archer. Black Images. p. 293
REVIEWS OF INDIVIDUAL MUSICALS:
Croesus and the Witch
    New Yorker 4 September 1971, p. 2
Don't Bother Me, I Can't Cope
    Barnes, C. New York Times, 8 October 1970,
        60: 3
    _____. New York Times, 20 April 1972, 51:
        1
    Kalen, T. E. "Jubilation." New York Times,
        8 May 1972, p. 75
    Kerr, W. New York Times, 30 April 1972, II,
        30: 2
    New York Theatre Critics' Reviews (1972): 304
The Ups and Downs of Theophilus Maitland Ward
    New Yorker 2 December 1974, p. 4
AWARDS:
Drama Desk, Outer Circle, Grammy, 1972
Mademoiselle Achievement Award, 1972
Girl Friends Achievement, 1972

Two Tony Nominations, 1972
N.A.A.C.P. Image Award, 1972

GRANT, RICHARD
    PLAY:
        [With Will Mercer] The Southerners, 1904

GRAY, ALFRED RUDOLPH, JR. (b. June 26, 1933)
    PLAYS:
        [With Maxwell Glanville] Dance to a Nosepicker's
           Drum
        The Dean
        Eye for an Eye, revised
        Lucy, My Rose Petal
        Open Night School
        Peeling to the Pain
        The Revenge
        Tryout

GREANE, DAVID
    PLAY:
        Martin Luther King--Man of God

GREAVES, DONALD (b. 1943)
    PLAY:
        The Marriage
    PLAYS PUBLISHED IN ANTHOLOGIES:
        The Marriage, in King and Milner, Black Drama
           Anthology

GREEN, JOHNNY L.
    PLAYS:
        Black on Black, one act. New York: Amuru, 1973
        The Night of Judgment, one act. New York: Amu-
           ru, 1973
        The Sign, two acts. New York: Amuru, 1973

GREENE, OTIS
    PLAY:
        A Different Part of the World, 1967

GREENWOOD, FRANK
    PLAY:
        Burn, Baby, Burn!
    CRITICISMS BY GREENWOOD:
        "Comment on Burn, Baby, Burn!" Freedomways 7
           (Summer 1967): 244-246

CRITICISMS OF INDIVIDUAL PLAYS:
Burn, Baby, Burn!
Whuldin, Donald. "The Situation in Watts Today."
Freedomways 7 (Winter 1967): 57

GREGGS, HERBERT D. (b. 1931)
PLAY:
The Ballad of a Riverboat Town, 1968

GRIMKE, ANGELINE WELD (February 27, 1880-June 10, 1958)
PLAYS:
Rachel. Boston: Cornhill, 1921 (Reprinted Washington, D.C.: McGrath, 1969).
PLAYS PUBLISHED IN ANTHOLOGIES:
Rachel, in Hatch and Shine, Black Theater USA;
Locke and Gregory, Plays of Negro Life
CRITICISMS BY GRIMKE:
"Rachel The Play of the Month: The Reason and
Synopsis by the Author." Competitor 1 (January 1920): 51-52
CRITICISMS OF GRIMKE:
Bond. The Negro and the Drama. pp. 189-190
Hatch and Shine. Black Theater, USA. pp. 137-138
Hicklin. The American Negro Playwright 1920-1964.
Part 1, p. 61; Part 2, p. 465
CRITICISMS OF INDIVIDUAL WORKS:
Rachel
Bradley, Gerald. "Goodbye, Mister Bones."
Drama Critique 7 (Spring 1964): 83, 84
McKinney, Ernest Rice. "Rachel: A Play by
Angeline W. Grimke." Competitor 3 (April 1921): 35

GUILLAUME, BOB
PLAY:
Montezuma's Revenge, 1971

GUNN, BILL
PLAY:
Black Picture Show
Johnnas
PLAYS PUBLISHED IN PERIODICALS:
Johnnas, in The Drama Review 12 (Summer 1968)
CRITICISMS OF GUNN:
Hughes and Meltzer. Black Magic. pp. 203, 214
"Interview with Bill Gunn." Essence 4 (October

1973): 27, 96

"Negro Playwrights: Young Chicagoan Is First with All-Negro Play on Broadway." Ebony 14 (April 1959): 100

REVIEWS OF INDIVIDUAL PLAYS:

Black Picture Show

New York Theatre Critics' Reviews (1975): 386-389

GUY, ROSA
    PLAY:
    Venetian Blinds, one act, 1954

HAIRSTON, WILLIAM
    PLAYS:
    The Honeymooners, 1967
    Walk in Darkness, 1963
    CRITICISMS OF HAIRSTON:
    Mitchell. Black Drama. p. 197
    CRITICISMS OF INDIVIDUAL WORKS:
    Walk in Darkness
        Ford, Clebert. "Theatre Review and Forecast." Liberator 4 (January 1964): 18
        Hicklin. The American Negro Playwright 1920-1964. Part 2, pp. 395-399

HALSEY, WILLIAM
    PLAY:
    Judgment
    PLAYS PUBLISHED IN PERIODICALS:
    Judgment, in Black Dialogue 4 (Spring 1969): 40-43

HAMILTON, KIILU ANTHONY
    PLAY:
    [With Otis Smith and Richard Dedeaux] The Rising Sons--Wisdom and Knowledge. Los Angeles: The Watts Prophets, 1973

HAMILTON, ROLAND
    PLAY:
    Crack of the Whip, one act

HANSBERRY, LORRAINE (May 1930-January 16, 1954)
    PLAYS:
    The Drinking Gourd
    Les Blancs: The Last Collected Plays of Lorraine

Hansberry. Edited by Robert Nemiroff. New
York: Random House, 1972. (Includes the tele-
vision play The Drinking Gourd, Les Blancs, and
What Use Are Flowers?)

A Raisin in the Sun. New York: Random House,
1961; New York: New American Library, 1961;
New York: Samuel French, 1961

A Sign in Sidney Brustein's Window. New York:
Random House, 1965; New York: Samuel French,
1965

To Be Young, Gifted and Black. Englewood Cliffs,
N.J.: Prentice-Hall, 1969; New York: Samuel
French, 1971

What Use Are Flowers?

PLAYS PUBLISHED IN ANTHOLOGIES:

The Drinking Gourd, in Hatch and Shine, Black Theater USA; Nemiroff, Les Blancs: The Collected
Last Plays of Lorraine Hansberry

A Raisin in the Sun, in Adams, Conn and Slepian,
Afro-American Literature: Drama; Barranger and
Dodson, Generations: An Introduction to Drama;
Cerf, Plays of Our Time; Cerf, Six American
Plays for Today; Chambers and Moon, Right On!;
Childress, Black Scenes (excerpts); Dietrich, The
Art of Drama; Kronenberger, The Best Plays of
1958-1959 (condensed); Oliver and Sills, Black
Drama; Patterson, Black Theatre; Simonson,
Quartet; White and Whiting, Playreader's Reper-
tory

The Sign in Sidney Brustein's Window, in Gassner
and Barnes, Best American Plays (sixth series);
Three Negro Plays, Harmondsworth, England:
Penguin, 1969

What Use Are Flowers?, in Nemiroff, Les Blancs:
The Collected Last Plays of Lorraine Hansberry;
Richards, The Best Short Plays of 1973, pp. 104-
130

PLAYS PUBLISHED IN PERIODICALS:

A Raisin in the Sun, in Theatre Arts 44 (October
1960): 27-58

CRITICISMS BY HANSBERRY:

"American Theatre Needs Desegregating Too."
Negro Digest 10 (June 1961): 28-33

"The Black Revolution and the White Backlash."
(transcript of a Town Hall Forum with Ossie
Davis, Ruby Dee, Lorraine Hansberry, LeRoi
Jones, John O. Killens, Paule Marshall, Charles

E. Silberman, James Wechsler, and David Susskind, moderator); Almost complete transcript: National Guardian, 26 (4 July 1964): 5-9. Partial excerpts: Black Protest, ed. with an introduction and commentaries by Joanne Grant, New York: Fawcett World Library, 1968

"A Challenge to Artists." Freedomways 3 (Winter 1963): 31-36

"Images and Essences: 1961 Dialogue with an Uncolored Egghead Containing Wholesome Intentions and Some Sass." The Urbanite 1 (May 1961): 10, 11, 36. (Dramatized version in To Be Young, Gifted and Black)

"A Letter from Lorraine Hansberry on Porgy and Bess." The Theatre, (August 1959): 10

"Me Tink Me Hear Sounds in de Night." Theatre Arts 44 (October 1960): 9-11, 69-70. Reprinted as "The Negro in the American Theatre" in American Playwrights on Drama. Horst Frenz, ed. New York: Hill and Wang, 1965

"Miss Hansberry on 'Backlash.'" Village Voice 23 July 1964, pp. 10, 16

"My Name Is Lorraine Hansberry; I Am a Writer." Esquire 72 (November 1969): 140

"The Nation Needs Your Gifts." Negro Digest 13 (August 1964): 26-29

"The Negro in American Culture" (symposium with James Baldwin, Emile Capouya, Lorraine Hansberry, Nat Hentoff, Langston Hughes, and Alfred Kazin). Printed in The Black American Writer, vol. 1: Fiction, C. W. E. Bigsby, ed. Baltimore: Pelican Book, 1971

"Negroes and Africa." Quoted extensively in this chapter in The New World of Negro Americans. Harold R. Isaacs, ed. New York: John Day Co., 1965

CRITICISMS OF HANSBERRY:

Abramson. Negro Playwrights in the American Theatre. pp. vii-viii, 3

Baldwin, James. "Sweet Lorraine." Esquire 72 (November 1969): 139-140

Bigsby, C. W. E. "Harold Cruse: An Interview." The Black American Writer, vol. 2: Poetry and Drama. p. 230-231

_____. "Lonne Elder III: An Interview." The Black American Writer, vol. 2: Poetry and Drama. p. 222

Davis, Ossie. "The Significance of Lorraine Hans-
    berry." Freedomways 5 (Summer 1965): 396-402
Farrison, W. Edward. "Lorraine Hansberry's Last
    Dramas." CLA Journal 16 (December 1972): 188-
    198
Isaacs, Harold. "Five Writers and Their African
    Ancestors: Part I." Phylon 21 (1960): 66-70
Killens, John O. "Broadway in Black and White."
    Forum I (1965): 66-70
Lahr. Up Against the Fourth Wall. p. 95
"Lorraine Hansberry's World." Liberator 4 (De-
    cember 1964): 9
Miller, Jordan. "Lorraine Hansberry." In Bigsby,
    The Black American Writer. vol. 2, pp. 157-
    170
"People Are Talking About...." Vogue 133 (June
    1959): 78-79
"Ten Playwrights Tell How It All Starts." New York
    Times Magazine, 6 December 1959
The Village Voice, 6 June 1963. (Interview)
Weales. The Jumping-Off Place. pp. 108-112
BIBLIOGRAPHIES OF HANSBERRY:
Gordon, Carolyn. "Lorraine Hansberry." CAAS
    Bibliography No. 1, Atlanta, Ga.: Center for
    African and African-American Studies, n.d.,
    (mimeographed)
Williams, Ora. American Black Women in the Arts
    and Social Sciences. Metuchen, N.J.: Scare-
    crow, 1973
CRITICISMS OF INDIVIDUAL PLAYS:
Les Blancs
    Kraus, Ted M. "Theatre East." Players 46
        (February-March 1971): 122
A Raisin in the Sun
    Abramson. "From Harlem to A Raisin in the
        Sun: A Study of Plays by Negro Playwrights."
        Ph.D. Dissertation. Columbia University,
        Teachers College, 1961
    _____. Negro Playwrights in the American
        Theatre, 1925-1959. pp. 69, 239-254, 258,
        263-266, 270, 274
    Ahman. Matthew H. The New Negro. pp. 110-
        111
    Atkinson, Broadway. pp. 445-446, 500
    Brownlee, L. "A Raisin in the Sun." Sepia 7
        (May 1959): 68-71
    Cameron and Hoffman. A Guide to Theatre Study.

p. 203

Driver, Tom F. "A Raisin in the Sun." New Republic 140 (13 April 1959): 21

Harrison. The Drama of Nommo. pp. 6-7, 200-202

Hays, Peter L. "A Raisin in the Sun and Juno and the Paycock." Phylon 33 (Summer 1972): 175-176

Hicklin. The American Negro Playwright 1920-1964. Part 2, pp. 409-414

"Inner City Repertory." Players 44 (December-January 1969): 52

Laufe, Abe. Anatomy of a Hit: Long Run Plays on Broadway from 1900 to the Present Day. pp. 297-302

Lewis. American Plays and Playwrights: Trends of the Decade. pp. 112, 252

Lewis, Emory. Stages: The Fifty Year Childhood of the American Theater. p. 155-157

Miller, Jordan. "Lorraine Hansberry." In Bigsby, The Black American Writer. vol. 2, pp. 165-168

Mitchell. Black Drama. pp. 180-182

"Negro Playwrights: Young Chicagoan Is First with All-Negro Play on Broadway." Ebony 14 (April 1959): 95-99

Pawley, Dr. Thomas D. "The Black Theatre Audience." Players 46 (August-September 1971): 259

"Playboy After Hours: Theatre." Playboy 6 (May 1959): 14, 16

"A Raisin in the Sun." The Theatre 1 (May 1959): 31

"A Raisin in the Sun." (Film) The Theatre 3 (April 1961): 28-29

"Raisin in the Sun Sets Record." Jet, 16 June 1970, p. 58

Rioch, W. A. D. "'Telling It Like It Is:' An Examination of Black Theater as Rhetoric." Quarterly Journal of Speech 46 (April 1970): 184

Sister Ann Edward. "Three Views on Blacks: The Black Woman in American Literature." The CEA Critic 37 (May 1975): 16

Talbot, William. "Every Negro in His Place." Drama Critique 7 (Spring 1964): 93

Turner, Darwin. "The Black Playwrights in the

Professional Theatre of the United States of
America 1858-1959." In Bigsby, The Black
American Writer. vol. 2, pp. 126-128
_____. "Negro Playwrights and the Urban
Negro." CLA Journal 12 (September 1968):
20-22
Weales. American Drama Since World War II.
pp. 231-233
Weales, Gerald. "Thoughts on A Raisin in the
Sun." Commentary 27 (June 1959): 527-530
Whitlow. Black American Literature. pp. 141-145

The Sign in Sidney Brustein's Window
Abramson. Negro Playwrights in the American
Theatre 1925-1959. pp. 270, 273
Adams, George R. "Black Militant Drama."
American Image 28 (Summer 1971): 109-115,
passim
Hicklin. The American Negro Playwright 1920-
1964. part 2, pp. 414-416
Holtan, Orley I. "Sidney Brustein and the Plight
of the American Intellectual." Players 46
(June-July 1971): 222-225
Lewis. American Plays and Playwrights: Trends
of the Decade. p. 257
Lewis, Emory. Stages: The Fifty Year Child-
hood of the American Theater. p. 157
Miller, Jordan. "Lorraine Hansberry." In Bigs-
by, The Black American Writer. vol. 2, pp.
168-170
Mitchell. Black Drama. pp. 202-204
Nemiroff, Robert. "The One Hundred and One
'Final' Performances of Sidney Brustein."
Introduction to Hansberry, Lorraine. The
Sign in Sidney Brustein's Window. New York:
Random House, 1965, pp. xiii-lxi
Smith, Milburn. "Producer's Schedules." The
Theatre (March 1959): 38
Weales. The Jumping-Off Place. pp. 38, 117-
122
Whitlow. Black American Literature. pp. 144-
145

REVIEWS OF INDIVIDUAL PLAYS:
Les Blancs
Barnes, C. New York Times, 16 November 1970,
48: 4
Gant, Liz. "Les Blancs." Black World 20
(April 1971): 46

Kerr, W. New York Times, 29 November 1970,
II, 3: 2

"Les Blancs." Nation 211 (30 November 1970):
573

New Yorker 7 November 1970, p. 2

New York Theater Critics' Reviews (1970) 152,
154

"Playboy After Hours: Theater." Playboy 18
(April 1971): 37

Riley, Clayton. "Theatre Review: Les Blancs."
Liberator 10 (December 1970): 19

_____. "Review: Les Blancs." New York
Times, 29 November 1970, II, 3: 5

Raisin in the Sun

America 101 (2 May 1959): 286-287

Catholic World 189 (May 1959): 159

Commentary 27 (June 1959): 527-30

Commonweal 70 (17 April 1959): 81

"Domestic Drama from the Top Drawer." Theatre Arts 43 (July 1959): 5

Essence 4 December 1973, p. 5

Life 46 (27 April 1959): p. 137-8

Ms. 2 December 1973, p. 40+

Nation 188 (4 April 1959): 301-2

New York Theatre Critics' Reviews (1959): 344;
(1973): 218-222

New York Times, 8 March 1959, II, p. 3; 12
March 1959, p. 27; 13 March 1959, p. 25;
29 March 1959, II, p. 1; 5 August 1959, p.
32; 27 July 1965, p. 19

New Yorker 35 (21 March 1959): 100-102

Newsweek 53 (23 March 1959): 76

"On Broadway: A Raisin in the Sun." Theatre
Arts 43 (May 1959): 22-23

"Playboy After Hours: Theater." Playboy 21
(February 1974): 38

"A Raisin in the Sun Basks in Praise." New
York Times, 14 November 1961, 47: 5

"A Raisin in the Sun to Close." New York
Times, 23 June 1960, 18: 6

"A Raisin in the Sun Staged in Soviet." New
York Times, 14 November 1961, 47: 5

Reporter 20 (16 April 1959): 34-5

Saturday Review 42 (4 April 1959): 28

Theatre Arts 43 (May 1959): 22-23; 43 (July
1959): 58-61

Time 73 (23 March 1959): 58

The Sign in Sidney Brustein's Window
America 111 (5 December 1964): 758
Barnes, Clive. "The Sign in Sidney Brustein's
Window." New York Times, 27 January 1972,
44: 1
Carter, John. "Hansberry's Potpourri." New
Yorker 40 (24 October 1964): 93
Commonweal 81 (6 November 1964): 197
Nation 199 (9 November 1964): 340
National Review 17 (23 March 1965): 250
Ness, D. E. Freedomways 11 (1971): 359-366
Neal, Lawrence P. "Theatre Review: The Sign
in Sidney Brustein's Window." Liberator 4
(December 1964): 25
New York Theatre Critics' Reviews (1964): 190;
1972: 382
New York Times, 11 October 1964, II, p. 1;
16 October 1964, p. 32; 1 November 1964, II,
p. 1
New Yorker 21 November 1964, p. 2
Newsweek 64 (26 October 1964): 101
Saturday Review 47 (31 October 1964): 31-
Taubman, Howard. "Theatre: 'Sidney Brustein's
Window.'" New York Times, 17 October 1964,
p. 18
Time 84 (23 October 1964): 67
To Be Young, Gifted and Black
Commonweal 90 (5 September 1969): 542-543
Duberman, Martin. "Theater 69: Black Theater."
Partisan Review 36 (1969): 490.
Nation 208 (28 April 1964): 548
New York Times, 3 January 1969, II, p. 15; 25
May 1969, II, p. 1; 22 September 1969, p. 36
New Yorker 4 January 1969, p. 2
Rudin, Seymour. "Theatre Chronicle: Fall
1970." The Massachusetts Review 12 (Winter
1971): 150-161
MEDIA RESOURCES:
Hansberry, Lorraine. Lorraine Hansberry on Her
Art and the Black Experience (discussing her
work and philosophy, the theater, the Black ex-
perience, and the challenge of the artist in mid-
century America). New York: Caedmon Records,
TC 1352 1-12" LP, $6.50; CDL 51352 cassette,
$7.95
_____. Lorraine Hansberry Speaks Out: Art and
the Black Revolution. Robert Nemiroff, ed. New

York: Caedmon Records, 1971

_____. A Raisin in the Sun (the complete play, 3 records with Ossie Davis, Ruby Dee, Claudia McNeil, Diana Sands, Leonard Jackson, Zakes Mokae, Sam Schacht, Harold Scott. Directed by Lloyd Richards). New York: Caedmon Records, 1972

_____. To Be Young, Gifted and Black (the complete play, 3 records with James Earl Jones, Barbara Baxley, Claudia McNeil, Tina Sattin, Camille Yarbrough, Garn Stevens, John Towey). New York: Caedmon Records, 1971

Raisin in the Sun. Audio-Film Center. 2138 E. 75th St., Mt. Vernon, New York 10550. 127 min.

AWARDS:

A Raisin in the Sun: New York Drama Critics' Circle Award for the Best American Play 1958-1959

HARRIS, BILL
   PLAY:
   No Use Crying, 1969

HARRIS, MRS. HELEN WEBB
   PLAYS:
   Frederick Douglass, three acts
   Ganifrede
   CRITICISMS OF INDIVIDUAL PLAYS:
   Frederick Douglass
      Hicklin. The American Negro Playwright 1920-1964. Part 2, pp. 308-309
      Woodson, Dr. Carter G. "Frederick Douglass." Negro History Bulletin 15 (February 1952): 97
   Ganifrede
      Hicklin. The American Negro Playwright 1920-1964. Part 1, pp. 135-136
   AWARDS:
   Howard University Award, First Prize, 1922, for Ganifrede

HARRIS, NEIL (b. February 20, 1936)
   PLAYS:
   Blues Changes
   Cop and Blow, 1972
   Off the Top
   Players Inn, 1972

The Portrait, 1969
[With Miguel Pinero] Straight from the Ghetto
Hernom

HARRIS, TOM
    PLAYS:
        The A Number One Family, 1958
        Always with Love, 1967
        Beverly Hills Olympics, 1964
        City Beneath the Skin, 1961
        Cleaning Day, 1969
        Daddy Hugs and Kisses, 1963
        The Dark Years, 1958
        Death of Daddy Hugs and Kisses, 1963
        Divorce Negro Style, 1968
        Fall of an Iron Horse, 1959
        The Golden Spear, 1969
        Moving Day, 1969
        Pray for Daniel Adams, 1958
        The Relic, 1967
        Shopping Day, 1969
        Woman in the House, 1958

HARRISON, PAUL CARTER (b. 1936)
    PLAYS:
        The Adding Machine
        Brer Soul, 1970
        The Great MacDaddy, 1972
        Pavane for a Dead-Pan Minstrel
        Pawns
        Tabernacle
        Top-Hat
    PLAYS PUBLISHED IN ANTHOLOGIES:
        The Adding Machine, in Hubenka and Garcia, The
            Design of Drama; Couch, New Black Playwrights
    PLAYS PUBLISHED IN PERIODICALS:
        Pavane for a Dead-Pan Minstrel, in Podium 20
            (November 1965)
    EDITOR:
        Kuntu Drama. N.Y.: Grove, 1974
    CRITICISMS BY HARRISON:
        "Black Theatre and the African Continuum." Black
            World 21 (August 1972): 42-48
        The Drama of Nommo. N.Y.: Grove, 1972
    REVIEWS OF INDIVIDUAL PLAYS:
        The Great MacDaddy
            Gottfried, Martin. Women's Wear Daily, 14

February 1974
The National Observer, 2 March 1974, p. 16
New York Theatre Critics' Reviews 35 (18 February 1974): 364-366
New Yorker 18 February 1974, p. 2
Watts, Richard. New York Post, 3 February 1974

HATCH, JAMES V. (b. 1928)
PLAY:
[With Larry Garvin and Aida Morales] The Conspiracy, 1970
MUSICALS:
[With Clarence Jackson] Fly Black Bird, 1960
Liar, Liar
MUSICALS PUBLISHED IN ANTHOLOGIES:
Fly Black Bird, in Hatch and Shine, Black Theater USA; Reardon and Pawley, The Black Teacher and the Dramatic Arts
EDITOR:
Black Images on the American Stage. N.Y.: DBS Publication, 1970
[With Ted Shine] Black Theater USA. N.Y.: Free Press, 1974
CRITICISMS BY HATCH:
"Theodore Ward, Black American Playwright." Freedomways 15 (First Quarter 1975): 37-41
CRITICISMS OF INDIVIDUAL MUSICALS:
Fly Black Bird
Hatch and Shine. Black Theater USA. p. 761
Lewis. American Plays and Playwrights: Trends of the Decade. p. 252
Reardon and Pawley. The Black Teacher and the Dramatic Arts. pp. 124-126
Weales. The Jumping-Off Place. pp. 124-125
AWARDS:
Fly Black Bird, Obie Award for the Best Off-Broadway Musical, 1961-62

HAYDEN, ROBERT (b. August 4, 1913)
PLAYS:
History of Punchinello (one act)
PLAYS PUBLISHED IN PERIODICALS:
History of Punchinello, in Nasda Encore, 1948
CRITICISMS OF INDIVIDUAL WORKS:
Hicklin. The American Negro Playwright 1920-1964. Part 2, pp. 310-312

HAZZARD, ALVIRA
    PLAYS:
        Little Heads
        Mother Liked It, one act, 1928
    PLAYS PUBLISHED IN PERIODICALS:
        Little Heads, in Saturday Evening Quill (April 1929)
        Mother Liked It, in Saturday Evening Quill (April
            1928)

HEYWOOD, DONALD
    PLAYS:
        How Come, Lawd?, 1937
        Ol' Man Satan, 1932
    CRITICISMS OF INDIVIDUAL PLAYS:
        How Come Lawd?
            Hicklin. The American Negro Playwright 1920-
                1964. Part 1, p. 230
        Ol' Man Satan
            Bond. The Negro and the Drama. pp. 176-177
            Hicklin. The American Negro Playwright 1920-
                1964. Part 1, p. 229
    REVIEWS OF INDIVIDUAL PLAYS:
        How Come, Lawd?
            Atkinson, Brooks. "'How Come, Lawd?'" New
                York Times, 1 October 1937
        Ol' Man Satan
            Atkinson, Brooks. "'Ol' Man Satan.'" New York
                Times, 4 October 1932

HIGHTOWER, CHARLES
    PLAY:
        Childrens' Games, 1969

HILL, ABRAM (b. 1911)
    PLAYS:
        [With Harry Wagstaff Gribble] Anna Lucasta.
            (Adaptation of Philip Yordan's Anna Lucasta)
        Hell's Half Acre, 1938
        [With John Silvera] Liberty Deferred, 1936
        Miss Mabel, 1951
        On Striver's Row: A Comedy about Sophisticated
            Harlem, 1945
        Power of Darkness, 1948
        So Shall You Reap, 1938
        Split down the Middle. New York: Simon and
            Schuster, 1970
        Stealing Lightning, 1937

Walk Hard (Walk Hard, Talk Loud), 1944
PLAYS PUBLISHED IN ANTHOLOGIES:
Walk Hard, in Hatch and Shine, Black Theater USA
CRITICISMS OF HILL:
Archer. Black Images. p. 19
Cotton, Letti Jo. "Negro in the American Theater."
    Negro History Bulletin 23 (May 1960): 176
Mitchell. Black Drama. pp. 110, 113
Williams. Stage Left. p. 230
CRITICISMS OF INDIVIDUAL PLAYS:
Anna Lucasta
    Gayle. Black Expression. p. 155
    "Harlem Meteor (Anna Lucasta)." Negro Digest
        3 (March 1945): 9-10
    Mitchell. Black Drama. pp. 122-123, 135
Hell's Half Acre
    Bond. The Negro and the Drama. p. 189
Liberty Deferred
    Abramson. Negro Playwrights in the American
        Theatre 1925-1959. pp. 65-66
On Striver's Row
    Abramson. Negro Playwrights in the American
        Theatre 1925-1959. pp. 95, 96-102, 159
    Gayle. Black Expression. p. 245
    Harrison. The Drama of Nommo. p. 166
    Hicklin. The American Negro Playwright 1920-
        1964. Part 2, pp. 322-324
    Kronenberger, Louis. "Critical and Amusements
        (On Striver's Row)." PM 11 March 1945
    _____. "On Striver's Row." PM 1 December
        1944
    Leonard, Claire. "The American Negro Theatre."
        Theatre Arts 28 (July 1944): 421-423
    _____. "Dark Drama." Negro Digest 2 (Au-
        gust 1944): 81-82
    Mitchell. Black Drama. p. 107
Power of Darkness
    Mitchell. Black Drama. p. 136
Walk Hard, Talk Loud
    Hatch and Shine. Black Theater USA. pp. 437-
        438
    Hicklin. The American Negro Playwright 1920-
        1964. Part 2, pp. 324-325
    Kronenberger, Louis. "Critical and Amusements."
        (Walk Hard, Talk Loud) PM 1 December 1944
REVIEWS OF INDIVIDUAL PLAYS:
On Striver's Row

Jefferson, Miles M. "The Negro on Broadway, 1945-1946." Phylon 7 (Second Quarter 1946): 191

The Power of Darkness
Jefferson, Miles M. "The Negro on Broadway: 1948-1949." Phylon 10 (Second Quarter 1949): 108

Walk Hard, Talk Loud
Jefferson, Miles M. "The Negro on Broadway, 1944." Phylon 6 (First Quarter 1945): 52
Nichols, Lewis. "The Play." (Walk Hard, Talk Loud) New York Times, 1 December 1944, 28: 2, 28 March 1946, 34: 2

HILL, ERROL (b. August 5, 1921)
PLAYS:
Dance Bongo, 1965
Dilemma, 1966
Oily Portraits, 1966
The Ping Pong, 1958
Strictly Matrimony, 1966
Wey-Wey, 1966
PLAYS PUBLISHED IN ANTHOLOGIES:
Dance Bongo, in Coulthard, Caribbean Literature
Strictly Matrimony, in King and Milner, Black Drama Anthology
MUSICAL:
Man, Better Man, folk musical
MUSICALS PUBLISHED IN ANTHOLOGIES:
Man, Better Man, in Gassner, Three Plays from The Yale School of Drama
EDITOR:
Caribbean Plays, vols. 1 and 2. Trinidad: Extramural Department, University of The West Indies, 1958, 1965
The Artist in West Indian Society: A Symposium. Trinidad: Extramural Department, University of The West Indies, 1964
CRITICISMS BY HILL:
"Calypso Drama." Theatre Survey 9 (November 1968)
"The Case for a National Theatre." Public Opinion (Jamaica), 20 September; 4 October, 1952
"Cultural Values and the Theatre Arts in the English-Speaking Caribbean." Resource Development in The Caribbean (McGill University), October 1972
"The Emergence of a National Drama in the West

Indies. Caribbean Quarterly 18 (December 1972)
The Trinidad Carnival: Mandate for a National
   Theatre. Austin, Texas: University of Texas
   Press, 1972
"The West Indian Artist." West Indian Review
   (Jamaica) 9 August 1952
"West Indian Drama." Trinidad Guardian Federa-
   tion Supplement, 20 April 1958
"The West Indian Theatre." Public Opinion 31 May,
   7 June, 21 June, 1958
[With Peter Greer] Why Pretend? New York:
   Chandler, 1973
REVIEWS OF INDIVIDUAL MUSICALS:
Man, Better Man
   New York Times, 3 July 1969, 22: 1; 13 July
      1969, II, 3: 6
AWARDS:
Theatre Guild of America Playwrighting Fellowship,
   1961-62

HILL, LESLIE PINKEY (May 14, 1880-February 16, 1960)
PLAYS:
Jethro
Toussaint D'Ouverture. Boston: Christopher, 1928
CRITICISMS OF INDIVIDUAL PLAYS:
Jethro
   Bond. The Negro and the Drama. p. 189

HILL, LEUBRIE (1873-1916)
MUSICALS:
[With Alex Rogers] Dark Town Follies
[With William LeBaron] Hello Paris, 1911
My Friend from Dixie
CRITICISMS OF INDIVIDUAL MUSICALS:
Dark Town Follies
   Isaacs, Edith J. R. "The Middle Distance:
      1890-1917--Heyday of Comedy and Dance."
      Theatre Arts 26 (August 1942): 531
   Mitchell. Black Drama. p. 68

HILL, MARS (b. November 18, 1927)
PLAYS:
The Buzzards
The Cage
First in War
House and Field
Huzzy

The Man in the Family
Occupation
Peck
The Street Walkers
To Have and to Have Not
A Very Special Occasion
The Visitors
You Ain't Got No Place to Put Yo Snow

HIMES, CHESTER (b. July 29, 1909)
    FILMSCRIPTS:
    Cotton Comes to Harlem
    If He Hollers, Let Him Go, adaptation of novel If
        He Hollers, Let Him Go, 1968
    CRITICISMS OF HIMES:
    Fuller, Hoyt W. "Traveler on the Long, Rough,
        Lovely Old Road: An Interview with Chester
        Himes." Black World 21 (March 1972): 4-24
    Reed, Ishmael. "Chester Himes: Writer." Black
        World 21 (March 1972): 24-39
    Williams, John A. "My Man Chester Himes."
        (Interview). Amistad 1 (1969): 25-93
    CRITICISMS OF INDIVIDUAL FILMSCRIPTS:
    Cotton Comes to Harlem
        Mapp. Black Women in Films. p. 45
        Mapp. Blacks in American Films. p. 244
    If He Hollers, Let Him Go.
        Mapp. Blacks in American Films. pp. 182-183
    REVIEWS OF INDIVIDUAL FILMS:
    Cotton Comes to Harlem
        Christian Century 87 (2 December 1970): 1454-
            1455
        Esquire 71 (October 1970): 67
        Life 69 (28 August 1970): 58-59
        Newsweek 75 (22 June 1970): 82
        Saturday Review 53 (18 July 1970): 22
        Time 96 (6 July 1970): 70

HOLDER, LAWRENCE
    PLAYS:
    Closed, 1972
    Grey Boy, 1973
    The Jackass, 1972
    The Journey, 1972
    The Mob, 1972
    Open, 1969
    The Prophylactic, 1970

The Shadows, 1970
Street Corners, 1972

HOLIFIELD, HAROLD
    PLAYS:
        Cow in the Apartment, 194?
        J. Toth, 1951
    CRITICISMS OF HOLIFIELD:
        Mitchell. Black Drama. pp. 136, 145

HOLMAN, M. CARL (b. 1919)
    PLAY:
        The Baptizing
    AWARDS:
        Blevins Davis Playwrighting Prize, Yale University
        The Baptizing, as performed by Tulsa Little Thea-
            tre, won first place in the 1971 National Com-
            munity Theatre Festival of the American Com-
            munity Theatre Association

HOPKINS, LINDA
    PLAY:
        Inner City
    CRITICISMS OF INDIVIDUAL PLAYS:
        Inner City
            Reische. The Performing Arts in America.
                vol. 45, p. 73

HOPKINS, PAULINE ELIZABETH (1859-August 13, 1930)
    PLAY:
        One Scene from the Drama of Early Days
    MUSICAL:
        Slaves' Escape: or The Underground Railroad, 1879;
            later revised and entitled Peculiar Sam, or The
            Underground Railroad

HOWARD, SALLIE
    PLAY:
        The Jackal, 195?
    CRITICISMS OF INDIVIDUAL PLAYS:
        The Jackal
            Mitchell. Black Drama. p. 162

HUGHES, BABETTE
    PLAYS:
        Murder! Murder! Murder!, 1933
    REVIEWS OF INDIVIDUAL PLAYS:

Murder! Murder! Murder!
Southern Workman 62 (May 1933): 234

HUGHES, LANGSTON (February 2, 1902-May 22, 1967)
PLAYS:
Angelo Herndon Jones, one act. Manuscript in the
Yale University Library
The Big Sea. New York: Alfred A. Knopf, 1945
Dear Lovely Death, 1932. (Juvenile)
[With James P. Johnson] De Organizer (Folk Opera),
1939. Manuscript in the Yale University Library
Don't You Want to Be Free?, 1937
The Dream Keeper. New York: Alfred A. Knopf,
1932
The Emfurher Jones (Em-fur-her), 1938
Five Wise, Five Foolish, work in progress as of
1958
For This We Fight, 1943
Front Porch, three act comedy drama, 1937
The Gold Piece, Juvenile, one act, 1921
I Wonder as I Wander. New York: Rinehart, 1956
Joy to My Soul, three act comedy, 1937
Limitations of Life, 1938
Little Eva's End, 1938
Little Ham, three act comedy, 1935
Love From a Tall Building
Mother and Child, one act
Mr. Jazz, 1960
Mulatto, three act tragedy, 1935
[With Nora Zeal Hurston] Mule Bone, 1931
A New Song, 1938
Outshines the Sun
Scottsboro Limited. New York: The Golden Stair
Press, 1932
[With Glenn Robert] Shakespeare in Harlem, 1959
Simply Heavenly, 1957. New York: Dramatists
Play Service, 1959
Soul Gone Home, one act fantasy
[With Bob Teague] Soul Yesterday and Today, 1959
Trouble with the Angels, one act
[With William Grant Still] Troubled Island, three
act tragedy, 1936
[With Arna Bontemps] When (the) Jack Hollers,
three act comedy, 1936
Wide, Wide River, work in progress as of 1958
PLAYS PUBLISHED IN ANTHOLOGIES:
Don't You Want to Be Free?, in Hatch and Shine,

Black Theater USA
Emperor of Haiti, in Turner, Black Drama in America
Limitations of Life, in Hatch and Shine, Black Theatre USA
Little Ham, in Five Plays by Langston Hughes
Mother and Child, in King and Milner, Black Drama Anthology
Mulatto, in Five Plays by Langston Hughes; Brasmer and Consolo, Black Drama; Watkins and David, To Be a Black Woman (excerpt)
Soul Gone Home, in Five Plays by Langston Hughes
PLAYS PUBLISHED IN PERIODICALS:
Don't You Want to Be Free?, in One Act Play Magazine 2 (October 1938): 359-393
Mule Bone, in Drama Critique 7 (Spring 1964): 103-107
Soul Gone Home, in One Act Play Magazine 1 (July 1937)
MUSICALS:
[With Margaret Bonds] Ballad of the Brown King, Christmas Cantata
[With Jan Meyerowitz] The Barrier, 1950, musical version of Mulatto
Black Nativity, Christmas song in two acts, 1961
Esther
Gospel Glory, 1962
Jericho-Jim Crow, 1963
[With Abby Mann and B. Drew] Just Around the Corner, 1951
Liar, Liar, children's musical
[With Jan Meyerowitz] Port Town, one act opera
The Prodigal Son
[With David Martin] Simply Heavenly, 1957, based on Simple Takes a Wife
St. Louis Woman, 1936. (Revision of the Bontemps-Cullen script)
[With Kurt Weill and Elmer Rice] Street Scene
The Sun Do Move, two act musical drama, 1942
Tambourines to Glory, two act gospel-singing play, 1963
MUSICALS PUBLISHED IN ANTHOLOGIES:
Simply Heavenly, in Five Plays by Langston Hughes; The Langston Hughes' Reader; Patterson, Black Theatre
MUSICALS PUBLISHED IN PERIODICALS:
The Prodigal Son, in Players 43 (October-November

1967): 16-21
FILM SCRIPT:
[With Clarence Muse] Way Down South, 1942
CRITICISMS BY HUGHES:
"Backstage." Ebony 4 (March 1949): 36-38
"Is Hollywood Fair to Negroes?" Negro Digest 1
(April 1943): 16-21
"The Need for an Afro-American Theatre." In
Anthology of the American Negro in The Thea-
tre, Lindsay Patterson, ed., pp. 163-164
"The Need for Heroes." Crisis 48 (June 1941): 184-
185, 206
CRITICISMS OF HUGHES:
Abramson. Negro Playwrights in the American
Theatre, pp. 67-88
Altick, Richard. The Art of Literary Research,
rev., p. 252, #70
Anon. "Langston Hughes and the Example of 'Sim-
ple'." Black World 19 (June 1970): 35-38
Atkinson. Broadway, pp. 348, 503
Bontemps. The Harlem Renaissance Remembered.
pp. 1-277, passim
Bradley, Gerald. "Goodbye, Mr. Bones: The
Emergence of Negro Themes and Characters in
American Drama." Drama Critique 8 (1964)
Broning, Eberhard. "'The Black Liberation Move-
ment' und Oas Amerikanische Drama." Zeit-
schrift Furanglistic und Amerikanistic 20 (1972):
46-58
Carey, Julian C. "Jessie B. Semple Revisited and
Revised." Phylon 32 (1971): 158-163
Coleman, Edwin Leon. Langston Hughes: As
American Dramatist. Ph.D. Dissertation, Uni-
versity of Oregon, 1971
Harrison. The Drama of Nommo, pp. 24, 113, 165
Kaufman and Henstell. American Film Criticism,
pp. 223, 227
Locke, Alain. "The Drama of Negro Life." Thea-
tre Arts Monthly 10 (1926), 701-706
"The Negro Artist and the Racial Mountain." The
Nation 122 (23 June 1926): 692-694
Parker, John. "Tomorrow in the Writing of Lang-
ston Hughes." College English 10 (May 1949):
438-441
Presley, James. "The American Dream of Lang-
ston Hughes." Southwest Review 48 (Autumn
1963): 380-386

Smalley, Webster, ed. "Introduction" to Five Plays of Langston Hughes, Bloomington: Indiana University Press, 1963

Smiley, Sam. The Drama of Attack. pp. 30, 34, 37, 53, 157, 163

Spencer, T. J. and Clarence J. River. "Langston Hughes: His Style and Optimism." Drama Critique 7 (Spring 1964): 99-102.

Staples, Elizabeth. "Langston Hughes' Malevolent Force." American Mercury 138 (January 1959): 46-50

Taylor, Patricia E. "Langston Hughes and the Harlem Renaissance: 1921-1931." In The Harlem Renaissance Remembered, Bontemps, ed. pp. 90-101

Tobin, Terrence. "Karamu Theater: Its Distinguished Past and Present Achievement." Drama Critique 7 (Spring 1964): 89

Turner, Darwin T. "Langston Hughes as Playwright." CLA Journal 11 (June 1968): 297-309
_____ . "Past and Present in Negro Drama." Negro American Literature Forum 2 (1968): 26-27

Turpin, Waters E. "The Contemporary American Negro Playwright." CLA Journal 9 (1965)

Van Vechten, Carl. "How The Theatre Is Represented in The Negro Collection at Yale." The Theatre Annual (1943): 33

Watkins, C. A. "'Simple,' Alter-Ego of Langston Hughes." Black Scholar 2 (June 1971): 18-26

Williams. Stage Left. pp. 46, 131, 230

Young. Black Writers of the Thirties, pp. 172-179, 216-219

CRITICISMS OF INDIVIDUAL PLAYS:
Don't You Want to Be Free?
Abramson. Negro Playwrights in the American Theatre 1925-1959. pp. 79-83, 88
Emanuel. Langston Hughes. pp. 39-40
Hicklin. The American Negro Playwright 1920-1964. Part 1, pp. 256-257
Mitchell. Black Drama. pp. 103-105
Drums of Haiti (Emperor of Haiti) (Troubled Island)
Emanuel. Langston Hughes. pp. 38, 42, 43
Hicklin. The American Negro Playwright 1920-1964. Part 1, pp. 283-285
Front Porch
Emanuel. Langston Hughes. p. 39

Hicklin. The American Negro Playwright 1920-
1964, Part 1, pp. 257-258
Joy to My Soul
Hicklin. The American Negro Playwright 1920-
1964, Part 1, pp. 256-257
Little Ham
Hicklin. The American Negro Playwright 1920-
1964, Part 1, pp. 250-252
Spencer and Rivers. "Langston Hughes: His
Style and Optimism." Drama Critique 7
(Spring 1964): 100
Turner, Darwin T. "Langston Hughes as Play-
wright." CLA Journal 11 (June 1968): 301-
304
Mulatto
Abramson. Negro Playwrights in the American
Theatre 1925-1959. pp. 69-79, 87
Bond. The Negro and the Drama. pp. 114-117
Cotton, Lettie Jo. "Negro in the American
Theatre." Negro History Bulletin 23 (May
1960): 177
Emanuel. Langston Hughes. pp. 37, 38, 43, 44
Hicklin. The American Negro Playwright 1920-
1964, Part 1, pp. 246-249
Hughes, Langston. Five Plays. pp. x-xl
Isaacs, Edith J. R. "The Negro in the American
Theater: A Record of Achievement." Thea-
ter Arts 26 (August 1942): 495
Locke, Alain. "Deep River." Opportunity 14
(January 1936): 6-10
Mitchell. Black Drama. p. 97
Spencer and Rivers. "Langston Hughes: His
Style and Optimism." Drama Critique 7
(Spring 1964): 100, 101
Turner, Darwin T. "Langston Hughes as Play-
wright." CLA Journal 11 (June 1968): 297-
301
Scottsboro Blues
Downer, Alan S. The American Theatre Today.
p. 30
Hicklin. The American Negro Playwright 1920-
1964. Part 1, pp. 245-246
Taylor. People's Theatre in Amerika. pp. 47-
50
Simply Heavenly
Emanuel. Langston Hughes. pp. 44, 155, 178
Hicklin. The American Negro Playwright 1920-

1964. Part 2, pp. 430-434
Hughes, Langston. Five Plays. pp. xiii-xv, 115
Spencer and Rivers. "Langston Hughes: His
    Style and Optimism." Drama Critique 7
    (Spring 1964): 100, 101
Turner, Darwin T. "Langston Hughes as Play-
    wright." CLA Journal 11 (June 1968): 305-307
    _____. "Negro Playwrights and the Urban
    Negro." CLA Journal 12 (September 1968): 20
Weales. American Drama Since World War II.
    pp. 210, 231
Soul Gone Home
    Emanuel. Langston Hughes. p. 83
    Hicklin. The American Negro Playwright 1920-
        1964. Part 1, pp. 249-250
    Hughes, Langston. Five Plays. pp. xi-xii
    Spencer and Rivers. "Langston Hughes: His
        Style and Optimism." Drama Critique 7
        (Spring 1964): 101-102
Street Scene
    Lewis. American Plays and Playwrights: Trends
        of the Decade. pp. 137, 255
When (the) Jack Hollers
    Hicklin. The American Negro Playwright 1920-
        1964. Part 1, pp. 252-253
    Isaacs, Edith J. R. The "Negroes in the Ameri-
        can Theater: The Hope Ahead." Theater Arts
        26 (August 1942): 541
CRITICISMS OF INDIVIDUAL MUSICALS:
    Ballad of the Brown King
        Emanuel. Langston Hughes. p. 168
    The Barrier
        Davis, Arthur P. "The Tragic Mulatto Theme
            in Six Works of Langston Hughes." Phylon
            (Winter 1955): 195-204
        Emanuel. Langston Hughes. p. 168
    Black Nativity
        Emanuel. Langston Hughes. p. 168
        Hicklin. The American Negro Playwright 1920-
            1964. Part 2, pp. 435-436
    Esther
        Emanuel. Langston Hughes. p. 43
    Gospel Glory (Gospel Glow)
        Emanuel. Langston Hughes. p. 168
        Hicklin. The American Negro Playwright 1920-
            1964. Part 2, pp. 438
    Jericho-Jim Crow

Emanuel. Langston Hughes. p. 169
Hicklin. The American Negro Playwright 1920-
    1964. Part 2, pp. 438-39
Lewis. American Plays and Playwrights: Trends
    of the Decade. p. 253
Lewis, Emory. Stages: The Fifty Year Child-
    hood of the American Theatre. p. 159

Mule Bone
    Spencer and Rivers. "Langston Hughes: His
    Style and Optimism." Drama Critique 7
    (Spring 1964): 99, 100

Port Town
    Emanuel. Langston Hughes. pp. 167-168

The Prodigal Son
    Emanuel. Langston Hughes. p. 169

The Sun Do Move
    Hicklin. The American Negro Playwright 1920-
    1964. Part 2, pp. 306-307
    Turner, Darwin T. "Langston Hughes as Play-
    wright." CLA Journal 11 (June 1968): 304-
    305

Tambourines to Glory
    Emanuel. Langston Hughes. pp. 168-169
    Henderson. The City and the Theatre. p. 283
    Hicklin. The American Negro Playwright 1920-
    1964. Part 2, pp. 436-438
    Nichols, Lewis. "Langston Hughes Describes the
    Genesis of His Tambourines to Glory." New
    York Times, 27 October 1963, 2: 3
    Turner, Darwin T. "Langston Hughes as Play-
    wright." CLA Journal 11 (June 1968): 308-309

REVIEWS OF INDIVIDUAL PLAYS:
Little Ham
    Atkinson, Brooks. "The Play" (Little Ham).
    New York Times, 25 October 1935, 25: 2
    Pullen, Glen C. "Gilpin Players Revive Lang-
    ston Hughes' Little Ham." Cleveland Plain
    Dealer, 26 May 1938

Mulatto
    Atkinson, Brooks. "The Play" (Mulatto). New
    York Times, 25 October 1935, 25: 2
    Belcher, Fannin S. J. "The Negro Theater: A
    Glance Backward." Phylon 11 (Second Quar-
    ter 1950): 126
    "Censors Tie on Mulatto." New York Times, 11
    February 1937, 18: 1
    "Lifts Ban on Mulatto." New York Times, 25

November 1939, 13: 2

"Mulatto." Cleveland Plain Dealer, 17 October
1936, 11: 5

"New Mulatto Hearing." New York Times, 10
February 1937, 19: 1

"Philadelphia Halts the Play Mulatto." New York
Times, 9 February 1937, 18: 5

"Philadelphia Keeps Ban on Play Mulatto." New
York Times, 12 February 1937, 27: 4

The Prodigal Son
America 113 (10 July 1965): 62
New York Times, 21 May 1965: 19
Riley, Clayton. "Prodigal Son." Liberator 5
(October 1965): 14
Zolotov, Sam. " 'St. Louis Woman' to Close
Saturday." New York Times, 3 July 1946, 20: 1

REVIEWS OF INDIVIDUAL MUSICALS:
The Barrier
Jefferson, Miles M. "The Negro on Broadway:
1949-1950." Phylon 11 (Second Quarter 1950):
110-111
————. "Empty Season on Broadway: 1950-
1951." Phylon (Second Quarter 1951): 128
"New Plays: The Barrier." Theatre Arts 35
(January 1951): 12
Black Nativity
Gordon, Charles. "Black Nativity." Black Thea-
tre 3 (1970): 34
"Gospel Abroad" (Black Nativity). Newsweek 60
(3 September 1962): 50
Shelton, Robert. "Theatre" (Black Nativity). Na-
tion 190 (5 January 1963): 20
Taubman, Howard. "Theatre" (Black Nativity).
New York Times, 12 December 1961, 54: 2
Simply Heavenly
New York Theater Critics' Reviews (1957): 264
Street Scene
New York Theater Critics' Reviews (1947): 490
Tambourines to Glory
Ivy, James. "Review: Tambourines to Glory,"
Crisis 64 (January 1957)
Parker, John. "Review: Tambourines to Glory."
Phylon 136 (Spring 1959)

CRITICISMS OF INDIVIDUAL FILMS:
Way Down South
Isaacs, Edith J. R. "The Negro in the American
Theater: The Foreground, 1917-1942." Thea-

ter Arts 26 (August 1942): 510
MEDIA RESOURCES:
Jericho-Jim Crow. Folkways, FL 9671. Musical
recording by the cast
Street Scene. Columbia, OL 4139. Musical record-
ing by the cast

HUGHLY, YOUNG
PLAY:
Place for the Manchild, 1972

HULT, RUBY
PLAY:
The Saga of George W. Bush, 1962

HUNKINS, LEECYNTH (Lee Hunkins) (b. January 8, 1930)
PLAY:
[With Steve Chambers] The Dolls, 1971

HUNTER, EDDIE
PLAYS:
The Battle of Who Run
Going to the Races
How Come?, 1923
The Lady, 1944
MUSICAL:
[With Alex Rogers] My Magnolia, 1926
CRITICISMS OF HUNTER:
Mitchell. Black Drama. pp. 65-67, 68, 92
CRITICISMS OF INDIVIDUAL PLAYS:
How Come?
Mitchell. Black Drama. pp. 70, 82

HUNTLEY, ELIZABETH MADDOX
PLAYS:
Legion, the Demoniac
What Ye Saw. New York: Court, 1955
PLAYS PUBLISHED IN ANTHOLOGIES:
Legion, the Demoniac, in Dreer, American Litera-
ture by Negro Authors

HURSTON, ZORA NEALE (January 7, 1903-January 38, 1960)
PLAYS:
Color Struck: A Play in Four Scenes
The First One, one act, 1927
Great Day, 1927
[With Langston Hughes] Mule Bone: A Comedy of

Negro Life in Three Acts, 1931
[With Dorothy Waring] Polk County, 1944
Spears
PLAYS PUBLISHED IN ANTHOLOGIES:
The First One, in Johnson, Ebony and Topaz
PLAYS PUBLISHED IN PERIODICALS:
Color Struck, in Fire, 1 (November 1926): 7-14
Mule Bone, in Drama Critique (Spring 1964): 1-3-
107, (Excerpts)
MUSICALS:
[With Clinton Fletcher and Tim Moore] Fast and
Furious
MUSICALS PUBLISHED IN ANTHOLOGIES:
Fast and Furious, in Burns, Mantle and Garrison
Sherwood, Best Plays of 1931-1932
AWARDS:
Honorable Mention for Spears, Opportunity Contest,
May 1925

ICEBERG SLIM see Robert Beck

IMAN, KASISI YUSEF
PLAYS:
Blowing Temptation Away, 1972
The Cause the Cure, 1971
The Joke on You, 1970
Libra, 1971
Mr. Bad, 1972
Nigger House, 1969
Praise the Lord, But Pass the Ammunition. Newark:
Jihad, 1967
The Price of Revolution, 1971
Resurrection, 1970
Santa's Last Ride, 1970
Sociology (700 Clean up Time), 1970
The Verdict Is Yours, 1970

JACKSON, C. GERNARD
MUSICAL:
[With James V. Hatch] Fly Blackbird, 1963
MUSICALS PUBLISHED IN ANTHOLOGIES:
The Blackbird, in Hatch and Shine, Black Theater
USA; Reardon and Pawley, The Black Teacher
and Dramatic Arts
REVIEWS OF INDIVIDUAL MUSICALS:

Fly Blackbird
New Yorker 24 February 1962, p. 2
Simon, John. "Play Reviews: Fly Blackbird."
Theatre Arts 46 (May 1962): 61-62
AWARDS:
Obie Award, 1962, for best musical: Fly Blackbird

JACKSON, ELAINE
PLAY:
Adaptation. Toe Jam
PLAYS PUBLISHED IN ANTHOLOGIES:
Toe Jam, in King and Milner, Black Drama Antholo-
gy
CRITICISMS OF JACKSON:
Lewis. American Plays and Playwrights of the Con-
temporary Theatre. p. 214

JACKSON, EUGENIA LUTCHER
PLAYS:
Everything Is Everything
Life

JACKSON, REV. JESSE
PLAY:
A New Day
AWARDS:
A New Day received an award from the National
Black Writers Conference

JACKSON, JO
PLAY:
Martin and Malcolm

JACKSON, REVEREND SPENCER
PLAYS:
Come Home, 1969
A New Day, 1969

JACKSON, WILLIAM
PLAY:
Burning the Mortgage, one act, 1931
Four Eleven
AWARDS:
Third Place for Four Eleven, Opportunity Contest
Award, June 1927

JEANETTE, GERTRUDE

PLAYS:
A Bolt from the Blue, 1952
Light in the Cellar
This Way Forward, 1951
CRITICISMS OF JEANETTE:
"Gertrude Jeanette in Hit." New York Amsterdam
News, 29 February 1964. p. 17
Hicklin. The American Negro Playwright 1920-
1964. Part 2, pp. 462-463
Mitchell. Black Drama. pp. 136, 139, 145, 208
CRITICISMS OF INDIVIDUAL PLAYS:
A Bolt from the Blue
Hicklin. The American Negro Playwright 1920-
1964. Part 2, p. 374
Light in the Cellar
Hicklin. The American Negro Playwright 1920-
1964. Part 2, pp. 374-375
This Way Forward
Hicklin. The American Negro Playwright 1920-
1964. Part 2, pp. 369-374
REVIEWS OF INDIVIDUAL PLAYS:
Bolt from the Blue
Jones, John Hudson. " 'Bolt from Blue' Pleases
Audiences in Harlem." Daily Worker, 10
April 1952

JOHNSON, EUGENE
PLAY:
Spaces in Between

JOHNSON, GEORGIA DOUGLAS (September 10, 1886-1966)
PLAYS:
Attucks
Blue Blood. New York: Appleton, 1927
Frederick Douglass
Plumes: Folk Tragedy. New York: French, 1927
The Starting Point
A Sunday Morning in the South: A One Act Play.
Washington, n.p., 1924?
William and Ellen Craft
PLAYS PUBLISHED IN ANTHOLOGIES:
Blue Blood, in Shay, Fifty More Contemporary One
Act Plays
Frederick Douglass, in Richardson and Miller, Negro
History in Thirteen Plays
Plumes, in Calverton, Anthology of American Negro
Literature; Locke and Gregory, Plays of Negro

Life
A Sunday Morning in the South, in Hatch and Shine,
    Black Theater USA
William and Ellen Craft, in Richardson and Miller,
    Negro History in Thirteen Plays
CRITICISMS OF JOHNSON:
Dover, Cedric. "The Importance of Georgia
    Douglas Johnson." Crisis 59 (December 1952):
    633-636, 674
CRITICISMS OF INDIVIDUAL PLAYS:
Attucks
    Hicklin. The American Negro Playwright 1920-
        1964. Part 1, p. 224
Frederick Douglass
    Bond. The Negro and the Drama. pp. 188-189
    Hicklin. The American Negro Playwright 1920-
        1964. Part 1, p. 223
A Sunday Morning in the South
    Hatch and Shine. Black Theater USA. pp. 211-
        212
William and Ellen Craft
    Hicklin. The American Negro Playwright 1920-
        1964. Part 1, pp. 223-224
AWARDS:
Plumes was chosen by Opportunity magazine as the
    best play in the 1927 contest

JOHNSON, HALL (March 12, 1888-1970)
MUSICALS:
Run, Little Chillun, 1933
CRITICISMS OF JOHNSON:
Archer. Black Images. p. 14
Arvey, Verna. "Hall Johnson and His Choir."
    Opportunity 19 (May 1941): 151, 158-159
"Negro Playwrights: Young Chicagoan First with
    All-Negro Play on Broadway." Ebony 14 (April
    1959): 100
CRITICISMS OF INDIVIDUAL MUSICALS:
Run, Little Chillun
    Beiswanger, George. "The Theatre Moves To-
        ward Music." Theatre Arts 25 (April 1941):
        295
    Carmer, Carl. "'Run, Little Chillun!': A Criti-
        cal Review." Opportunity 11 (April 1933): 113
    Eustis, Morton. "The Optimist on Broadway:
        Broadway in Review." Theatre Arts Monthly
        17 (May 1933): 337

Flanagan. Arena. p. 290
Gayle. Black Expression. p. 153
Harrison. The Drama of Nommo. pp. 98-102
Hicklin. The American Negro Playwright 1920-
1964. Part 1, pp. 235-239
Isaacs, Edith J. R. "The Negro in the American
Theatre: The Foreground 1917-1942." Thea-
tre Arts 26 (August 1942): 526
Quin. A History of American Drama from the
Civil War to the Present Day. p. 289
"Run, Little Chillun!" Theatre Arts Monthly 12
(April 1933): 307
REVIEWS OF INDIVIDUAL MUSICALS:
Run, Little Chillun
Downes, Olin. "Run, Little Chillun!" New York
Times, 2 April 1933, IX, 5: 1
Nichols, Lewis. "The Play." (Run, Little Chil-
lun). New York Times, 2 March 1933, 21: 3
AWARDS:
Harmon Award, 1931

JOHNSON, HERMAN
PLAYS:
Nowhere to Run, Nowhere to Hide
REVIEWS OF INDIVIDUAL PLAYS:
Nowhere to Run, Nowhere to Hide
New Yorker 25 March 1974, p. 4
Willis, John. Theatre World: 1973-1974 Season.
Vol. 30. N.Y.: Crown, 1975, p. 118

JOHNSON, J. ROSAMOND
MUSICALS:
[With Bob Cole] Red Moon, 1908
[With Bob Cole] The Shoofly Regiment, 1906
CRITICISMS OF JOHNSON:
Atkinson. Broadway. p. 337
Cotton, Lettie Jo. "Negro in the American Thea-
tre." Negro History Bulletin 23 (May 1960): 173
Fisher, Rudolph. "The Caucasian Storms Harlem."
American Mercury 11 (August 1927): 397-
Gayle. The Black Aesthetic. p. 297
      . Black Expression. p. 151
Mitchell. Black Drama. pp. 41, 46, 47, 84, 109
CRITICISMS OF INDIVIDUAL MUSICALS:
Red Moon
Isaacs, Edith J. R. "The Middle Distance:
1890-1917--Heyday of Comedy & Dance."

Theatre Arts 26 (August 1942): 527
Johnson. Black Manhattan. p. 109
Shoofly Regiment
Isaacs, Edith J. R. "The Middle Distance:
1890-1917--Heyday of Comedy & Dance."
Theatre Arts 26 (August 1942): 527
Johnson. Black Manhattan. p. 109
A Trip to Coontown
Isaacs, Edith J. R. "The Middle Distance:
1890-1917--Heyday of Comedy and Dance."
Theatre Arts 26 (August 1942): 527

JOHNSTON, PERCY
PLAYS:
DaWitt II. N.Y.: Rinjohn Productions, 1973
Emperor Dessalines. N.Y.: Rinjohn Productions,
1973
John Adams, A Historical Drama, Parts I and II.
N.Y.: Rinjohn Productions, 1972

JONES, E. H. (July 8, 1925)
PLAY:
Our Very Best Christmas

JONES, GENE-OLIVAR
PLAY:
No Church Next Sunday

JONES, ROBERT
PLAYS:
Patriot's Dream; or, The Past, the Present, and
the Future, 1861
The Hidden Hand, 1859. Boston: W. H. Baker,
1889
Through Black and Black
White Terror, 1882

JONES, WALTER
PLAYS:
Dudder Lover, 1972
The Boston Party at Annie Mae's House, 1970
Fish 'n Chips
Jazz Nite, one act, 1968
Mae's House, 1970
Nigger Nightmare, 1969
Reverend Brown's Daughter, 1972
REVIEWS OF INDIVIDUAL PLAYS:

Jazz Nite
    Barnes, C. New York Times, 19 April 1971,
      52: 1
    Kerr, W. New York Times, 25 April 1971, II,
      3: 1
    New Yorker 1 May 1971, p. 4
    Rudin, Seymour. "Theatre Chronicle: Winter-
      Spring 1971." Massachusetts Review 12
      (Autumn 1971): 821-833

JONES, WILLA SAUNDERS (b. February 22, 1904)
    PLAYS:
      The Birth of Christ
      The Call to Arms
      Just One Hour to Live (For the Dope Addict)
      The Life Boat
      The Passion Play. (1973 Passion Play was the
        44th Annual Production, Chicago, Illinois)
      Up from Slavery

JOPLIN, SCOTT (1868-1917)
    OPERAS:
      Guest of Honor, a Ragtime Opera, 1903. (Joplin
        scholars have been unable to locate a copy of
        this work.)
      The Ragtime Dance, Folk Ballet, 1903
      Treemonisha, Ragtime Opera, 1911. World pre-
        miere held in Atlanta, January 28-29, 1972,
        under the direction of Robert Shaw with Katherine
        Dunham as stage director
    OPERAS PUBLISHED IN ANTHOLOGIES:
      Treemonisha
      Lawrence, Vera Brodsky. The Collected Works
        of Scott Joplin. Vol. 2. N.Y.: New York
        Public Library, 1971
    CRITICISMS OF INDIVIDUAL OPERAS:
      Treemonisha
      "An Old Ragtime Man Goes to the Opera."
        Ebony 27 (April 1972): 90
      Bolcom, William. "Orchestrating 'Treemonisha.'"
        The Performer Magazine at Wolf Trap, (Sec-
        ond Season, 1972). Vol. 2, Book 3, p. 9
      Brodsky, Vera Laurence. "The Opera and Its
        Composer." The Performer Magazine at
        Wolf Trap. (Second Season, 1972). Vol. 2,
        Book 3, p. H
            . "Scott Joplin's 'Treemonisha.'" High

Fidelity/Musical America (May 1972): MA-10

Drimmer, Melvin. "Joplin's Treemonisha in Atlanta." Phylon 34 (June 1973): 197-202

Kolodin, Irving. "Carry Me Back to Treemonisha." Saturday Review (2 September 1972): 62

Kriegsman, Alan M. " 'Treemonisha:' Cheers and Contagious Zest." The Washington Post, 11 August 1972

Reed, Addison W. "The Life and Works of Scott Joplin." Ph.D. Dissertation. University of North Carolina at Chapel Hill, 1973

Rowley-Rotunno, Virginia. "Scott Joplin's Renascence of a Black Composer of Ragtime and Grand Opera." Negro History Bulletin 37 (January 1974): 188-193

Schafer, William J. and Johannes Riedel. "Scott Joplin's Treemonisha," in The Art of Ragtime. Baton Rouge: Louisiana State University Press, 1973, pp. 205-225

BOOK:
The School of Ragtime. n.p., 1908

JORDON, NORMAN (b. July 30, 1938)
PLAYS:
Cadillac Dreams, 1972
Destination Ashes, 1971
In the Last Days, 1971
MEDIA RESOURCES:
The Life and Works of Norman Jordon, English Dept. Case Western Reserve, Cleveland, Ohio

JUA, CHAKULA CHA
PLAYS:
[With Leppaigne Chiphe] A Black Experience
Langston & Company
Langston Hughes: A Poet of the People
REVIEWS OF INDIVIDUAL PLAYS:
Langston & Company
"Langston & Company Comes to F.S.T." FST Voice 1 (August 1974): 1

JULIAN, MAX
FILM SCRIPT:
Thomasine and Bushrod
REVIEWS OF INDIVIDUAL FILMS:
Thomasine and Bushrod
"Playboy After Hours: Movies." Playboy 7 (July 1974): 35

KAIN, GYLAN
    PLAY:
        Epitaph to a Coagulated Trinity

KELLY, JO-ANN (b. April 16, 1949)
    PLAYS:
        A Gift for Aunt Sarah, 1970
        Where the Sun Don't Shine

KEMP, ARNOLD
    PLAY:
        White Wound, Black Scar

KENNEDY, ADRIENNE (b. September 13, 1931)
    PLAYS:
        A Beast Story, 1966
        Boats, 1969
        Cities in Bezique: Two One-Act Plays. New York:
           Samuel French, 1970; Includes A Beast Story and
           The Owl Answers
        An Evening with Dead Essex, 1973
        Funnyhouse of a Negro
        [With John Lennon and V. Spinetti] The Lennon
           Play: In His Own Write. New York: Simon
           and Schuster, 1972
        A Lesson in Dead Language
        The Owl Answers
        A Rat's Mass
        The Son, 1970
        Sun
    PLAYS PUBLISHED IN ANTHOLOGIES:
        A Beast Story, in Kennedy, Cities in Bezique
        Funnyhouse of a Negro, in Brasmer and Consolo,
           Black Drama; Oliver and Sills, Contemporary
           Black Drama; Patterson, Anthology of the Negro
           in American Theatre; Richards, Best Short Plays
           of 1970
        A Lesson in Dead Language, in Parone, Collision
           Course
        The Owl Answers, in Harrison, Kuntu Drama; Hatch
           and Shine, Black Theater USA; Hoffman, New
           American Plays, vol. 2; Kennedy, Cities in
           Bezique
        A Rat's Mass, in Couch, New Black Playwrights;
           Poland and Mailman, The Off-Broadway Book;
           Smith, More Plays from Off Off-Broadway
        Sun, in Owens and Feingold, Spontaneous Combustion:
           Eight New American Plays

CRITICISMS OF KENNEDY:
  Abramson. Negro Playwrights in the American
    Theatre. pp. 279, 281, 283
  Harrison. The Drama of Nommo. pp. 216-220
  Little. Off-Broadway. pp. 233, 282
  Mitchell. Black Drama. pp. 198-199, 216
  Weales. The Jumping-Off Place. p. 117
CRITICISMS OF INDIVIDUAL PLAYS:
  Funnyhouse of a Negro
    Hicklin. The American Negro Playwright 1920-
      1964. Part 2, pp. 417-418
    Lewis. American Plays and Playwrights: Trends
      of the Decade. pp. 233, 253
    Lewis, Emory. Stages: The Fifty Year Child-
      hood of the American Theater. p. 158
    Little. Off-Broadway. p. 233
    Patterson. Anthology of the American Negro in
      the Theatre. pp. 281-290
    Talbot, William. "Every Negro in His Place."
      Drama Critique 7 (Spring 1964): 94
    Turner, Darwin T. "Negro Playwrights and the
      Urban Negro." CLA Journal 12 (September
      1968): 24
  Cities in Bezique
    Duberman, Martin. "Theater 69: Black Theater."
      Partisan Review (1969): 490-491
  The Owl Answers
    Hatch and Shine. Black Theater USA. p. 756
  A Rat's Mass
    Scott, John. "Teaching Black Drama." Players
      47 (February-March 1972): 131
REVIEWS OF INDIVIDUAL PLAYS:
  Cities in Bezique
    New York Times, 13 January 1969, p. 26; 19
      January 1969, II, p. 3
    New Yorker 44 (25 January 1969): 77
    Rudin, Seymour. "Theatre Chronicle: Winter-
      Spring 1969." The Massachusetts Review 10
      (Summer 1969): 583-593
  Cities in Bezique: The Owl Answers
    New York Times, 13 January 1969, p. 26: 1;
      19 January 1969, II, p. 3: 5
  Cities in Bezique: A Beast Story
    New York Times, 13 January 1969, 26: 1
      _____, 19 January 1969, II, p. 3: 5
  Funnyhouse of a Negro
    " 'Funnyhouse' Is Reprieved." New York Times,

28 January 1964, 24: 4

Sontag, Susan. "Going to the Theatre (and the
Movies)." Partisan Review 31 (Spring 1964):
284-293

Taubman, Howard. "The Theatre: Funnyhouse
of a Negro." New York Times, 15 January
1964, p. 25

In His Own Write
New York Times, 20 June 1968, p. 50; 9 July
1968, p. 30; 14 July 1968, II, p. 4

A Rat's Mass
New York Times, 1 November 1969, 39: 1

AWARDS:
Obie Award for Funnyhouse of a Negro; Stanley
Award for Playwrighting

KENYATTA, DAMON
PLAY:
The Black Experience, 1971

KILLENS, JOHN OLIVER (b. 1916)
PLAYS:
[With Loften Mitchell] Ballad of the Winter Soldiers,
1965

Lower than the Angels, 1965

FILM SCRIPTS:
Odds Against Tomorrow
[With Herbert Bibeman] Slaves

CRITICISMS BY KILLENS:
"Another Time When Black Was Beautiful." Black
World 20 (1970): 20-36

"The Black Writer and the Revolution." Arts in
Society 5 (1968): 395-399

"The Black Writer vis-à-vis His Country." In
Gayle, The Black Aesthetic. pp. 379-396

"Broadway in Black and White." African Forum 1
(Winter 1966): 66-70

"New Creative Writers." Library Journal 79 (15
February 1974): 374

"Opportunities for Development of Negro Talent."
American Negro Writer and His Roots. pp. 64-
70

"Rappin' With Myself." In Williams and Harris,
Amistad 2. pp. 97-136

CRITICISMS OF KILLENS:
Gayle. The Black Aesthetic. p. 257
Mitchell, Loften. "Three Writers and a Dream."

Crisis 72 (April 1965): 219-223

Russell, Charles L. "John O. Killens: Tell It Like It Is." Liberator 4 (April 1964): 10

CRITICISMS OF INDIVIDUAL PLAYS:

Ballad of the Winter Soldiers

Bigsby. The Black American Writer. Vol II, p. 144

Mitchell. Black Drama. p. 202

CRITICISMS OF INDIVIDUAL FILM SCRIPTS:

Odds Against Tomorrow

Bogle. Toms, Coons, Mulattoes, Mammies and Bucks. pp. 225-226

Mapp. Blacks in American Films. p. 49

Slaves

Mapp. Blacks in American Films. pp. 211-212

KILPATRICK, LINCOLN

PLAY:

[With Loretta Leverse] Deep Are the Roots

KING, WOODIE, JR. (b. July 27, 1937)

PLAYS:

Simple Blues, 1967 (adaptation from Langston Hughes)

The Weary Blues, 1966 (adaptation from Langston Hughes)

CRITICISMS BY KING:

"Black Theatre: Present Condition." Drama Review 12 (Summer 1968): 117-124; also in King and Anthony, Black Poets and Prophets

"Black Theater: Weapon for Change." Negro Digest 16 (April 1967): 35-39

"Black Writer's View of Literary Lions and Values." Negro Digest 18 (January 1968): 26

"The Dilemma of a Black Theater." Negro Digest 19 (April 1970): 86-87

"Educational Theater and the Black Community." Black World 21 (April 1972): 25-29

"Leading Man at the Met." Ebony 21 (January 1966): 84-90

"Problems Facing Negro Actors." Negro Digest 16 (April 1966): 53. Also in Patterson, Anthology of the American Negro in the Theater

"Remembering Langston." Negro Digest 18 (April 1969): 27-32

"The Theater: a Weapon for Change." Negro Digest 14 (April 1967): 35

CRITICISMS OF KING:
> Bailey, Peter A. "Woodie King, Jr.: Renaissance Man of Black Theatre." Black World 26 (April 1975): 4-12
>
> Fuller, Hoyt W. "Stage, Screen and Black Hegemony: Black World Interviews Woodie King, Jr." Black World 26 (April 1975): 4-12

FILMSCRIPT:
> [With Herbert Dunska] Right On!, 1971

CRITICISMS OF FILMS:
> Right On!
>> Mapp. Blacks in American Films. p. 250

DRAMA CRITIC:
> Detroit Tribune, 1959-1962

EDITOR:
> [With Ron Milner] Black Drama Anthology. New York: Columbia University Press, 1972; New York: New American Library, 1972

PRODUCER:
> Plays by Ben Caldwell, Ed Bullins, Ronald Milner and LeRoi Jones in A Black Quartet
> Black Girl, J. E. Franklin
> Behold! Cometh the Vanderkellans, William Mackay
> In New England Winter, Ed Bullins
> Slave Ship, Le Roi Jones

KIRKSEY, VAN
> PLAY:
>> The Hassle

KNUDSEN, K.
> PLAY:
>> There Were Two Tramps, Now There Are None

KOENIG, LAIRD
> PLAY:
>> The Dozens, 1969

LAMB, ARTHUR CLIFTON (b. May 5, 1909)
> PLAYS:
>> Black Woman in White, 1941; updated in 1964 for Off-Broadway
>> The Breeders
>> Christy's Citadel
>> The Faith Cure Man, one act, 1930
>> God's Great Acres, three acts, 1939

The New Window
Portrait of a Pioneer, one act
Reaching for the Sun, one act
Shades of Cotton Lips, one act, 1933
She Died for a Prince, one act farce
The Two Gifts: A Christmas Play for Negroes, 1932
PLAYS PUBLISHED IN ANTHOLOGIES:
The Two Gifts, in Grinnell Plays
PLAYS PUBLISHED IN PERIODICALS:
Christy's Citadel, in Intercollegian, April 1956
Portrait of a Pioneer, in Negro History Bulletin
12 (April 1949): 162-164
MUSICAL:
Roughshod up the Mountain, 1956
TELEVISION SCRIPTS:
Mistake into Miracle, ninety minutes, 1961
CRITICISMS OF INDIVIDUAL PLAYS:
God's Great Acres
Hicklin. The American Negro Playwright 1920-
1964. Part 1, pp. 272-273
CRITICISMS OF INDIVIDUAL MUSICALS:
Roughshod up the Mountain
"Musical Play Going to Festival in Paris." New
York Times, 14 December 1963, 21: 4
AWARDS:
Sergel's Prize in Regional Playwrighting, State Uni-
versity of Iowa.
Roughshod Up the Mountain was selected as the
American entry in the International Festival Sarah
Bernhardt Theatre, Paris, June 1964
Shades of Cotton Lips won first prize in the Henry
York Steiner Memorial Playwrighting Prize

LANGE, TED
PLAYS:
Day Zsa Voo
A Foul Movement
Pig, Male and Young
Sounds from a Flute
FILM SCRIPTS:
Booker's Back
Boss Rain Bow
Little Brother
Passing Thru
Pig, Male and Young
Sounds from a Flute
Tuned In

LAYTON, J. TURNER
    MUSICAL:
        [With Henry S. Creamer] Strut Miss Lizzie, (1922)

LEAGUE, RAYMOND
    PLAY:
        Mrs. Carrie B. Phillips, 1971

LEAKS, SYLVESTER (b. August 11, 1927)
    PLAY:
        Trouble, Blues 'n' Trouble

LeBLANC, WHITNEY J. (b. June 20, 1931)
    PLAYS:
        Dreams Deferred
        It's a Small World
        The Killing of an Eagle

LEE, BILLY (b. February 23, 1942)
    PLAY:
        The Rag Pickers

LEE, LESLIE
    PLAYS:
        The First Breeze of Summer, 1975
    REVIEWS OF INDIVIDUAL PLAYS:
        New York Times, 3 March 1975, 37: 1
        Ward, D. T. "The First Breeze of Summer."
           New York Times, 2 March 1975, II, 1: 2

LEE, MARY AT.
    PLAYS:
        Dope, revised edition, 1965
        Four Men and a Monster, 1969

LeROY, LESLIE HURLEY
    PLAY:
        Festivities for a New World

LEVERSE, LORETTA
    PLAY:
        [With Lincoln Kilpatrick] Deep Are the Roots

LEWIS, DAVID (b. January 14, 1939)
    PLAYS:
        Georgia Man and Jamaican Woman, 1969
        Heaven--I've Been There; Hell--I've Been There Too.

Bronx, N.Y.: By Author, 1972
Miss America of 1910
One Hundred Is a Long Number
Sporty
Those Wonderful Folks (of The First Baptist Church
   of Jerusalem)
Wally Dear
AWARDS:
New American Playwriting Series Award, Brooklyn
   College, 1959

LINCOLN, ABBEY
   PLAY:
   A Steak o' Lean
   PLAYS PUBLISHED IN ANTHOLOGIES:
   A Steak o' Lean, in Childress, Black Scenes

LINDSAY, POWELL
   PLAYS:
   Flight from Fear
   Young Man from Harlem, 1938
   CRITICISMS OF LINDSAY:
   Abramson. Negro Playwrights in the American
      Theatre 1925-1959. p. 92
   Negro Playwrights Company. "Perspective." A
      Professional Theatre with an Idea, 1940, unpaged.
      (New York Public Library)

LIPSCOMB, G. D.
   PLAY:
   Frances, one act
   PLAYS PUBLISHED IN PERIODICALS:
   Frances, in Opportunity 3 (May 1925)
   AWARDS:
   First place for Frances, Opportunity Contest, May
      1925

LIVINGSTON, MYRTLE A. SMITH (b. 1901)
   PLAY:
   For Unborn Children, 1926
   PLAYS PUBLISHED IN ANTHOLOGIES:
   For Unborn Children, in Hatch and Shine, Black
      Theater USA
   PLAYS PUBLISHED IN PERIODICALS:
   For Unborn Children, in Crisis 31-33 (July 1926):
      122
   CRITICISMS OF INDIVIDUAL WORKS:

For Unborn Children
    Hatch and Shine, Black Theater USA, p. 184
AWARDS:
    Third Prize, For Unborn Children, Crisis contest,
        October, 1925

LOMAX, PEARL CLEAGE (b. December 7, 1948)
    PLAYS:
        Duet for Three Voices, one act, 1969
        Hymn for the Rebels, one act, 1968
        The Sale, one act, 1972
    CRITICISMS OF LOMAX:
        Kent. Outstanding Works. pp. 323-324

LONG, RICHARD (Ric Alexander) (b. February 9, 1927)
    PLAYS:
        Black Is Many Hues, 1969
        Pilgrim's Price, sketches, 1963
        Reasons of State, 1966
    MUSICALS:
        Joan of Arc, folk opera, 1964
        Stairway to Heaven, gospel opera, 1964
    CRITICISMS BY LONG:
        "Alain Locke: Cultural and Social Mentor." Black
            World 20 (November 1970): 87-90
        "Crisis of Consciousness: Reflections of the Afro-
            American Artist." Negro Digest 17 (May 1968):
            88-92
    REVIEWS BY LONG:
        Published in Phylon

LYLE, K. CURTIS (Kansas Curtis Lyle) (b. May 13, 1944)
    PLAYS:
        Days of Thunder, Nights of Violence, 1970
        Guerrilla Warfare, 1970
        Minstrel Show, 1970
        The Processes of Allusion
        Wichita

MACBETH, ROBERT
    PLAYS:
        A Black Ritual
    PLAYS PUBLISHED IN ANTHOLOGIES:
        A Black Ritual, in Simmons and Hutchinson, Black
            Culture
    PLAYS PUBLISHED IN PERIODICALS:

A Black Ritual, in TDR: The Drama Review 13
(Summer 1969): 129-130
CRITICISMS BY MACBETH:
"A Theatre Uptown Please." The Probe 1 (May
1967): 12
CRITICISMS OF MACBETH:
"Interview with Bob MacBeth: Director of New
Lafayette Theatre." Black Theatre 6 (Fall 1972):
14-21

McBROWN, GERTRUDE PARTHENIC
PLAY:
Birthday Surprise, 1953
PLAYS PUBLISHED IN ANTHOLOGIES:
Birthday Surprise, (Paul L. Dunbar), 1953, in
Negro History Bulletin 16 (February 1953): 102-
104

McCLENDON, ROSE
PLAY:
[With Richard Bruce] Taxi Fare, one act

McCORMACK, TOM
PLAY:
American Roulette, 1969

McDONALD, WARREN A.
PLAY:
Humble Instrument
AWARDS:
Won 2nd Place for Humble Instrument, May 1925
Opportunity Contest

McGRIFF, MILTON
PLAY:
And Then We Heard Thunder, 1968 (based on a
novel by John O. Killens)

McGUIRE, LOIS
PLAY:
The Lion Writes, 1970

McIVER, RAY
PLAY:
God Is a (Guess What?), 1968
CRITICISMS OF McIVER:
Duberman, Martin. "Theatre 69: Black Theatre."
Partisan Review (1969): 488

REVIEWS OF INDIVIDUAL PLAYS:
God Is a (Guess What?)

> Harris, Leonard. WCBS TV 2 17 December 1968
>
> Kerr, Walter. The New York Sunday Times, 29 December 1968
>
> New York Daily News, 18 December 1968
>
> New York Post, 18 December 1968
>
> New York Theatre Critics' Reviews (1968): 129
>
> New Yorker 21 December 1968, p. 2
>
> Probst, Leonard. NBC 4 TV 17 December 1968
>
> Sullivan, Dan. New York Times, 18 December 1968
>
> Women's Wear Daily, 18 December 1968

MACK, ETHEL
PLAY:
Phyllis
PLAYS PUBLISHED IN PERIODICALS:
Phyllis, in Dasein 1 (March 1961): 15-28

MACK, RON
PLAY:
Black Is ... We Are, 1969

McKETNEY, EDWIN CHARLES
PLAYS:
Mr. Big, three acts. New York: Pageant, 1954
Virgin Islands, three acts. New York: William-Frederick, 1951

MACKEY, WILLIAM WELLINGTON
PLAYS:
Behold! Cometh the Vanderkellons. New York: Azaziel Books, 1967
Death of Charlie Blackman
Family Meeting. New York: Dramatists Play Service, 1973
Love Me, Love Me, Daddy--Or I Swear I'm Gonna' Kill You
Requiem for Brother X. Saga, five act musical drama, forthcoming
PLAYS PUBLISHED IN ANTHOLOGIES:
Family Meeting, in Couch, New Black Playwrights
Requiem for Brother X, in King and Milner, Black Drama Anthology
MUSICAL:
Billy No Name, 1970

CRITICISMS OF INDIVIDUAL PLAYS:
Family Meeting
Scott, John S. "Teaching Black Drama." Players 47 (February-March 1972): 130
CRITICISMS OF INDIVIDUAL MUSICALS:
Billy No Name
"Playboy After Hours: Theatre." Playboy 17 (June 1970): 42
REVIEWS OF INDIVIDUAL PLAYS:
Behold! Cometh the Vanderkellans
Barnes, Clive. New York Times, 1 April 1971, 50: 1
Fuller, Hoyt. Negro Digest 16 (April 1967): 51-52
New Yorker 10 April 1971

MADDOX, GLORIA DEMBY
PLAY:
Black Monday's Children

MALONEY, CLARENCE J. (CHAKA JO)
PLAY:
The Sun Force, 1970

MARCUS, FRANK
PLAY:
Bamboula
CRITICISMS OF INDIVIDUAL PLAYS:
Bamboula
Tutt, Whitney. "Smarter Set Company Presents New Vehicle." Competitor 2 (August-September 1920): 157

MARTIN, HERBERT WOODWARD (b. October 4, 1933)
PLAY:
Dialogue
PLAYS PUBLISHED IN ANTHOLOGIES:
Dialogue, in Cahill and Cooper, The Urban Reader

MARTIN, SHARON see Stockard, Sharon

MASON, CLIFFORD (b. March 5, 1932)
PLAYS:
Gabriel
Jimmy X, one act, 1971
Midnight Special
Sister Sadie, 1970

PLAYS PUBLISHED IN ANTHOLOGIES:
Gabriel, in King and Milner, Black Drama Anthology
CRITICISMS BY MASON:
"Black Writers' Views on Literary Lions and Values."
Negro Digest 17 (January 1968): 47
"The Electronic Nigger Meets the Gold Dust Twins:
Clifford Mason Talks with Robert Macbeth and Ed
Bullins." Black Theatre No. 1 (1968): 24-30
REVIEWS BY MASON:
Published in New York Magazine; New York Amster-
dam News
REVIEWS OF INDIVIDUAL PLAYS:
Gabriel
Riley, Clayton. "Gabriel." Liberator 8 (Decem-
ber 1968): 21
AWARDS:
$1,000 first prize for Gabriel

MATHEUS, JOHN FREDERICK (b. September 10, 1887)
PLAYS:
Black Damp
'Cruiter
[With Clarence C. White] Ouanga, a drama and a
libretto, 1929-31. World premiere held in South
Bend, Indiana, June 10 and 11, 1949
Ti Yvette
PLAYS PUBLISHED IN ANTHOLOGIES:
'Cruiter, in Cromwell, Turner and Dykes, Readings
from Negro Authors; Hatch and Shine, Black Thea-
ter USA; Locke and Montgomery, Plays of Negro
Life
Ti Yvette, in Richardson, Plays and Pageants from
the Life of the Negro
PLAYS PUBLISHED IN PERIODICALS:
Black Damp, in Caroline Magazine 49 (April 1927)
CRITICISMS BY MATHEUS:
"The Theatre of Jose Joaquin Gamboa." College
Language Association Bulletin. (Spring 1951)
CRITICISMS OF INDIVIDUAL PLAYS:
'Cruiter
Bond. The Negro and the Drama. p. 193
Hatch and Shine. Black Theater USA. p. 225
Ouanga
Brawley. The Negro Genius. p. 302
Ti Yvette
Bond. The Negro and the Drama. p. 112
Brawley. The Negro Genius. p. 284

AWARDS:
'Cruiter: 2nd prize in 1926 Opportunity Contest

MATURA, MUSTAPHA
PLAYS:
As Time Goes By
[With Clader and Boyars] Black Pieces

MAYFIELD, JULIAN (b. June 6, 1928)
PLAYS:
417
The Other Foot, one act, 1950
A World Full of Men, one act, 1952
PLAYS PUBLISHED IN ANTHOLOGIES:
417, in Childress, Black Scenes
FILMSCRIPTS:
Christophe
Uptight. Jules Dassin wrote the script with help
from Julian Mayfield and Ruby Dee, 1968. Para-
mount Pictures
CRITICISMS BY MAYFIELD:
"Explore Black Experience." New York Times, 2
February 1969, D: 9. (A rebuttal to Renata Ad-
ler's position on Uptight. Cf. Reviews in this
entry)
"Lorraine Hansberry." in The Black Aesthetic.
Addison Gayle, p. 30
"You Touch My Black Aesthetic and I'll Touch Yours."
in The Black Aesthetic. Addison Gayle, pp. 24-
31
CRITICISMS OF MAYFIELD:
Gayle. The Black Aesthetic. p. 301
CRITICISMS OF INDIVIDUAL PLAYS:
The Other Foot
Gayle. Black Expression. p. 156
Mitchell. Black Drama. pp. 155-156
CRITICISMS OF INDIVIDUAL FILMS:
Uptight
Bluestone, George. Novels into Film. p. 62
Bogle. Toms, Coons, Mulattoes, Mammies and
Bucks. pp. 223-224
REVIEWS ON INDIVIDUAL FILMS:
Uptight
Adler, Renata. "Critic Keeps Her Cool on 'Up-
tight.'" New York Times, 29 December 1968,
D I: 29
Alpert, Hollis. Saturday Review 28 June 1969, p.
23

Ebony 23 (November 1968): 48, 52, 54
Knight, Arthur. Saturday Review 28 June 1969,
    p. 23
New York Times, 24 March 1972, 28: 3; 30
    April 1972, II, 13: 1

MERCER, WILL
    PLAY:
        [With Richard Grant] The Southerners, 1904

MERRIAM, EVE
    MUSICAL:
        [With Helen Miller] Inner City

MEYER, ANNIE NATHAN
    PLAY:
        Black Souls, 1932

MILES, CHERRILY
    PLAYS:
        Eleanora
        To Each His Own
        X Has No Value, 1970

MILLER, CLIFFORD LEONARD
    PLAYS:
        Wings over Dark Waters. New York: Great-
           Concord, 1954

MILLER, FLOURNOY
    PLAY:
        [With Aubrey Lyles] Runnin' Wild
    CRITICISMS OF INDIVIDUAL PLAYS:
        Runnin' Wild
           Isaacs, Edith J. R. "The Negro in the American
               Theater: The Foreground, 1917-1942." Thea-
               ter Arts 26 (August 1942): 500

MILLER, HELEN
    MUSICAL:
        [With Eve Merriam] Inner City

MILLER, JEFFREY
    PLAYS:
        The Last Ditch Junkie
        Who Dreamed of Attica

MILLER, LAURA ANN
    PLAYS:
        The Cricket Cries, one act, 1967
        The Echo of Sound, one act, 1967
        Fannin Road, Straight Ahead, 1968
        Git Away from Here Irvine, Now Git, 1969

MILLER, MAY (Mrs. John Sullivan)
    PLAYS:
        The Bog Guide
        Christophe's Daughters, one act, 1935
        The Cuss'd Thing
        Graven Images, one act, 1929
        Harriet Tubman, one act
        Riding the Goat, one act, 1929
        Samory, one act, 1935
        Scratches, one act, 1929
        Sojourner Truth, one act, 1935
    PLAYS PUBLISHED IN ANTHOLOGIES:
        Christophe's Daughters, in Richardson and Miller,
            Negro History in Thirteen Plays
        Graven Images, in Hatch and Shine, Black Theater
            USA; Richardson and Miller, Negro History in
            Thirteen Plays
        Harriet Tubman, in Richardson and Miller, Negro
            History in Thirteen Plays
        Riding the Goat, in Richardson, Plays and Pageants
            from the Life of the Negro
        Samory, in Richardson and Miller, Negro History
            in Thirteen Plays
        Sojourner Truth, in Richardson and Miller, Negro
            History in Thirteen Plays
    PLAYS PUBLISHED IN PERIODICALS:
        Scratches, in "Negro Play Numbers." Carolina
            Magazine 59 (April 1929)
    EDITOR:
        [With Willis Richardson] Negro History in Thirteen
            Plays. Washington, D.C.: Associated Publish-
            ers, 1935
    CRITICISMS OF INDIVIDUAL PLAYS:
        Christophe's Daughters
            Hicklin. The American Negro Playwright 1920-
                1964. Part 1, pp. 222-223
        Graven Images
            Brawley. The Negro Genius. p. 284
            Hatch and Shine. Black Theater USA. p. 353
            Hicklin. The American Negro Playwright 1920-

1964. Part 1, p. 139
Harriet Tubman
    Hicklin. The American Negro Playwright 1920-
        1964. Part 1, p. 223
Riding the Goat
    Brawley. The Negro Genius. p. 284
    Hicklin. The American Negro Playwright 1920-
        1964. Part 1, p. 140
Scratches
    Hicklin. The American Negro Playwright 1920-
        1964. Part 1, p. 139
AWARDS:
    Third prize in the 1925 Opportunity Contest for The
    Bog Guide
    Honorable mention in the May 1926 Opportunity Con-
    test for The Cuss'd Thing

MILNER, RON (b. 1938)
    PLAYS:
        How's the World Treating You?
        (M) Ego and the Green Ball of Freedom, 1972
        The Monster
        Nommo
        The Warning--A Theme for Linda, 1969
        What the Winesellers Buy, 1972
        Who's Got His Own, 1966
    PLAYS PUBLISHED IN ANTHOLOGIES:
        The Monster, in Alhamisi and Wangara, Black Arts;
            Robinson, Nommo
        The Warning--A Theme for Linda, in Caldwell, A
            Black Quartet
        Who's Got His Own, in King and Milner, Black
            Drama Anthology
    PLAYS PUBLISHED IN PERIODICALS:
        The Monster, in Drama Review 12 (Summer 1968):
            94-105; Negro Digest 19 (November 1969): 63
        The Warning--A Theme for Linda, in Negro Digest
            18 (April 1969): 53-68 (excerpt)
    CRITICISMS BY MILNER:
        "Black Majic: Black Art." Negro Digest 16 (April
            1967): 8-12
        "Black Theatre-Go Home." Negro Digest 17 (April
            1968): 5-10; also in Gayle, The Black Aesthetic
        "Black Writers' Views on Literary Lions and
            Values." Negro Digest 17 (January 1968): 45
    CRITICISMS OF MILNER:
        Bigsby. The Black American Writer. vol. 2, pp.

199-200
Harrison. The Drama of Nommo. p. 26
Mitchell. Black Theatre. p. 223
"A New Playwright." Negro Digest 15 (October 1966): 49-50
Sadler, Jeanne E. "Ron Milner: The People's Playwright." Essence, November 1974, p. 20

CRITICISMS OF INDIVIDUAL WORKS:

The Monster
    Riach, W. A. D. " 'Telling It Like It Is': An Examination of Black Theater as Rhetoric." Quarterly Journal of Speech 46 (April 1970): 183-184

The Warning--A Theme for Linda
    Eckstein, George. "The New Black Theater" Dissent 20 (Winter 1973): 112

What the Winesellers Buy
    Atkinson. Broadway. pp. 490, 493

Who's Got His Own
    Browne, E. Martin. "Theatre Abroad." Drama Survey 5 (Summer 1966): 194
    Campbell, Dick. "Is There a Conspiracy Against Black Playwrights?" Negro Digest 17 (April 1968): 12
    Jeanpierre, Wendell A. "Ron Milner's Who's Got His Own." Crisis 74 (October 1967): 423
    Lewis, Emory. Stages: The Fifty Year Childhood of the American Theater. p. 160
    Mitchell, Loften. "The Season is Now (Who's Got His Own and My Sweet Charlie)." Crisis 74 (January-February 1967): 31-34

REVIEWS OF INDIVIDUAL WORKS:

Warning--A Theme for Linda
    New York Times, 27 April 1969, 92: 1; 3 August 1969, II, 1: 4; 22 September 1969, 36: 1

What the Winesellers Buy
    Gottfried, Martin. Women's Wear Daily, 19 February 1974
    The National Observer 2 March 1974, p. 16
    New York Theatre Critics' Reviews (February 1974): 386-388
    New York Time Magazine, 7 March 1974, p. 62
    New York Times, 22 May 1973, 49: 1
    New Yorker 19 May 1973, 4; 11 February 1974, p. 4
    Wilson, Edwin. The Wall Street Journal 21 February 1974

Who's Got His Own
New York Times, 13 October 1966, 52: 1; 14
October 1967, 13: 3
New Yorker 27 October 1966, p. 4
Orman, Roscoe. "The New Lafayette Theater."
Black Theater Magazine 4 (April 1970): 6
Riley, Clayton. "Who's Got His Own." Liber-
ator 6 (November 1966): 20
Willis, John. Theatre World: 1966-1967 Season.
vol. 23. N.Y.: Crown, 1967, p. 114

MITCHELL, JOSEPH A.
PLAYS:
The Elopement, one act
Help Wanted, one act
Son Boy, one act
PLAYS PUBLISHED IN PERIODICALS:
The Elopement, in Saturday Evening Quill (April
1930)
Help Wanted, in Saturday Evening Quill (April 1928)
Son Boy, in Saturday Evening Quill (June 1928)

MITCHELL, LOFTEN (b. April 15, 1919)
PLAYS:
The Afro Philadelphian, 1970
And the Walls Came Tumbling Down
Ballad of the Blackbird, 1968
[With John Oliver Killens] Ballad of the Winter
Soldiers, 1964
The Bancroft Dynasty, 1948
Blood in the Night
The Cellar, 1952
City Called Norfolk!
The Depression Years
The Final Solution to the Black Problem in the
United States of America, or The Fall of the
American Empire, 1970
Horse's Play
Land Beyond the River, 1957. Cody, Wyoming:
Pioneer Drama Service, 1963
Of Mice and Men (adaptation of John Steinbeck's
novel. Ms. only)
The Phonograph, 1961
Sojourn to the South of the Wall
Star of the Morning. New York: Free Press, 1965
Tell Pharaoh, 1967. New York: Negro University
Press, 1970

The World of a Harlem Playwright, 1968

PLAYS PUBLISHED IN ANTHOLOGIES:

Land Beyond the River, in Adams, Conn, and
Slepian, Afro-American Literature: Drama;
Childress, Black Scenes (excerpt); Reardon and
Pawley, The Black Teacher

The Phonograph, in Hatch and Shine, Black Theater
USA

Star of The Morning, in Hatch and Shine, Black
Theater USA; King and Milner, Black Drama
Anthology

Tell Pharaoh, in Reardon and Pawley, The Black
Teacher and the Dramatic Arts

MUSICALS:

[With Irving Burgie] Ballad for Bimshire, 1963
Ballad of a Blackbird, 1968
[With Rosetta LaNoire] Bubbling Brown Sugar, 1975

FILMSCRIPTS:

I'm Sorry, 1962
Integration: Report One, 1961
The Vampires of Harlem, 1973. (To be filmed by
Vanguard Productions)
Young Man of Williamsburg, 1954

TELEVISION SCRIPTS:

Come Back to Harlem. A benefit performance at
Loew's Victoria, produced by Brock Peters
Readings from the Work of a Harlem Playwright.
Performed by Ossie Davis, in Westchester Coun-
ty, November 1972

RADIO SCRIPTS:

The Later Years. A Weekly WYNC Radio Program

BOOKS:

CRITICISM:

Black Drama: The Story of the American Negro
in the Theatre. New York: Prentice-Hall,
1967

Voices of the Black Theater. Clifton, N.J.:
James White, 1975

COLLECTIONS:

Loften Mitchell Collection established at Talladega
College; Loften Mitchell Collection of Plays and
Essays at Schomburg Collection (New York City
Library); Collection of Plays for the State Univer-
sity of New York at Binghamton

CRITICISMS BY MITCHELL:

"Alligators in the Swamp." [On Black Theater].
Crisis 72 (February 1965): 84-88

"A Long Way from 125th Street." Crisis 75 (December 1968): 351-359

"An Informal Memoir for Langston Hughes and Stell Holt." Negro Digest 17 (April 1968): 41-43, 74-

"Black Drama." Negro Digest 16 (April 1967): 75-87

Black Drama: The Story of the American Negro in the Theatre. New York: Hawthorne, 1967

"Death of a Decade: Black Drama in the Sixties." Crisis 77 (March 1970): 87-93

"Fishing--On and Off Broadway." Crisis 76 (June-July 1969): 250-253

"Harlem Has Broadway on Its Mind." Theatre Arts 37 (June 1953)

"The Negro Theatre and the Harlem Community." Freedomways 3 (Summer 1963): 384-394; also in Gayle, Black Expression, pp. 148-158; Patterson, Anthology of the American Negro in the Theatre, pp. 178-184

"The Negro Writer and His Materials." In The American Negro Writer and His Roots, pp. 55-60

"On Images and The Theatre." The Talladegan 79 (1962): 68-70

"On the 'Emerging' Playwright." In Bigsby. The Black American Writer. vol. 2, pp. 129-136

"Raisin in the Sun." In A Guide to Theatre Study, Kenneth Cameron and Theodore Hoffman, p. 203

"The Season is Now (Who's Got His Own and My Sweet Charlie)." Crisis 74 (January-February 1967): 31-34

"Three Writers and a Dream." The Crisis 72 (1965): 219-223

CRITICISMS OF MITCHELL:

Abramson. Negro Playwrights in the American Theater. 1925-1959, pp. 204-221

Archer. Black Images. p. 22

Arts in Society 5 (1968): 230-232

Bigsby, C. W. E. "Three Black Playwrights: Loften Mitchell, Ossie Davis, Douglas Turner Ward." In Bigsby, The Black Writer in America, vol. 2, pp. 137-155

"Mitchell Wins Drama Prize." New York Times, 6 November 1958

Redding, Saunders. "Literature and the Negro." Contemporary Literature 9 (Winter 1968): 130-135

CRITICISMS OF INDIVIDUAL WORKS:

Ballad for Bimshire
  Hicklin. The American Negro Playwright 1920-
    1964. Part 2, p. 378
  Lewis. American Plays and Playwrights: Trends
    of the Decade. pp. 253
Blood in the Night
  Hicklin. The American Negro Playwright 1920-
    1964. Part 2, p. 329
The Cellar
  Hicklin. The American Negro Playwright 1920-
    1964. Part 2, p. 329
The Depression Years
  Hicklin. The American Negro Playwright 1920-
    1964. Part 2, p. 329
A Land Beyond the River
  Abramson. Negro Playwrights in the American
    Theatre. pp. 204-221, 254-256
  Campbell, Dick. "Is There a Conspiracy against
    Black Playwrights?" Negro Digest 7 (April
    1968): 15
  Driver, Tom F. "A Land Beyond the River."
    Christian Century 74 (24 July 1957): 895
  Hicklin. The American Negro Playwright 1920-
    1964. Part 2, pp. 376-378
  Mitchell. Black Drama. pp. 7, 170-180
  Turner, Darwin T. "Negro Playwrights and the
    Urban Negro." CLA Journal 12 (September
    1968): 24
  Whitlow. Black American Literature. p. 142
Star of Morning
  Hicklin. The American Negro Playwright 1920-
    1964. Part 2, p. 378
REVIEWS OF INDIVIDUAL WORKS:
Ballad for Bimshire
  New York Times, 16 (October 1963) 54: 1
Land Beyond the River
  Driver, Tom. "'A Land Beyond the River.'"
    Christian Century 74 (1957): 26
  New York Post, 20 March 1957
  New York Times, 29 March 1957, 15: 7; 2 June,
    II, 1: 1
  Raymond, Harry. "Theatre: Moving Desegrega-
    tion Play at Greenwich Mews." Daily Worker,
    1 April 1957
  Walker, Barbara. "Theater: Bedford Stuyvesant
    Theater." Black Creation 3 (Summer 1972):
    22

Of Mice and Men (Adaptation of J. Steinbeck's novel)
  Hicklin. The American Negro Playwright 1920-
    1964. Part 2, pp. 375-376
AWARDS:
  John Simon Guggenheim Memorial Award for Cre-
  ative Writing in the Drama, 1958-59

MITCHELL, MELVIN L.
  PLAY:
  The American Dream, one act
  PLAYS PUBLISHED IN PERIODICALS:
  The American Dream, in Black Creation 1 (Summer
    1970): 8-10

MOLETTE, BARBARA (b. 1940)
  PLAYS:
    [With Carlton Molette] Booji Wooji, 1971, revised
      as a screen play
    [With Carlton Molette and Charles Mann] Doctor
      B. S. Black
    [With Carlton Molette] Rosalee Pritchett. New
      York: Dramatists Play Service, 1973
  PLAYS PUBLISHED IN ANTHOLOGIES:
  Rosalee Pritchett, in Barksdale and Kinnamon,
    Black Writers of America
  PLAYS PUBLISHED IN PERIODICALS:
  Doctor B. S. Black, in Encore 13 (1970)
  CRITICISMS OF INDIVIDUAL PLAYS:
  Barksdale and Kinnamon. Black Writers of America.
    p. 824
  REVIEWS OF INDIVIDUAL PLAYS:
  Rosalee Pritchett
    Gussow, M. New York Times, 22 January 1971,
      19: 1
    Kerr, Walter. New York Times, 7 February
      1971, II, 3: 1
    New Yorker 30 January 1971, p. 2
    Riley. New York Times, 7 February 1971, II,
      3: 5
    Willis, John. Theatre World: 1970-1971 Season.
      Vol. 27. N.Y.: Crown, 1971, p. 138

MOLETTE, CARLTON W. III (b. August 23, 1939)
  PLAYS:
    [With Barbara Molette] Booji Wooji, 1971, revised
      as screenplay
    [With Barbara Molette and Charles Mann] Doctor

B. S. Black
[With Barbara Molette] Rosalee Pritchett. New
York: Dramatists Play Service, 1973
Rosche, 1970
PLAYS PUBLISHED IN ANTHOLOGIES:
Rosalee Pritchett, in Barksdale and Kinnamon,
Black Writers of America
PLAYS PUBLISHED IN PERIODICALS:
Doctor B. S. Black, in Encore 13 (1970)
CRITICISMS BY MOLETTE:
"Afro-American Ritual Drama." Black World 22
(April 1973): 4-12
"Black Theatre in Atlanta." Players 45 (April-May
1969): 162-165
CRITICISMS OF INDIVIDUAL PLAYS:
Rosalee Pritchett
Barksdale and Kinnamon. Black Writers of
America. p. 824
REVIEWS OF INDIVIDUAL PLAYS:
Rosalee Pritchett
Gussow, M. New York Times, 22 January 1971,
19: 1
Kerr, Walter. New York Times, 7 February
1971, II, 3: 1
New Yorker 30 January 1971, p. 2
Riley, C. New York Times, 7 February 1971,
II, 3: 5
Willis, John. Theater World: 1970-1971 Season.
Vol. 27. N.Y.: Crown, 1971, p. 138
AWARDS:
Graduate Fellowship in Theatre, University of Kan-
sas City, 1959-60

MONTE, ERIC
PLAY:
Revolution
FILMSCRIPT:
Cooley High
T.V. SCRIPTS:
For "All in The Family"; "Sanford and Son."
Creator of "Good Times."
CRITICISMS OF INDIVIDUAL FILMSCRIPTS:
Siskel, Gene. "Four Stars Graduate in 'Cooley
High'." Chicago Tribune, 15 June 1975, pp. 2-3

MOORE, ELVIE
PLAYS:

Angela Is Happening, 1971
Bring the House Down

MORALES, AIDA
    PLAY:
        [With James V. Hatch and Larry Garvin] The Con-
           spiracy, 1970

MORE, MAL
    PLAY:
        Where? 1971

MORRIS, ISAAC
    PLAY:
        The Secret Place

MOSES, GILBERT (b. August 20, 1942)
    PLAYS:
        Roots
    PLAYS PUBLISHED IN ANTHOLOGIES:
        Roots, in Dent, Scheckner and Moses, The Free
           Southern Theater
    EDITOR:
        [With Thomas C. Dent and Richard Scheckner] The
           Free Southern Theater by The Free Southern
           Theater
    CRITICISMS BY MOSES:
        [With John O'Neal] "Dialogue: The Free Southern
           Theater." Tulane Drama Review 9 (Summer
           1965): 63-76
    CRITICISMS OF MOSES:
        Jones, Martha M. "Interview with Gil Moses."
           Black Creation 3 (Winter 1972): 19-26
        Peterson, Maurice. "Gilbert Moses: Re-Paving
           the Yellow Brick Road." Essence (December
           1974): 24
    AWARDS:
        Obie Award
        Drama Desk Award
        Tony Nomination

MOSS, F. CARLTON
    PLAY:
        Sacrifice, one act, 1931

MUHAJIR, EL (Marvin X; Marvin Jackman)
    PLAYS:

The Black Bird, a Parable. San Francisco: Julian
  Richardson, n.d.
Come Next Summer
Flowers for the Trashman, or Take Care of Business
The Resurrection of the Dead: A Ritual
The Trial
PLAYS PUBLISHED IN ANTHOLOGIES:
  The Black Bird, in Bullins, New Plays from the
    Black Theatre
  Flowers for the Trashman, in Jones and Neal, Black
    Fire
PLAYS PUBLISHED IN PERIODICALS:
  Flowers for the Trashman, in Black Dialogue 1
    (Spring 1966); Drama Review 12 (Summer 1968)
  The Resurrection of the Dead, in Black Theatre 3
    (1969)
CRITICISMS BY EL MUHAJIR:
  "Interview with Ed Bullins" in New Plays from Black
    Theatre
  "Interview with LeRoi Jones." Black Theatre 1
    (October 1968)
  "Manifesto: The Black Educational Theatre of San
    Francisco." Black Theatre 6 (1972): 30-35
CRITICISMS OF INDIVIDUAL PLAYS:
  The Black Bird
    Killinger. The Fragile Presence. p. 128
    Eckstein, George. "The New Black Theater."
      Dissent 20 (Winter 1973): 111
  Take Care of Business
    Riach, W. A. D. "'Telling It Like It Is': An
      Examination of Black Theater as Rhetoric."
      Quarterly Journal of Speech 46 (April 1970):
      183

MULET, PAUL
  PLAYS:
    Jimmy, Jr.
    Portraits in Blackness
    The Scabs
    This Piece of Land

MURRAY, JOHN
  PLAYS:
    The Prince of Mandalore
    Room Service
  CRITICISMS OF INDIVIDUAL PLAYS:
    The Prince of Mandalore

Tobin, Terence. "Karamu Theater: Its Dis-
tinguished Past and Present Achievement."
Drama Achievement." Drama Critique 7
(Spring 1964): 89

MYERS, GAYTHER
    PLAY:
      Teachers Teaching

NAYO (Barbara Malcomb)
    PLAY:
      Fourth Generation, 1969

NEAL, LARRY (b. 1937)
    PLAY:
      The Suppression of Jazz, 1970
    EDITOR:
      [With LeRoi Jones] Black Fire: An Anthology of
        Afro-American Writing. New York: Morrow,
        1968
    CRITICISMS BY NEAL:
      "Any Day Now: Black Art and Black Liberation."
        Ebony 24 (August 1969); 54-58, 62
      "Beware of the Tar Baby." New York Times, 3
        August 1969, p. 13-D
      "The Black Arts Movement." Drama Review 12
        (Summer 1968): 29-39; also in Bigsby, The Black
        American Writer, vol. 2, pp. 187-202; Davis
        and Redding, Cavalcade, pp. 797-810; Singer and
        Fellowes, Black Literature in America; Gayle,
        The Black Aesthetic, pp. 272-290
      "Black Writers' Views of Literary Lions and Values."
        Negro Digest 17 (January 1968): 35
      "Cultural Nationalism and Black Theatre." Black
        Theatre, no. 1 (1968): 8-10
      "The Development of LeRoi Jones." Liberator 6
        (January 1966): 20; 6 (February 1966): 18
      "Theatre Review: LeRoi Jones 'The Slave and The
        Toilet'." Liberator 6 (February 1965): 22
      "Theatre Review: The Sign in Sidney Brustein's
        Window." Liberator 4 (December 1964): 25
      "Towards a Relevant Black Theatre." Black Thea-
        tre, no. 4 (1970): 14-15
    CRITICISMS OF NEAL:
      Anderson, Jervis. "Black Writing--The Other
        Side." Dissent 14 (May-June 1968): 233-242

Bigsby. The Black American Writer. vol. 2, pp. 104, 106, 107

Harrison. The Drama of Nommo. pp. 145, 203-204, 228-229

NEELY, BENNIE E.
PLAY:
Sue

NICHOL, JAMES W.
PLAY:
Home, Sweet Home, 1969

NODELL, ALBERT CHARLES
PLAY:
A River Divided, 1964

NORFORD, GEORGE
PLAYS:
Head of the Family, 1950
Joy Exceeding Glory, 1939
CRITICISMS OF NORFORD:
"Negro Playwrights: Young Chicagoan Is First with All-Negro Play on Broadway." Ebony 14 (April 1959): 95, 100
CRITICISMS OF INDIVIDUAL PLAYS:
Head of the Family
Hicklin. The American Negro Playwright 1920-1964. Part 1, p. 260
Joy Exceeding Glory
Hicklin. The American Negro Playwright 1920-1964. Part 1, pp. 260-263
Mitchell. Black Drama. p. 107
REVIEWS OF INDIVIDUAL PLAYS:
Head of the Family
Jefferson, Miles M. "Empty Season on Broadway, 1950-1951." Phylon 12 (Second Quarter 1951): 135

OKPAKU, JOSEPH O. O. (b. March 24, 1943)
PLAYS:
Born Aside the Grave, 1966
The Frogs on Capitol Hill, an adaptation of Aristophanes' The Frogs
The Virtues of Adultery, 1966
PLAYS PUBLISHED IN PERIODICALS:

Born Aside the Grave, in The Journal of the New
   African Literature (Spring 1966): 21, 57
REVIEWS BY OKPAKU:
Published in Black World and Essence
CRITICISMS OF INDIVIDUAL PLAYS:
Born Aside the Grave
   Nwozomudo, B. "An Epoch: A Critique of Born
      Aside the Grave." The Journal of the New
      African Literature (Spring 1966): 12-13
AWARDS:
Second Prize, BBC African Drama Competition for
   Virtues of Adultery, 1966

O'NEAL, JOHN
   PLAYS:
      Black Power, Green Power, Red in The Eye, 1972
      Going Against the Tide
      Hurricane Season, 1973
      When the Opportunity Scratches, Itch It
      [With The Southern Free Theatre Workshop] Where
         Is The Blood of Your Fathers, 1971

ORMES, GWENDOLYN
   PLAYS:
      Ome-Nka
      Untitled

OWENS, DANIEL WALTER (b. July 14, 1948)
   PLAYS:
      Acceptance, 1973
      The Box, 1969
      Bus Play, 1972
      Clean, 1970
      Imitatin' Us, Imitatin' Us, Imitatin' Death, 1971
      Joined, 1970
      Misunderstanding
      Nigger, Nigger, Who's the Bad Nigger
      What Reasons Could I Give, 1973
   AWARDS:
      One of 12 playwrights selected for the Eugene O'Neill
         Theatre Program, 1973

OYAMO (Charles F. Gordon) (b. 1943)
   PLAYS:
      The Advantage of Dope
      The Barbarians
      The Breakout

The Chimpanzee
The Entrance--A Journey
His First Step
Lovers, 1969
The Revelation
The Thieves, 1970
Willie Bignigga
PLAYS PUBLISHED IN ANTHOLOGIES:
The Breakout, in King and Milner, Black Drama
 Anthology
His First Step, in Bullins, The New Lafayette Thea-
 tre Presents
PLAYS PUBLISHED IN PERIODICALS:
The Thieves, in Black Dialogue 4 (Summer 1970):
 22-25
CRITICISMS BY OYAMO:
 "Review: Black Nativity" (Langston Hughes). Black
  Theatre. no. 3 (1970): 34
REVIEWS OF INDIVIDUAL PLAYS:
His First Step
 Willis, John. Theatre World: 1972-1973 Season.
  Vol. 29. N.Y.: Crown, 1974, p. 143

OYEDELE, OBAMOLA
 PLAY:
 The Struggle Must Advance to a Higher Level, one
  act, 1970
 PLAYS PUBLISHED IN PERIODICALS:
 The Struggle Must Advance to a Higher Level, in
  Black Theatre 5 (Fall 1972): 12-13

PANNEL, LYNN
 PLAYS:
 Conversation
 It's a Shame, 1971

PARKER, LEWIS M.
 PLAYS:
 Pomander, Walk, a three act costume play

PARKS, GORDON (b. November 30, 1912)
 FILM SCRIPTS:
 The Learning Tree
 CRITICISMS OF PARKS:
 Archer. Black Images. pp. 265-66, 305
 "Gordon Parks Releases Second Movie" (Shaft).

Crisis 78 (July 1971): 162

Harnan, Terry. Gordon Parks: Black Photographer and Film Maker. Champaign, Ill.: Garrard, 1972

Interview. Black Creation (Winter 1972)

Turk, Midge. Gordon Parks. New York: Crowell, 1971

CRITICISMS OF INDIVIDUAL FILM SCRIPTS:

The Learning Tree

Archer. Black Images. p. 300

Bogle. Toms, Coons, Mulattoes, Mammies and Bucks. pp. 226-227, 240

Gayle. The Black Aesthetic. pp. 56-57; (Val Ferdinand's Criticism of The Learning Tree, written for The Plain Truth, a newspaper published by one of the Free Southern Theatre workshops in New Orleans); pp. 57-58

Mapp. Blacks in American Films. pp. 212-215, 248

"Playboy After Hours: Movies." Playboy 16 (October 1969): 48, 52

AWARDS:

Spingarn Medal, 1972

Image Awards for Best Director and Best Producer, The Learning Tree

PATTERSON, CHARLES (b. October 29, 1941)

PLAYS:

Black Ice

Legacy

The Super

PLAYS PUBLISHED IN ANTHOLOGIES:

Black Ice, in Jones and Neal, Black Fire

Legacy, in Reed, 19 Necromancers from Now

PAWLEY, THOMAS (b. August 5, 1917)

PLAYS:

Crispus Attucks, 1947

FFV (First Family of Virginia), 1963

Freedom in My Soul, one act, 1938; written for Master's thesis

Judgment Day, one act, 1938; written for Master's thesis

Smokey, one act, 1939, written for Master's thesis

The Tumult and the Shouting, 1969

Zebedee, 1949

PLAYS PUBLISHED IN ANTHOLOGIES:

Judgment Day, in Brown Davis and Lee, The Negro
Caravan
The Tumult and the Shouting, in Hatch and Shine,
Black Theater USA
EDITOR:
[With William R. Reardon] The Black Teacher and
the Dramatic Arts: A Dialogue, Bibliography and
Anthology. New York: Negro Universities Press,
1970
CRITICISMS BY PAWLEY:
"The Black Theatre Audience." Players 46 (August-
September 1971): 257-261
"Dunbar as Playwright." Black World 26 (April
1975): 70-88
"The First Black Playwrights." Black World 21
(April 1972): 16-25
"I Am a Fugitive from a Play." National Theatre
Conference 10 (July 1948): 9-12
"Stage Craft in Negro Colleges." Negro College
Quarterly 4 (December 1946): 193-199, 217
"Theatre Arts and the Educated Man." Central
States Speech Journal 8 (Spring 1957): 5-11
CRITICISMS OF PAWLEY:
"Jamestown Awards for Plays: Dr. T. D. Pawley."
New York Times, 23 November 1954, 26: 8
CRITICISMS OF INDIVIDUAL PLAYS:
Crispus Attucks
Hicklin. The American Negro Playwright 1920-
1964. Part 2, pp. 315-319
FFV (First Family of Virginia)
Hicklin. The American Negro Playwright 1920-
1964. Part 2, pp. 362-367
Judgment Day
Hicklin. The American Negro Playwright 1920-
1965. Part 1, pp. 273-275
Messiah
Hicklin. The American Negro Playwright 1920-
1964. Part 2, pp. 319-322
"Jamestown Awards for Plays: Dr. T. D. Paw-
ley." New York Times, 23 November 1954,
26: 8
Smokey
Hicklin. The American Negro Playwright 1920-
1964. Part 1, pp. 275-277
The Tumult and the Shouting
Hatch and Shine. Black Theater USA. p. 475
AWARDS:

Messiah won first prize of $1000.00 for being the
best play dealing with a person or an event in
Virginia history. The contest was sponsored by
Jamestown Corporation, Williamsburg, Va.

PERKINS, EUGENE (b. September 13, 1932)
PLAYS:
Black Is So Beautiful
Cry of the Black Ghetto
Fred
Ghetto Fairy (A play for children)
God Is Black But He's Dead
The Image Makers, 1972
Maternity Ward
Our Street
Turn a Black Cheek
CRITICISMS BY PERKINS:
"Black Theatre and Community Expression." Inner
City Studies Journal (North Eastern State College),
Summer 1970
"Black Theatre as Image Maker." Black Books
Bulletin 1 (Spring-Summer 1972): 24
"Black Writers and Liberation Movement." Illinois
English Bulletin, 1968
"Changing Status of Black Writers." Black World
19 (June 1970): 18-23
"New Voices in Black Culture." Panorama Maga-
zine Chicago Daily News, 7 December 1968
CRITICISMS OF PERKINS:
Washington, Cleve. "Perkins Pulls the Plug on
Electric Niggers." Black Books Bulletin 1
(1973): 21-23
CRITICISMS OF INDIVIDUAL PLAYS:
Our Street
"Black Theatre in America." Black World 26
(April 1975): 34
AWARDS:
Special Award, Council on Interracial Books for
Children, for Ghetto Fairy, 1972

PERRY, LESLIE
PLAYS:
The Minstrel Show, 1970
The Side Show, 1971

PERRY, MANOKAI

PLAY:
The House That Was a Country

PERRY, SHAUVNEILLE
PLAY:
Mio, 1971

PETERSON, LOUIS (b. 1922)
PLAYS:
Count Me for a Stranger
Crazy Horse Have Jenny Now
Entertain a Ghost, 1962
Take a Giant Step. New York: French, 1954
PLAYS PUBLISHED IN ANTHOLOGIES:
Take a Giant Step in Ford, Black Insights; Hatch
and Shine, Black Theater USA; Kronenberger,
The Best Plays of 1953-54 (condensation); Patter-
son, Black Theatre; Turner, Black Drama in
America
FILM SCRIPTS:
Take a Giant Step
TELEVISION SCRIPTS:
Joey
CRITICISMS OF PETERSON:
Mitchell. Black Drama, pp. 163-166, 170
CRITICISMS OF INDIVIDUAL PLAYS:
Entertain a Ghost
Hicklin. American Negro Playwrights 1920-1964.
Part 2, p. 401
Take a Giant Step
Abramson. Negro Playwrights in the American
Theatre 1925-1959. pp. 170-171, 221-238,
260-263
Atkinson, Brooks. New York Times, 29 March
1957
Bellows, Saul. "Theatre Chronicle: Pleasures
and Pains of Playgoing." Partisan Review 21
(May-June 1954): 312-317
Bogle. Toms, Coons, Mulattoes, Mammies and
Bucks. p. 196
Cotton, Lettie Jo. "The Negro in the American
Theatre." Negro History Bulletin 23 (May
1960): 178
Ebony 9 (January 1954): 24; 14 (September 1959):
48-51
Hicklin. The American Negro Playwright 1920-
1964. Part 2, pp. 399-401

"Louis Takes a Giant Step." Our World 9 (January 1954): 45-48

Mapp. Blacks in American Film. p. 50

"Negro Playwrights: Young Chicagoan Is First with All-Negro Play on Broadway." Ebony 14 (April 1959): 95

Talbot, William. "Every Negro in His Place." Drama Critique 7 (Spring 1964): 93

Taubman, Howard. "The Theater: Peterson's Work." New York Times, 10 April 1962, 48: 1

Turner, Darwin T. "Negro Playwrights and the Urban Negro." CLA Journal 12 (September 1968): 19

Weals. American Drama Since World War II. p. 231

CRITICISMS OF INDIVIDUAL FILMS:

Take a Giant Step

"Take a Giant Step" (movie). Ebony 14 (June 1950): 22-25

REVIEWS OF INDIVIDUAL PLAYS:

Entertain a Ghost

Taubman, Howard. "Theatre: Peterson's Work." New York Times, 10 April 1962, p. 48: 1

Take a Giant Step

America 90 (17 October 1953): 81; 96 (13 October 1956): 56

Catholic World 178 (November 1953): 148

Commonwealth 59 (16 October 1953): 38

Hawkins, William. "'Giant Step' Shows Mature Touch." New York World Telegram 26 September 1953

Jefferson, Miles M. "The Negro on Broadway, 1952-1953." Phylon 14 (Third Quarter 1953): 277

_____. "The Negro on Broadway, 1953-54: A Baffling Season." Phylon 15 (Third Quarter 1954): 253, 254-255

Kerr, Walter. New York Herald Tribune, 25 September 1953

Marja, Fern. "'Giant Step' Off-Broadway." New York Post, 18 November 1956

Nation 177 (19 October 1953): 298

New York Times, II 20 September 1953, p. 1; 25 September 1953, p. 16; 4 October 1953, p. 1; 26 September 1956, p. 30; 11 November 1956, p. 31

New York Theater Critics' Reviews. 1953, p.
274
New Yorker 29 (3 October 1953): 79
Newsweek 42 (5 October 1953): 54
Saturday Review 36 (10 October 1953): 33; 36 (12
December 1953): 47
Theatre Arts 37 (November 1953): 24
Time 62 (5 October 1953): 78

PIPES, WILLIAM
PLAY:
Say Amen, Brother!

PITCHER, OLIVER
PLAYS:
The Bite, 1970
The One
Snake! Snake! A Play, 1961
So How're You Wearing Your Straight Jacket?
PLAYS PUBLISHED IN ANTHOLOGIES:
The One, in King and Milner, Black Drama Anthology
PLAYS PUBLISHED IN PERIODICALS:
So How're You Wearing Your Straight Jacket?, in
Umbra 1 (Winter 1963): 13-16

PITTS, LUCIA MAE
PLAY:
Let Me Dream

PLANT, PHILIP PAUL
PLAYS:
Different Strokes for Different Folks
Switcharoo

PLOMER, WILLIAM
PLAYS:
I Speak of Africa: Two Plays for a Puppet Theatre
(The Triumph of Justice, and The Man in The
Corner)
PLAYS PUBLISHED IN PERIODICALS:
I Speak of Africa: Two Plays for a Puppet Theatre,
in Drama Critique 7 (Spring 1964): 110-114

PONTIFLET, SUDAN
PLAYS:
Five Black Men
The Preacher's Son

PORTMAN, JULIE
    PLAY:
        [With Bryant Rollins] Riot, 1968

PRESTON, TONY
    PLAYS:
        Rags and Old Iron, 1972

PRICE, DORIS
    PLAYS:
        The Bright Medallion, one act.   University of
            Michigan Plays, Publisher, 1932
        The Eyes of the Old, one act.   University of
            Michigan Plays, Publisher, 1932
        Two Gods, a "minaret"
    PLAYS PUBLISHED IN PERIODICALS:
        Two Gods, in Opportunity, December 1932

PRIMUS, MARC
    PLAY:
        [With B. Banks]   High John de Conquer,   1969

PRINGLE, RONALD J.
    PLAYS:
        Dead Flowers on a Dead Man's Grave
        Deep Roots
        The Fall of the Chandelier
        Feed the Lion
        The Finger Meal
        The Lesser Sleep
        The Price
    PLAYS PUBLISHED IN ANTHOLOGIES:
        The Finger Meal, in Reed, 19 Necromancers from
            Now

RAHMAN, AISHAH
    PLAY:
        [With Archie Shepp] Lady Day, 1972
    REVIEWS OF INDIVIDUAL PLAYS:
        Lady Day
            Barnes, E.   New York Times, 26 October 1972,
                39: 1
            Kerr, W.   New York Times, 5 November 1972,
                II, 5: 1
            New York Theater Critics' Reviews (1972): 165

RANDLE, ANNIE K.
  PLAY:
    The Voice on the Wire. Waco, Texas: Counselor
      Print, 1919

RANDOLPH, JEREMY
  PLAYS:
    Blow Up in A Major, N.Y.: Amuru, 1972
    Cartouche. N.Y.: Amuru, 1973
    Negro Mama, Black Son. N.Y.: Amuru, 1973
    Rock Baby Rock While de Darkies Sleep. N.Y.:
      Amuru, 1973
    To the Slave Mountain Alone. N.Y.: Amuru, 1973

RAPHAEL, LENNOX
  PLAYS:
    Blue Soap
    Che! North Hollywood, California: Contact Books,
      1969
  CRITICISMS BY RAPHAEL:
    "Notes from the Underground." Evergreen Review
      67 (June 1969): 20-1, 92
  CRITICISMS OF RAPHAEL:
    Bigsby. The Black American Writer. Vol. 2, p.
      101
    McPherson. Blacks in America. p. 259
  CRITICISMS OF INDIVIDUAL WORKS:
    Che!
      Gilman. Common and Uncommon Masks. pp.
        193-198
  REVIEWS OF INDIVIDUAL WORKS:
    Che!
      New York Times, 24 March 1969, 56: 1; 25 March
        1969, 41: 2; 27 March 1969, 56: 1; 28 March
        1969, 38: 7; 1 April 1969, 46: 2

RAVELOMANANTSOA, GLEN ANTHONY (b. July 12, 1948)
  PLAYS:
    19th Nervous Break Down
    Obsolete Bird
    Resurrection and Kingly Rites

RAZAF, ANDY (Andreamanentania Paul Razafinkeriefo)
  (b. 1895)
  MUSICAL:
    Hot Chocolates, 1929
  CRITICISMS OF RAZAF:

"Do You Remember ... Andy Razaf?" Negro Digest 9 (October 1951): 11-12
"Mr. Tin Pan Alley." Our World 8 (July 1953): 38-39

REARDON, WILLIAM R.
PLAY:
Never Etch in Acid, 1969
EDITOR:
[With Thomas Pawley] The Black Teacher and the Dramatic Arts: A Dialogue, Bibliography and Anthology. New York: Negro Universities Press, 1970
CRITICISMS BY REARDON:
[With Theodore Hatlen] "The Black Teacher and the Drama." (pamphlet). University of California, Santa Barbara, Calif. (October 1968): 28 pp.

REDMOND, EUGENE B. (b. December 1, 1937)
PLAYS:
The Face of the Deep, 1971
The Night John Henry Was Born, 1972
[With Katherine Dunham] Ode to Taylor Jones, 1967-68
Poets with the Blues, 1971
River of Bones, 1971
Shadows Before the Mirror, 1965
Will I Still Be Here Tomorrow? A Eulogistic Ritual, 1972
Zwanza: A Poetic Ritual in 7 Movements, 1973
EDITOR:
Sides of the River: A Mini-Anthology of Black Writing. Oberlin, Ohio: By the Author, 1969
CRITICISMS OF REDMOND:
Elelstein, Steward I. "Artists in Their Residences." Oberlin Alumni Magazine (May 1970): 20-21
Gorman, Bertha. "Aiwa! Aiwa! Aiwa!" Sacramento Bee, 12 February 1971, p. 2
Slattery, Tom. "Redmond at C.C.C." The Computer (Cuyahoga Community College), 6 November 1970, pp. 6-7
CRITICISMS OF INDIVIDUAL PLAYS:
The Face of the Deep
Price, Ann. "'Face of the Deep' Stunning Work." Morning Advocate (Baton Rouge, La.), 28 July 1971, 13-A

REDWOOD, JOHN
    PLAY:
        But I Can't Go Alone

REID, HAZEL
    PLAYS:
        H.E.W. down the People
        Midnight Maze

REID, IRA A.
    PLAY:
        John Henry, 1937
    CRITICISMS OF INDIVIDUAL PLAYS:
        Hicklin. The American Negro Playwright 1920-1964.
            Part 1, p. 282

REILLY, J. TERRANCE (b. February 16, 1945)
    PLAYS:
        Black. Poughkeepsie, N.Y.: Myry House, 1973
        Bogey
        Enter at Your Own Risk
        JeJune Ju Ju
        Montage: An All-Black Play
        Waiting on the Man
    AWARDS:
        Playwright in Residence, Black Masquers Guild

RHONE, TREVOR
    PLAY:
        Smile Orange

RICHAM, CARL
    PLAY:
        Brown Buddies, 1930

RICHARDS, BEAH
    PLAY:
        One Is a Crowd, 1971

RICHARDS, STANLEY
    PLAY:
        District of Columbia, one act
    PLAYS PUBLISHED IN ANTHOLOGIES:
        District of Columbia, in Hatch and Shine, Black
            Theater USA
    PLAYS PUBLISHED IN PERIODICALS:
        District of Columbia, in Opportunity 23 (January-

March 1945): 88-91

RICHARDSON, MEL
PLAY:
The Breach, 1969
REVIEWS OF INDIVIDUAL PLAYS:
The Breach
Miller, Adam David. "News from the San Fran-
cisco East Bay." Black Theater Magazine 14
(April 1970): 5

RICHARDSON, WILLIS (b. November 5, 1889-)
PLAYS:
Alimony Rastus. N.Y.: Willis Bugbee Co., n.d.
The Amateur Prostitute
Antonio Maceo, one act
Attucks, the Martyr
The Black Horseman, 1929
Bold Love, one act
Bootblack Lover
The Broken Banjo
The Brown Boy
The Brownies Book, 1921
[With E. C. Williams] Chase
The Chip Woman's Fortune
Compromise, a folk play
The Curse of the Shell Road Witch
The Danse Calinda
The Dark Haven, one act
The Deacon's Awakening, one act, 1921
Dragon's Tooth, one act
The Elder Dumas, 1935
Fall of the Conjurer
The Flight of the Natives, 1927
A Ghost of the Past. Dayton, O.: Paine Publ.
Co., n.d.
The Gypsy's Finger Ring, 1956
Hope of the Lonely
The House of Sham, 1928
The Idle Head
Imp of the Devil
In Menelik's Court, 1935
The Jail Bird
Joy Rider
The King's Dilemma, 1929
Man of Magic, 1956
Miss or Mrs., 1941

Mortgaged, 1923
Near Calvary, Easter play for children, 1935
The New Generation
The New Santa Claus, 1956
The Nude Siren
The Peacock's Feathers, 1928
A Pillar of the Church
Protest
The Rider of the Dream
Rooms for Rent
Sacrifice, 1930
The Victims
The Visiting Lady

PLAYS PUBLISHED IN ANTHOLOGIES:
Antonio Maceo, in Richardson and Miller, Negro
   History in Thirteen Plays
The Broken Banjo, in Barksdale and Kinnamon,
   Black Writers of America; Cromwell, Readings
   from Negro Authors; Locke and Montgomery,
   Plays of Negro Life
The Chip Woman's Fortune, in Patterson, Anthology
   of the American Negro in the Theatre; Shay, Fifty
   More Contemporary One Act Plays; Turner, Black
   Drama in America
Compromise, in Locke, The New Negro
The Danse Calinda, in Locke and Gregory, Plays of
   Negro Life
The Flight of the Natives, in Hatch and Shine, Black
   Theater USA; Locke and Montgomery, Plays of
   Negro Life
The House of Sham, in Dreer, American Literature
   by Negro Authors
Mortgaged, in Cromwell, Readings from Negro
   Authors
The Rider of the Dream, in Locke and Gregory,
   Plays of Negro Life

PLAYS PUBLISHED IN PERIODICALS:
The Broken Banjo, in Crisis 31 (1926): 167-225
The Deacon's Awakening, in Crisis 21 (1920): 10-15
The Idle Head, in Carolina Magazine 49 (April 1929)

CRITICISMS BY RICHARDSON:
"Characters." Opportunity 3 (June 1925): 183
"The Hope of a Negro Drama." Crisis 19 (1919):
   338
"The Negro and the Stage." Opportunity 2 (October
   1924): 310
"Poetry and Drama." Crisis 27 (1927)

"The Unpleasant Play." Opportunity 3 (September 1925): 282

CRITICISMS OF RICHARDSON:

Barksdale and Kinnamon. Black Writers of America. pp. 638-639

Bond. The Negro and The Drama. pp. 76, 166-167

Brawley. The Negro Genius. pp. 271, 282-284

Hicklin. The American Negro Playwright 1920-1964. Part 1, p. 213; Part 2, pp. 459-460

Mitchell. Black Drama. pp. 83-84

Peterson, Bernard L., Jr. "Willis Richardson: Pioneer Playwright." Black World 26 (April 1975): 40-48, 86-88

CRITICISMS OF INDIVIDUAL WORKS:

Alimony Rastus

Peterson, Bernard L. "Willis Richardson: Pioneer Playwright." Black World 26 (April 1975): 44

Antonio Maceo

Hicklin. The American Negro Playwright 1920-1964. Part 1, p. 222

Peterson, Bernard L. "Willis Richardson: Pioneer Playwright." Black World 26 (April 1975): 86

Attucks, the Martyr

Peterson, Bernard L. "Willis Richardson: Pioneer Playwright." Black World 26 (April 1975): 86

The Black Horseman

Peterson, Bernard L. "Willis Richardson: Pioneer Playwright." Black World 26 (April 1975): 86

The Broken Banjo

Hicklin. The American Negro Playwright 1920-1964. Part 1, pp. 133-134

The Chip Woman's Fortune

Bigsby. The Black American Writer. Vol. 2, p. 117

Gayle. Black Expression. pp. 126, 132, 152

Hicklin. The American Negro Playwright 1920-1964. Part 1, pp. 129-131

Isaacs, Edith J. R. "The Negro in The American Theater: The Foreground, 1917-1942." Theater Arts 26 (August 1942): 510

Johnson. Black Manhattan. p. 191

Locke and Gregory. Plays of Negro Life. p. 420

Peterson, Bernard L. "Willis Richardson:
Pioneer Playwright." Black World 26 (April
1975): 41, 44-46, 48

Williams. Stage Left. p. 15

Compromise

Archer. Black Images. p. 134-138

Hicklin. The American Negro Playwright 1920-
1964. Part 1, pp. 133-134

Peterson, Bernard L. "Willis Richardson:
Pioneer Playwright." Black World 26 (April
1925): 46-47

The Deacon's Awakening

Peterson, Bernard L. "Willis Richardson:
Pioneer Playwright." Black World 26 (April
1975): 44

The Elder Dumas

Hicklin. The American Negro Playwright 1920-
1964. Part 1, pp. 221-222

Peterson, Bernard L. "Willis Richardson:
Pioneer Playwright." Black World 26 (April
1975): 86

A Ghost of the Past

Peterson, Bernard L. "Willis Richardson:
Pioneer Playwright." Black World 26 (April
1975): 44

The House of Sham

Hicklin. The American Negro Playwright 1920-
1964. Part 1, pp. 226-228

Peterson, Bernard L. "Willis Richardson:
Pioneer Playwright." Black World 26 (April
1975): 48

The Idle Head

Peterson, Bernard L. "Willis Richardson:
Pioneer Playwright." Black World 26 (April
1975): 48

In Menelik's Court

Hicklin. The American Negro Playwright 1920-
1964. Part 1, p. 227

Peterson, Bernard L. "Willis Richardson:
Pioneer Playwright." Black World 26 (April
1975): 86

The King's Dilemma

Peterson, Bernard L. "Willis Richardson:
Pioneer Playwright." Black World 26 (April
1975): 48

Meek Mose

Bigsby. The Black American Writer. vol. 2,
p. 117

Miss or Mrs.
  Hicklin. The American Negro Playwright 1920-
    1964. Part 2, p. 307
  Peterson, Bernard C. "Willis Richardson:
    Pioneer Playwright." Black World 26 (April
    1975): 87
Mortgaged
  Peterson, Bernard L. "Willis Richardson:
    Pioneer Playwright." Black World 26 (April
    1975): 46
Near Calvary
  Hicklin. The American Negro Playwright 1920-
    1964. Part 1, p. 221
  Peterson, Bernard L. "Willis Richardson:
    Pioneer Playwright." Black World 26 (April
    1975): 86-87
REVIEWS OF INDIVIDUAL WORKS:
  The Chip Woman's Fortune
    New York Times, 8 May 1923, 22: 2; 16 May
      1923, 22: 5; 20 May, VII. 1: 1
MEDIA RESOURCES:
  Taped Interview. N.Y.: Cohen Library of the City
    College of New York; Schomburg Collection, N.Y.
    1972
AWARDS:
  The Amy Spingarn Prize for Drama: 1925 and 1926
  First Prize for Bootblack Lover: Crisis, October
    26, 1926
  First Prize for Broken Banjo: Crisis, 1925
  Honorable Mention for Fall of the Conjurer: Oppor-
    tunity, May 1925

RIVERS, CONRAD KENT (1933-1968)
  PLAY:
  To Make a Poet Black

RIVERS, LOUIS (Paul Mulet, pseud.) (b. September 18, 1922)
  PLAYS:
  Madam Odum, 1973
  Mr. Randolph Brown
  Purple Passages
  A Rose for Lorraine
  The Scabs
  Seeking
  PLAYS PUBLISHED IN ANTHOLOGIES:
  The Scabs, in First Stage: A Quarterly of New
    Drama. (Purdue University), Fall 1962

ROACH, FREDDIE
    PLAY:
      Soul Pieces, 1969

ROBERSON, ARTHUR
    PLAYS:
      Don't Leave Go My Hand, 1965
      In the Shadow of Ham, 1968
      Melanosis, one act, 1969
      Run Sweet Child to Silence, 1968
    MUSICALS:
      Two Years, No Fears

ROBERSON, WILLIAM
    PLAYS:
      The Anger of One Young Man, 1959
      The Passing Grade, 1958

ROBERTS, VICTORIA
    PLAY:
      A Time to Laugh, 1971

ROBINSON, GARRETT
    PLAY:
      Land of Lem, 1971

ROGERS, ALEX
    MUSICALS:
      [With J. A. Shipp] Abyssinia, 1906
      Baby Blues, 1919
      [With J. A. Shipp] Bandanna Land, 1908
      [With Harry Cort] Charlie, 1923
      [With Leubrie Hill] Dark Town Follies, 1913
      [With Harry Cort and George Stoddard] Go-Go, 1923
      [With J. A. Shipp and Paul Laurence Dunbar] In
        Dahomey, 1902
      [With J. A. Shipp and Bert Williams] Mr. Lode of
        Koal, 1909
      [With Eddie Hunter] My Magnolia, 1926
      [With Henry Creamer] The Old Man's Boy, 1914
      [With James J. Vaughn] Sultan of Zulu
      This and That, 1919
      [With Henry Creamer] The Traitor, 1912
    PLAYS PUBLISHED IN ANTHOLOGIES:
      Go-Go, in Mantle. Best Plays of 1922-1923
    CRITICISMS OF ROGERS:
      Hughes and Meltzer. Black Magic. p. 88

Hughes and Meltzer. Black Magic. p. 88
Johnson. Black Manhattan. pp. 107, 115, 176, 177, 178
Mitchell. Black Drama. pp. 40, 48, 71
CRITICISMS OF INDIVIDUAL MUSICALS:
Abyssinia
    Mitchell. Black Drama. pp. 50-51, 61
Bandanna Land
    Johnson. Black Manhattan. p. 107
    Mitchell. Black Drama. pp. 8, 51-53
Dark Town Follies
    Mitchell. Black Drama. p. 68
In Dahomey
    Mitchell. Black Drama. p. 49
Mr. Lode of Koal
    Mitchell. Black Drama. p. 53

ROGERS, DAVID
    PLAY:
    If That's Where It's At Baby, I'm Not Going, 1969

ROGERS, W. F.
    PLAY:
    Judge Lynch
    PLAYS PUBLISHED IN ANTHOLOGIES:
    Judge Lynch, in Locke and Gregory, Plays of Negro Life

ROLLINS, BRYANT (13 December, 1937-)
    PLAY:
    [With Julie Portman] Riot. 1968
    AWARDS:
    Obie Award, 1969 for Riot

ROOS, JOANNA
    MUSICAL:
    [With Lehman Engel] Golden Ladder
    CRITICISMS OF INDIVIDUAL MUSICALS:
    Golden Ladder
        Tobin, Terrence. "Karamu Theater: Its Distinguished Past and Present Achievement." Drama Critique 7 (Spring 1964): 86-91

ROSS, JOHN M.
    PLAYS:
    Aztec Qzin, 1968
    Dog's Place

Half Caste Moon
House or No House, 1967
I Will Repay, 1963
One Clear Call. Nashville, Tenn.: Fisk University, 1936
The Purple Lily
Rho Kappa Epsilon. Nashville, Tenn.: Fish University, 1935
Strivin', 1937
The Sword, 1948
Wanga Doll. New Orleans, La.: Dillard University, 1954
CRITICISMS OF INDIVIDUAL PLAYS:
The Purple Lily
Hicklin. The American Negro Playwright 1920-1964. Part 2, pp. 313-314
Wanga Doll
Hicklin. The American Negro Playwright 1920-1964. Part 2, pp. 312-313

ROY, JESSIE H.
TELEVISION SCRIPT:
Bridging a Gap
CRITICISMS OF INDIVIDUAL SCRIPTS:
Bridging a Gap
"Bridging a Gap: A Documentary by Geneva C. Turner and Jessie H. Roy." The Negro History Bulletin 20 (March 1957): 133-137

RUSSELL, CHARLIE (b. March 10, 1932)
PLAYS:
Five on the Back Hand Side. New York: Samuel French, 1970
[With Barbara Ann Teer] Revival!
FILM SCRIPTS:
Five on the Back Hand Side, 1973 (Adaptation of play Five on the Back Hand Side)
T.V. SCRIPTS:
The Black Church (For ABC-TV)
A Man Is Not Made of Steel (For WGBH-TV)
CRITICISMS BY RUSSELL:
"John O. Killens: Tell It Like It Is." Liberator 4 (April 1964): 10
"LeRoi Jones Will Get Us All in Trouble." Liberator 4 (August 1964): 18
"The Wide World of Ossie Davis: Exclusive Interview." Liberator 3 (December 1963): 11-12

CRITICISMS OF RUSSELL:
Harris, Jessica B. "The Sun People of 125th
Street--The National Black Theatre." Drama
Review 16 (4 December 1972): 39-45
CRITICISMS OF INDIVIDUAL PLAYS:
Five on the Back Hand Side
Harrison. The Drama of Nommo. pp. 176, 223
Revival
Harris, Jessica B. "The Sun People of 125th
Street--The National Black Theatre." Drama
Review 16 (4 December 1972): 39-45
REVIEWS OF INDIVIDUAL PLAYS:
Five on the Back Hand Side
Barnes, Clive. "Review: Five on the Back Hand
Side." New York Times, 2 January 1970, 32:
2
Kerr, W. "Review: Five on the Back Hand
Side." New York Times, 11 January 1970,
II, p. 3: 5
Riley, Clayton. "Theatre Review: Five on the
Back Hand Side." Liberator 10 (January
1970): 21

ST. CLAIR, WESLEY
PLAY:
The Station, 1969

SALAAM, KALAMU YA (Val Ferdinand) (b. March 3, 1947)
PLAYS:
Black Liberation Army, one act, 1969
Blk Love Song #1, 1969
Black Love Song #2
Cop Killer, one act, 1968
The Destruction of the American Stage
Happy Birthday, Jesus, one act, 1968
Homecoming, one act, 1969
Mama, one act, 1968
The Picket, one act, 1968
[With Tom Dent] Song of Survival, one act, 1969
PLAYS PUBLISHED IN ANTHOLOGIES:
Blk Love Song #1, in Hatch and Shine, Black Thea-
tre USA
PLAYS PUBLISHED IN PERIODICALS:
Homecoming, in Nkombo 8 (August 1972): 2-15
CRITICISMS BY SALAAM:
"The Dashiki Project Theatre; We Are the Thea-

tre." Black Theatre No. 3 (1969): 4-6
"News from Blkartsouth." Black Theatre No. 4
(1970): 4
CRITICISMS OF INDIVIDUAL PLAYS:
Blk Love Song #1
Hatch and Shine. Black Theater USA. p. 864

SALIMU (Nettie McGray)
PLAY:
Growin' into Blackness
PLAYS PUBLISHED IN ANTHOLOGIES:
Growin' into Blackness, in Bullins, New Plays from
the Black Theatre

SAMPSON, JOHN PATTERSON (b. 1837)
PLAYS:
The Disappointed Bride; or Love at First Sight.
Hampton, Va.: Hampton School Steam Press,
1883
Jolly People
PLAYS PUBLISHED IN ANTHOLOGIES:
Jolly People, in Plays, Poems, and Miscellany.
The Schomburg Collection

SANCHEZ, SONIA (b. September 9, 1934)
PLAYS:
The Bronx Is Next, one act
Malcolm/Man Don't Live Here No Mo
Sister Son/Ji, one act, 1969
Un Huh, But How Do It Free Us, 1973
PLAYS PUBLISHED IN ANTHOLOGIES:
The Bronx Is Next, in Davis and Redding, Cavalcade
Sister Son/Ji, in Bullins, New Plays from the Black
Theatre
Un Huh, But How Do It Free Us, in Bullins, The
New Lafayette Theatre Presents
PLAYS PUBLISHED IN PERIODICALS:
The Bronx Is Next, in Drama Review 12 (Summer
1968): 78-83
Malcolm/Man Don't Live Here No Mo, in Black
Theatre 6 (Fall, 1972): 24-27
CRITICISMS BY SANCHEZ:
"Uh Huh But How Do It Free Us." In The New
Lafayette Theatre Presents, Ed Bullins, ed. pp.
161-163
CRITICISMS OF SANCHEZ:
Cameron and Hoffman. A Guide to Theatre Study.
p. 204

Clarke, Sabastian. "Sonia Sanchez and Her Work."
Black World 20 (June 1971): 44-46
Davis and Redding. Cavalcade. pp. 569-70
Gayle. The Black Aesthetic. p. 368
Kent. Struggle for the Image. p. 315
Walker, Barbara. "Sonia Sanchez Creates Poetry
for the Stage." Black Creation 5 (Fall 1973): 12-
13
CRITICISMS OF INDIVIDUAL PLAYS:
The Bronx Is Next
Riach, W. A. D. "Telling It Like It Is: An
Examination of Black Theatre as Rhetoric."
Quarterly Journal of Speech 46 (April 1970):
183

Sister Son/Ji
Harrison. The Drama of Nommo. p. 145
Whitlow. Black American Literature. p. 175
Uh Huh, But How Do It Free Us
McElroy, Hilda Njoki. "Books Noted." Black
World 26 (April 1975): 80-81
REVIEWS OF INDIVIDUAL PLAYS:
Sister Son/Ji
New York Times, 26 March 1972, II, 3: 1;
5 April 1972, 27: 1

SAUNDERS, RUBY CONSTANCE (b. August 29, 1939)
PLAY:
Goddam, Judy, one act, 1969

SCOTT, JIMMIE
PLAY:
Money, 1969
REVIEWS OF INDIVIDUAL PLAYS:
Money
Miller, Adam David. "News from the San
Francisco East Bay." Black Theatre Maga-
zine 14 (April 1970): 5

SCOTT, JOHN
PLAYS:
The Alligator
Black Sermon Rock
I Talk with the Spirits
Karma's Call
Play Division
Ride a Black Horse, 1971
Time Turns Black

PLAYS PRINTED IN DISSERTATION:
Black Sermon Rock
Ride a Black Horse
Time Turns Black
CRITICISMS BY SCOTT:
The Black Spirit: A Trilogy of Original Plays and
a Treatise on Dramatic Theory in Contemporary
Black Drama. Ph.D., Bowling Green State Uni-
versity, 1972, p. 168
"Teaching Black Drama." Players 47 (February-
March 1972): 130-131
REVIEWS OF INDIVIDUAL PLAYS:
Ride a Black Horse
Oliver, Edith. "Also Ran 'Ride a Black Horse.'"
New Yorker 5 June 1971, p. 100
Willis, John. Theatre World: 1970-1971 Season.
Vol. 27. N.Y.: Crown, 1971, p. 139

SCOTT, SERET (b. September 1, 1947)
PLAYS:
Funny Time, 1972
No, You Didn't, 1972
Wine and Cheese, 1970
CRITICISMS OF SCOTT:
"Unsigned Interview with Seret Scott." (Star of
My Sister, My Sister) New York Times, 2 July
1974, 28: 1

SEBREE, CHARLES (b. 1914)
PLAYS:
The Dry August, 1949
[With W. Greer Johnson] Mrs. Patterson, 1954
PLAYS PUBLISHED IN ANTHOLOGIES:
Dry August, in Hatch and Shine, Black Theater USA
Mrs. Patterson, in Hewes, Best Plays of 1954-1955
CRITICISMS OF INDIVIDUAL PLAYS:
Dry August
Hatch and Shine. Black Theater USA. p. 658
Mrs. Patterson
Hicklin. The American Negro Playwright 1920-
1964. Part 2, pp. 401-402
Mitchell. Black Drama. p. 167
"Negro Playwrights: Young Chicagoan Is First
with All-Negro Play on Broadway." Ebony
14 (April 1959): 99
REVIEWS OF INDIVIDUAL PLAYS:
Mrs. Patterson

New York Theater Critics' Reviews (1954): 231

SEILER, CONRAD
PLAYS:
Darker Brother
End of the World
Sweet Land, 1935

SEJOUR, VICTOR (Juan Victor Sejour Marcon-Ferrand)
(1817-1874)
PLAYS:
Les Aventuriers. Paris: Michel-Lévy frères,
1860. (The Adventurers)
André Gérard. Paris: Michel-Lévy frères, 1857
L'Argent du Diable. Paris: Michel-Lévy frères,
1857. (The Devil's Corn)
La Chute de Séjan. Paris: Michel-Lévy frères,
1849. (The Fall of Sejanus)
Compère Guillery. Paris: Michel-Lévy frères,
1860. (Friend Guillery)
Diégarias. Paris: C. Tresse, 1844
[With Théodore Barrière] Les Enfants le la Louvre.
Paris: Michel-Lévy frères, 1856. (The Kids of
The Louvre)
Les Fils de Charles-Quint. Paris: Michel-Lévy
frères, 1864. (The Sons of Charles the Fifth)
Les Fils de la Nuit. Paris: Michel-Lévy frères,
1856. (Sons of the Night)
Les Grands Vassaux. Paris: Michel-Lévy frères,
1859.
La Madone des Roses. Paris: Michel-Lévy frères,
1869. (Our Lady of the Roses)
Le Marquis Caporal. Paris: Michel-Lévy frères,
1856. (The Corporal is a Marquis)
[With Jules Brésil] Le Martyr du Coeur. Paris:
Michel-Lévy frères, 1858.
Les Massacres de la Syrie, 1856; Paris: J. Bar-
bre, 1960. (Syrian Massacre)
Les Mystères du Temple. Paris: Michel-Lévy
frères, 1862.
Les Noces Venitiennes. Paris: Michel-Lévy frères,
1855. (The Venetian Wedding)
Le Paletot Brun. Paris: Michel-Lévy frères, 1860.
(The Brown Overcoat)
Richard III, 1852; Paris: Michel-Lévy frères, 1870.
La Tireuse de Cartes. Paris: Michel-Lévy frères,
1860. (The Fortune Teller)

Le Vampire
Les Volontaires de 1814. Paris: Michel-Lévy
    frères, 1862. (The 1814 Volunteers)
PLAYS PUBLISHED IN ANTHOLOGIES:
The Brown Overcoat (Le Paletot Brun), in Hatch
    and Shine, Black Theater USA
PLAYS PUBLISHED IN PERIODICALS:
Les Mystères du Temple. In La Renaissance (New
    Orleans) 21 September 1862
Richard III. In La Semaine (New Orleans). 1853
CRITICISMS OF SEJOUR:
Bisbane, Era Mae. Théâtre de Victor Séjour.
    Master's thesis, Hunter College, 1942
Daley, T. A. "Victor Séjour." Phylon 4 (First
    Quarter 1943): 5-16
Gautier, Theophile. Histoire de l'art dramatique
    en France depuis vingt-cinq ans. Paris: Magnin,
    Blanchard, 1858-1859. 6 vols.
McElroy, Hilda Njoki. "Books Noted." Black
    World 26 (April 1975): 62
Tinker, Ed. L. Les Ecrits de Langue Française
    en Louisiane au XIX siècle. Paris: H. Cham-
    pion, 1932
Van Vechten, Carl. "How the Theatre is Repre-
    sented in The Negro Collection at Yale." The
    Theatre Annual (1943): 32-33
CRITICISMS OF INDIVIDUAL PLAYS:
The Brown Overcoat, in Hatch and Shine. Black
    Theater USA
REVIEWS OF INDIVIDUAL PLAYS:
The Brown Overcoat
    Barnes, Clive. "The Brown Overcoat." New
    York Times, 7 December 1972, 73: 1

SELF, CHARLES
    PLAY:
    Tite Smokers, 1968

SHEPP, ARCHIE (b. May 24, 1937)
    PLAYS:
    Junebug Graduates Tonight!, 1967
    Revolution, 1968
    PLAYS PUBLISHED IN ANTHOLOGIES:
    Junebug Graduates Tonight!, in King and Milner,
        Black Drama Anthology
    CRITICISMS OF SHEPP:
    Nation 206 (27 March 1967): 411-412

Patterson. "A Profile-Interview: Archie Shepp."
Black World 23 (November 1973): 58-61
Williams, M. "Problematic Mr. Shepp." Saturday
Review 12 (November 1966): 90
CRITICISMS OF INDIVIDUAL WORKS:
Junebug Graduates Tonight!
Abramson. Negro Playwrights in the American
Theatre. pp. 281-283
Gayle. The Black Aesthetic. pp. 143, 238
_____. Black Expression. pp. 139-140

SHERMAN, JIMMIE
PLAYS:
A Ballad from Watts
CRITICISMS OF SHERMAN:
Schulberg. Black Phoenix. p. 280

SHIPMAN, WILLIE B.
PLAY:
Pepper, 1972

SHINE, TED
PLAYS:
Bats out of Hell, 1955
The Coca-Cola Boys, one act, 1969
Cold Day in August, one act, 1950
Come Back after the Fire, 1969
Contribution, one act, 1969
Dry August, 1952
Epitaph for a Bluebird, 1958
Flora's Kisses, one act, 1968
Hamburgers at Hamburger Haven Are Impersonal,
one act, 1969
Herbert III
Idabel's Fortune, one act, 1969
Miss Victoria, one act, 1965
Morning, Noon and Night, 1964
Plantation, one act, 1970
Pontiac, one act, 1967
A Rat's Revolt, 1959
Revolution, 1968
Shoes, one act, 1969
Sho' Is Hot in the Cotton Patch, one act, 1951
Waiting Room, one act, 1969
MUSICALS:
Entourage Royale, 1958
Jeanne West, 1968

PLAYS PUBLISHED IN ANTHOLOGIES:
Contribution, in Brasmer and Consolo, Black
Drama; Richards, The Best Short Plays of 1972
Herbert III, in Hatch and Shine, Black Theater USA
Morning, Noon and Night, in Reardon and Pawley,
The Black Teacher and the Dramatic Arts
Shoes, in Childress, Black Scenes (one scene)
PLAYS PUBLISHED IN PERIODICALS:
Sho' Is Hot in the Cotton Patch, in Encore Maga-
zine 12 (1967)
Shoes, in Encore Magazine 12 (1969)
CRITICISMS OF INDIVIDUAL WORKS:
Contribution
Rich, Dennia. "The Kuumba Workshop."
Players 47 (December-January 1972): 68-70
Morning, Noon and Night
Pawley, Dr. Thomas D. "The Black Theatre
Audience." Players 46 (August-September
1971): 258
REVIEWS OF INDIVIDUAL WORKS:
Contribution
New York Theatre Critics' Reviews (1970): 282
Willis, John. Theatre World: 1968-1969 Season.
Vol. 25. N.Y.: Crown, 1969, p. 163

SHIPP, J. A.
MUSICALS:
[With Alex Rogers] Abyssinia, 1906
[With Alex Rogers] Bandanna Land, 1908
[With Alex Rogers and Paul Laurence Dunbar] In
Dahomey, 1902
[With Alex Rogers and Bert Williams] Mr. Lode of
Koal, 1909
[With Will Marion Cook] The Policy Players, 1900
[With Alex Rogers] Senegambian Carnival, 1898
CRITICISMS OF SHIPP:
Gayle. The Black Aesthetic. pp. 297-298
_____. Black Expression. pp. 149, 151
Johnson. Black Manhattan. pp. 102, 178
Mitchell. Black Drama. pp. 40, 42, 47, 48
CRITICISMS OF INDIVIDUAL MUSICALS:
Abyssinia
Mitchell. Black Drama. pp. 50-51, 61
Bandanna Land
Johnson. Black Manhattan. p. 107
Mitchell. Black Drama. pp. 8, 51-53
In Dahomey

Mitchell. Black Drama. p. 49
Mr. Lode of Koal
   Mitchell. Black Drama. p. 53

SILVERA, FRANK
   PLAYS:
   Unto the Least, 1938
   CRITICISMS BY SILVERA:
   "Toward a Theatre of Understanding." Negro Digest 18 (April 1969): 33-35
   CRITICISMS OF SILVERA:
   Hughes and Meltzer. Black Magic. pp. 203, 214, 227, 236, 295
   Mitchell. Black Drama. pp. 114, 122, 144, 163-64, 204

SILVERA, JOHN
   PLAYS:
   [With Abram Hill] Liberty Deferred, 1936
   CRITICISMS BY SILVERA:
   "Still in Blackface." Crisis 46 (March 1939): 76-77
   CRITICISMS OF SILVERA:
   Hicklin. The American Negro Playwright, 1920-1964. Part 2, p. 452
   CRITICISMS OF INDIVIDUAL PLAYS:
   Liberty Deferred
      Abramson. Negro Playwrights in the American Theatre 1925-1959. pp. 65-66

SISSLE, NOBLE (b. 1889)
   MUSICALS:
   [With Lew Payton] Chocolate Dandies, 1924
   [With Ed Sullivan] Harlem Cavalcade
   MUSICAL MELANGE:
   [With Eubie Black, Audrey Lyles and Flournay Miller] Shuffle Along of 1933, 1932
   CRITICISMS BY SISSLE:
   "How Jo Baker Got Started." Negro Digest 9 (August 1951): 15-19
   CRITICISMS OF SISSLE:
   Fisher, Rudolph. "The Caucasian Storms Harlem." American Mercury 11 (August 1927): 397-398
   Hughes and Meltzer. Black Magic. pp. 69, 71, 88, 97, 99, 101
   Isaacs, Edith J. R. "The Negro in The American Theater: The Foreground, 1917-1942." Theater Arts 26 (August 1942): 501

Kimball, Robert and William Balcom. Reminiscing with Sissle and Blake. New York: Viking, 1973

"Sissle and Blake (40 Years in Vaudeville)." Ebony 10 (March 1955): 112-118

CRITICISMS OF INDIVIDUAL MUSICALS:

Chocolate Dandies

Johnson. Black Manhattan. p. 190

Mitchell. Black Drama. p. 83

Shuffle Along of 1933

Archer. Black Images. p. 11

Isaacs, Edith J. R. "The Negro in The American Theater: The Foreground, 1917-1942." Theater Arts 26 (August 1942): 498, 501

Johnson. Black Manhattan. pp. 187-189

Mitchell. Black Drama. pp. 76-77

REVIEWS OF INDIVIDUAL MUSICALS:

Chocolate Dandies

Isaacs, Edith J. R. "The Negro in The American Theater: The Foreground, 1917-1942." Theater Arts 26 (August 1942): 501

Walrond, Eric D. "Review of The Chocolate Dandies." Opportunity 2 (November 1924): 345

Harlem Cavalcade

New York Theatre Critics' Reviews (1942): 296

Shuffle Along of 1933

Belcher, Fannin S. "The Negro Theater: A Glance Backward." Phylon 11 (Second Quarter 1950): 123

SMITH, AUGUSTUS J.

PLAYS:

[With Peter Morrell] Just Ten Days, Louisiana, 1933

[With Peter Morrell] Turpentine, 1936

Voodooism, 1933

CRITICISMS OF INDIVIDUAL PLAYS:

Turpentine

Abramson. Negro Playwrights in the American Theatre. pp. 63-64

Flanagan, Hallie. Arena. p. 75

Gayle. Black Expression. p. 114

Hicklin. The American Negro Playwright 1920-1964. Part 1, pp. 231-232

Locke, Alain. "God Save Reality." Opportunity 15 (January 1937): 12

Nichols, Lewis. "The Play." New York Times, 27 June 1936, 21: 6

Pullen, Glenn C. " 'Turpentine, ' Saga of Modern
Negro in the South." Cleveland Plain Dealer,
15 January 1937, 9: 1
Voodooism
    Hicklin. The American Negro Playwright 1920-
    1964. Part 1, pp. 230-231
REVIEWS OF INDIVIDUAL WORKS:
Nichols, Lewis. "The Play" (Turpentine). New
York Times, 27 June 1936, 21: 6

SMITH, DEMON
    PLAY:
    Private Huckle Berry, 1972

SMITH, DJENI BA
    PLAY:
    Please, Reply Soon, 1971

SMITH, JEAN
    PLAY:
    O.C.'s Heart, 1970
    PLAYS PUBLISHED IN PERIODICALS:
    O.C.'s Heart, in Black World 19 (April 1970): 56-76

SMITH, OTIS
    PLAY:
    [With Kiiln Anthony Hamilton and Richard Dedeaux]
        The Rising Sons--Wisdom and Knowledge. Los
        Angeles: The Watts Prophets, 1973

SMITH, WELTON
    PLAY:
    The Roach Riders

SNAVE, ELMAS
    PLAY:
    Little DoDo

SPENCE, EULALIE
    PLAYS:
    Being Forty
    Fool's Errand. New York: Samuel French, 1927
    Foreign Mail. New York: Samuel French, 1927
    Help Wanted
    Her, one act, 1927
    Hot Stuff, 1927
    The Hunch, one act, 1927

La Divinia Pastora, 1929
The Starter
Undertow
The Whipping, 3 act comedy based on a novel by
    Ray Flannagan
PLAYS PUBLISHED IN ANTHOLOGIES:
The Starter, in Locke and Gregory, Plays of Negro
    Life
Undertow, in Hatch and Shine, Black Theater USA
PLAYS PUBLISHED IN PERIODICALS:
Episode, in The Archive, April 1928
Help Wanted, in Saturday Evening Quill (April 1929)
The Hunch, in The Carolina Magazine 47 (May 1927);
    Opportunity (1927)
Undertow, in The Carolina Magazine 49 (April 1929)
FILMSCRIPT:
The Whipping, Sold to Paramount Pictures, 1934
CRITICISMS BY SPENCE:
"A Criticism of the Negro Drama." Opportunity 6
    (June 1928): 180
CRITICISMS OF SPENCE:
Mitchell. Black Drama. p. 88
CRITICISMS OF INDIVIDUAL PLAYS:
The Whipping
    Hicklin. The American Negro Playwright 1920-
        1964. Part 2, pp. 225-226
REVIEWS OF INDIVIDUAL WORKS:
Being Forty
    Walrond, Eric D. "Review of Being Forty."
        Opportunity 2 (November 1924): 346
AWARDS:
Fool's Errand, Samuel French Prize
Second Prize for Foreign Mail, 25 October 1926
Third Prize for The Starter: Opportunity Contest,
    1927
Third Place for Hot Stuff and Undertow: Crisis Con-
    test, December 1927

SPENSLEY, PHILIP
    PLAY:
    The Nitty Gritty of Mr. Charlie, 1969

STANBACK, THURMAN W.
    PLAY:
    A Change Has Got to Come, 1969

STAVIS, BARRIE

PLAYS:
The Man Who Never Died
The Sun and I
CRITICISMS OF INDIVIDUAL PLAYS:
The Man Who Never Died
Mitchell. Black Drama. p. 180
The Sun and I
Himelstein. Drama Was a Weapon. p. 101

STEELE, RICHARD
PLAYS:
The Matter of Yo Mind

STEWART, JAMES T.
PLAYS:
Abganli and the Hunter (Why No One Ever Tells the
Truth to Women)
The Gourd Cup (A Play Spoken with Song and Dance
for Little Children)
How Men Came into the World (How the Lesser
Gods Came into the World)
JoJo, the Story Teller: A Play for Children
The Messenger of God (Mama's Ways Are Just)
PLAYS PUBLISHED IN PERIODICALS:
Abganli and the Hunter, in Black Lines 2 (Fall 1971):
43-45
The Gourd Cup, in Black Lines 2 (Fall 1971): 51-52
How Men Came into the World, in Black Lines 2
(Fall 1971): 48-51
JoJo, the Story Teller, in Black Lines 2 (Fall 1971):
52-54
The Messenger of God, in Black Lines 2 (Fall 1971):
45-58

STEWART, FON
MUSICALS:
[With Neal Tate] Sambo, a Nigger Opera, 1969
REVIEWS OF INDIVIDUAL MUSICALS:
Sambo
NBC 4 TV, 21 December 1969
New York Post, 22 December 1969
New York Theatre Critics' Reviews 30 (22 Decem-
ber 1969): 130-131
New York Times, 22 December 1969
WCBS TV 2, 21 December 1969
Women's Wear Daily, 22 December 1969

STILES, THELMA JACKSON (b. December 10, 1939)
PLAY:
No One-Man Show, one act, 1972

STOCKARD, SHARON
PLAYS:
Edifying Further Elaborations on the Mentality of a
Chore, 1972
Proper and Fine, 1969

STOKES, HERBERT (DAMU)
PLAYS:
The Man Who Trusted the Devil Twice
The Uncle Toms
PLAYS PUBLISHED IN ANTHOLOGIES:
The Man Who Trusted the Devil Twice, in Bullins,
New Plays from the Black Theatre
PLAYS PUBLISHED IN PERIODICALS:
The Uncle Toms, in The Drama Review 12 (Sum-
mer 1968): 58-60

STOREY, RALPH
PLAY:
Down, 1971

STREATOR, GEORGE
PLAYS:
New Courage
A Sign
PLAYS PUBLISHED IN PERIODICALS:
New Courage and A Sign, in Crisis 41 (January
1934): 9+

STRONG, ROMANER JACK
PLAYS:
A Date with the Intermediary, 1968
A Direct Confrontation in Black, one act, 1968
Mesmeriam of a Maniac, 1967
Metamorphism, one act, 1966
The Psychedelic Play of a Happening, one act, 1967

SUBLETTE, WALTER (S. W. Edwards, pseud.) (b. Septem-
ber 6, 1940)
PLAY:
Natural Murder, 1973

SUDAN, NAZZAM AL. (b. 1944)

PLAY:
 Flowers for the Whiteman, or, Take Care of Business, 1967

SUTHERLAND, EFUA
 PLAY:
  Ananse Swore an Oath, 1972

SWANN, DARIUS LEANDER
 PLAYS:
  A Choral Drama: The Circle Beyond Fear. N.Y.:
   Friendship, 1960
  The Crier Calls: A Drama for Verse Choir. N.Y.:
   Friendship, 1956
  A Desert, a Highway: A One-Act Play. N.Y.:
   Friendship, 1963
  I Have Spoken to My Children: A One-Act Play for
   Verse Chorus. N.Y.: Friendship, 1957
  A House for Marvin: A One-Act Play about Discrimination in Housing. N.Y.: Friendship, 1957

TAPIA, JOSE (b. September 12, 1942)
 PLAY:
  Welcome to the Space Ship O.R.G.Y.
 MUSICALS:
  Ego, comedy
  Kenya, mystery
  Outrage
  Satin Man

TATE, NEAL
 PLAY:
  No More Dragons to Kill
 MUSICALS:
  [With Ron Steward] Sambo: A Black Opera with
   White Spots, 1969
  Searchin'
  Surprise
  You Gotta Deal with It

TAYLOR, JACKIE
 PLAY:
  The Other Cinderella
 CRITICISMS OF INDIVIDUAL PLAYS:
  The Other Cinderella
   "Jackie Taylor: A Cinderella Story." Chicago

Tribune: Arts and Fun, 15 June 1975, p. 2

TAYLOR, JEANNE
PLAY:
House Divided, 1968

TAYLOR, MARGARET FORD
PLAYS:
Hotel Happiness, 1972
I Want to Fly

TEAGUE, BOB
PLAY:
[With Langston Hughes] Soul Yesterday and Today,
1969

TEER, BARBARA ANN (b. June 18, 1937)
PLAYS:
A Revival: Change! Love! Organize!, 1972
FILM SCRIPTS:
Rise/A Love Poem for a Love People
CRITICISMS BY TEER:
"The Great White Way Is Not Our Way." Negro
Digest 17 (April 1968): 21-29
"To Black Artists, with Love." Negro Digest 18
(April 1969): 4-8
"We Are Liberators, Not Actors." Essence 1
(March 1971): 56-59
CRITICISMS OF TEER:
Harrison. The Drama of Nommo. pp. xxiii, 85-
86, 88, 191, 198
Jones, Martha Ann. "Barbara Ann Teer's National
Black Theatre." Black Creation 3 (Summer 1972):
18-20
"Needed: A New Image." In Black Power Revolt,
Floyd Barbour, ed., Boston: Porter Sargent,
1968
CRITICISMS OF INDIVIDUAL PLAYS:
Revival
Harris, Jessica B. "The Sun People of 125th
Street--The National Black Theatre." Drama
Review 16 (4 December 1972): 39-45
REVIEWS OF INDIVIDUAL PLAYS:
Revival
Thompson, Howard. "Black Theater Stages 'Re-
vival'." New York Times, 30 July 1972, 43:
3

TERRELL, VINCENT
    PLAYS:
        Sarge, 1970
        Will It Be Like This Tomorrow, 1972

THIBODEAUX, RICHARD
    PLAY:
        No 'Count Boy
    CRITICISMS OF THIBODEAUX:
        Pierce, Evelyn Miller. "Jim Crow Dons the Buskin."
           Theatre Magazine 49 (May 1929): 50-51

THOMAS, FATISHA
    PLAYS:
        Choice of Worlds Unfilled
        It's Been a Long Time Comin'
        Twenty Year Nigger

THOMAS, STAN
    PLAY:
        In the City of Angels

THOMPSON, ELOISE BIBB
    PLAY:
        Cooped Up
    AWARDS:
        Honorable Mention for Cooped Up, May 1925: Op-
           portunity Contest

THOMPSON, GARLAND LEE (Aquarius) (b. February 14,
    1938)
    PLAYS:
        Sisyphus and the Blue-Eyed Cyclops
        Papa Bee on the D Train
    AWARDS:
        Prize for Sisyphus from the 42nd Annual One Act
           Tournament, Washington, D.C.

THOMPSON, LARRY (b. 1950)
    PLAY:
        A Time to Die: A Skit

THORUE, ANNA V.
    PLAY:
        Black Power Every Hour, 1970

THUNA, LEE

PLAY:
Natural Look
REVIEWS OF INDIVIDUAL PLAYS:
Natural Look
New York Theatre Critics' Reviews (1967): 348

THURMAN, WALLACE (1901-1934)
PLAYS:
[With William Jourdan Rapp] Harlem: A Melodrama
of Negro Life in Harlem (originally called Black
Belt), 3 acts, 1929. In the James Weldon John-
son Collection of Yale University Library
[With William Jourdan Rapp] Jeremiah, the Magnifi-
cent, 3 acts, 1930
Savage Rhythm, 1932
Singing the Blues, 1931
CRITICISMS BY THURMAN:
See The Messenger, April to September 1926
"Negro Artists and the Negro." New Republic 52
(31 August 1927): 37-39
"Nephews of Uncle Remus." Independent 119 (4
September 1927): 296-298
Rapp, William Jourdan and Wallace Thurman. "De-
touring Harlem to Times Square." New York
Times, 7 April 1929, 10: 4
Young. Black Writers of the Thirties, pp. 134,
142, 143, 205, 209-212, 214
CRITICISMS OF THURMAN:
Barksdale and Kinnamon. Black Writers of America.
pp. 604-606
Bontemps. The Harlem Renaissance Remembered.
pp. 15, 19, 46, 48, 50, 64, 97-98, 101, 147-
170, 194, 213, 234, 268
Harrison. The Drama of Nommo. pp. 178-180
Hicklin. The American Negro Playwright, 1920-
1964. Part 1, p. 260
CRITICISMS OF INDIVIDUAL PLAYS:
Harlem
Abramson. Negro Playwrights in the American
Theatre. pp. 32-43
Bond. The Negro and the Drama. pp. 117-118
Edmonds, Randolph. "Some Reflections on the
Negro in American Drama." Opportunity 8
(October 1930): 303-305
Hicklin. The American Negro Playwright, 1920-
1964. Part 1, pp. 190-193
Hughes, Langston. "Harlem Literati in the

Twenties." Saturday Review of Literature 22 (22 June 1940): 13

Isaacs, Edith J. R. "The Negro in the American Theatre: A Record of Achievement." Theatre Arts 26 (August 1942)

Mitchell. Black Drama. pp. 86-87

Whitlow. Black American Literature. p. 89

Jeremiah, the Magnificent

Hicklin. The American Negro Playwright, 1920-1964. Part 1, p. 260

REVIEWS OF INDIVIDUAL PLAYS:

Harlem

Atkinson, Brooks. "The Play." (Harlem). New York Times, 21 February 1929

————. "Up 'Harlem' Way." New York Times, 3 March 1929

Lewis, Theophilus. Opportunity 7 (April 1929)

New Yorker 2 March 1929

Skinner, R. Dana. Commonweal 6 March 1929

TILLMAN, KATHERINE DAVIS

PLAYS:

Aunt Betsy's Thanksgiving. Philadelphia: A.M.E. Book Concern, n.d.

Fifty Years of Freedom; or, From Cabin to Congress. Philadelphia: A.M.E. Book Concern, 1910

Thirty Years after Freedom

TOLSON, MELVIN BEAVNORUS (February 6, 1900-August 29, 1966)

PLAYS:

Black Boy

Black No More, 1952

The Fire in the Flint, 1952, an adaptation of Walter White's book

The Moses of Beale Street

Southern Front

CRITICISMS OF TOLSON:

Bigsby. The Black American Writer. Vol. 2, p. 101

McPherson. Blacks in America. pp. 248-49

TOOMER, JEAN (December 26, 1894-March 30, 1967)

PLAYS:

Balo, 1924

Kabnis (In Toomer's Cane). New York: Boni and Liveright, 1923

PLAYS PUBLISHED IN ANTHOLOGIES:
    Balo, in Hatch and Shine, Black Theater USA; Locke
        and Montgomery, Plays of Negro Life
CRITICISMS OF TOOMER:
    Fullinwider, S. P. "Jean Toomer: Lost Generation
        or Negro Renaissance." Phylon 27 (1966): 396-
        403
    Turner, Darwin T. "The Failure of a Playwright."
        CLA Journal 10 (June 1967): 308-318
CRITICISMS OF INDIVIDUAL PLAYS:
    Balo
        Hatch and Shine. Black Theater USA. p. 218
        Hicklin. The American Negro Playwright 1920-
            1964. Part 1, pp. 140-142
        Krasny, Michael J. "Design in Jean Toomer's
            Balo." Negro American Literature Forum 7
            (Fall 1973): 103-106
    Kabnis
        Harrison. The Drama of Nommo. pp. 114-118

TOUSSAINT, RICHARD
    PLAY:
    Three Black Ghettos, 1969

TOWNS, GEORGE A.
    PLAY:
    The Sharecroppers

TOWNSEND, WILLA A.
    PLAY:
        Because He Lives. Nashville: Sunday School Pub-
            lishers, Board of Baptist Convention, 1924

TRENIER, DIANE
    PLAY:
    Rich Black Heritage, 1970

TROY, HENRY
    MUSICAL:
        [With Lester A. Walton and Will Marion Cook]
            Darkeydom, 1914?

TURNER, DENNIS
    PLAY:
    Charlie Was Here and Now He's Gone
    CRITICISMS OF INDIVIDUAL PLAYS:
    Charlie Was Here and Now He's Gone

Rudin, Seymour. "Performing Arts: 1971-1972."
Massachusetts Review 14 (Winter 1973): 215

TURNER, GENEVA C.
TELEVISION SCRIPT:
[With Jessie H. Roy] Bridging a Gap
CRITICISMS OF INDIVIDUAL SCRIPTS:
Bridging a Gap
"Bridging a Gap: A Documentary by Geneva C.
Turner and Jessie H. Roy." The Negro His-
tory Bulletin 20 (March 1957): 133-137

TURNER, JOSEPH
PLAY:
The Scheme

TUTT, J. HOMER
PLAYS (with Salem Whitney):
Children of the Sun
Darkest Americans
De Gospel Train, 1941
Expresident of Liberia
George Washington Bullion Abroad
His Excellency the President
Mayor of Newton
My People
Oh Joy
Up and Down
MUSICALS (with Salem Whitney):
Deep Harlem

ULLMAN, MARVIN
PLAY:
... And I Am Black, 1969

VAN PEEBLES, MELVIN (b. August 21, 1932)
PLAYS:
Don't Play Us Cheap. New York: Bantam, 1973
MUSICALS:
Ain't Supposed to Die a Natural Death. New York:
Bantam, 1973
FILMSCRIPTS:
Don't Play Us Cheap
Serious as a Heart Attack
Story of a Three Day Pass
Sweet Love Bitter (Based on John A. Williams'

novel, Night Song)
Sweet Sweetback's Baadasssss Song
Watermelon Man
CRITICISMS OF VAN PEEBLES:
Archer. Black Images. p. 266
Botto, Louis. "Melvin Van Peebles: Work in
Progress." Black Times 2 (1972): 12-13
Coleman, Horace W. "Melvin Van Peebles."
Journal of Popular Culture 5 (Fall 1972): 368-
384. (Interview with Introduction)
Higgins, C. "Meet the Man behind the Sweetback."
Jet (2 July 1971): 11-D
"Interview." Black Creation 2 (Fall 1971)
Murray, James P. "Black Movies/Black Theatre."
Drama Review 16 (December 1972): 56-61
"On the Scene: Melvin Van Peebles: 'Brer Soul'."
Playboy 17 (September 1970): 195
Riley. Contemporary Literary Criticism. pp. 447-
448
CRITICISMS OF INDIVIDUAL WORKS:
Ain't Supposed to Die a Natural Death
Archer. Black Images. p. 291
Bailey, Peter. "Annual Round-Up: Black Thea-
tre in America." Black World 21 (April 1972):
31-36
Collier, Eugene. "Drama Review." Black World
21 (April 1972): 79-81
Eckstein, George. "The New Black Theater."
Dissent 23 (Winter 1973): 112
Harrison. The Drama of Nommo. pp. 169, 226-
228
Henry, Hewes. "The Aints and the Am Nots."
Saturday Review (13 November 1971): 10-12
Kraus, Ted M. "Theatre East." Players 47
(February-March 1972): 133
New York Times 29 July 1972, 13: 7
"Playboy After Hours--Theater." Playboy 18 (Au-
gust 1972): 42, 44
Reische. The Performing Arts in America. pp.
72-73
Rudin, Seymour. "Arts in Review: The Per-
forming Arts 1971-72." Massachusetts Review
14 (Winter 1973): 209
Don't Play Us Cheap
"Playboy After Hours--Theater." Playboy 18 (Au-
gust 1972): 42, 44
Reische. The Performing Arts in America. pp.
72-73

Rudin, Seymour. "Performing Arts: 1971-1972."
Massachusetts Review 14 (Winter 1973): 209
CRITICISMS OF INDIVIDUAL FILMSCRIPTS:
Don't Play Us Cheap
Simon, John. "Don't Play Us At All." New
York Magazine, 5 June 1972, p. 72
Stasio, Marilyn. "Don't Play Us Cheap." Cue
27 May 1972
The Story of a Three Day Pass
Archer. Black Images. p. 300
Bogle. Toms, Coons, Mulattoes, Mammies and
Bucks. p. 232
Sweet Sweetback's Baadasssss Song
Archer. Black Images. pp. 304-306, 308
Bennett, Lerone. "The Emancipation Orgasm:
Sweetback in Wonderland." Ebony (September
1971): 106
Bogle. Toms, Coons, Mulattoes, Mammies and
Bucks. pp. 16-17, 232-235
Gussow, M. "Badasssss Success of Melvin Van
Peebles." New York Times Magazine, 20
August 1972, pp. 14-15
Harrison. The Drama of Nommo. pp. 145-147
Lee, Don L. "The Bittersweet of Sweetback/or
Shake Yo Money Maker." Black World 21 (No-
vember 1971): 43-54
Mapp. Blacks in Films. p. 251
_____. Black Women in Films. p. 45
"Playboy After Hours--Movies." Playboy 18 (Au-
gust 1971): 30, 32
Riley, Clayton. "What Makes Sweetback Run?"
New York Times, 9 May 1971, 11-D
Scobie, W. "Supernigger Strikes." London
Magazine, (April-May 1972): 111-116
Wolf, William. "B**da****s Peebles." Mil-
waukee Journal Magazine, 17 September 1972,
pp. 33-35
Watermelon Man
Bogle. Toms, Coons, Mulattoes, Mammies and
Bucks. p. 232
Harrison. The Drama of Nommo. pp. 148-149
Mapp. Blacks in Films. pp. 224, 251
REVIEWS OF INDIVIDUAL PLAYS:
Ain't Supposed to Die a Natural Death
New York Theatre Critics' Reviews (1971): 229
New York Times, 29 July 1972, 13: 7
Don't Play Us Cheap

Barnes, C. New York Times, 17 May 1972,
39: 1
Giovanni, Nikki. New York Times, 28 May
1972, II, 1: 1
New York Theatre Critics' Reviews (1971): 279

VAN SCOTT, GLORY
PLAY:
Miss Truth, a poetic suite on Sojourner Truth

VANCE, BOBBYE MARIE BOOKER (b. June 16, 1943)
FILM SCRIPT:
[With Samuel Vance] Rip Off

VANCE, SAMUEL (b. March 15, 1939)
FILM SCRIPTS:
The Measure of a Man
[With Bobbye Vance] Rip Off

VOTEUR, FERDINAND
PLAY:
The Right Angle Triangle, 1939

VROMAN, MARY ELIZABETH (1923-1967)
FILM SCRIPT:
Bright Road, MGM (Based on her short story, "See
How They Run." Ladies Home Journal (June
1951)
CRITICISMS OF VROMAN:
"Writing School Marm: Alabama Teacher Finds
Literary Movie Success with First Short Story."
Ebony 8 (July 1952): 23-28

WALCOTT, BRENDA (b. July 12, 1938)
PLAYS:
The Black Puppet Show
Fantastical Funny
Look Not Upon Me
Temporary Lives

WALCOTT, DEREK
PLAYS:
Dream on Monkey Mountain, 1971
Malcochon
REVIEWS OF INDIVIDUAL PLAYS:
Dream on Monkey Mountain

Willis, John. Theatre World: 1970-1971 Season.
    Vol. 27. N.Y.: Crown, 1971, p. 139
Malcochon
    Willis, John. Theatre World: 1968-1969 Season.
    Vol. 25. N.Y.: Crown, 1969, p. 163

WALKER, DRAKE (b. February 15, 1936)
    FILM SCRIPTS:
        Buck and the Preacher. Columbia Pictures, 1969-
        70
        Henry O. and Jimmy D. Drapat Productions, 1974-
        75
        The Joust. Drapat Productions, 1975-76
        The Prodigals. Drapat Productions, 1974

WALKER, EVAN
    PLAYS:
        Coda for the Blues, 1968
        Dark Light in May, one act, 1960
        East of Jordan, 1969
        The Message, one act, 1969
        A War for Brutus, 1958

WALKER, GEORGE
    PLAY:
        [With Bert Williams] Sons of Ham, 1899

WALKER, JOSEPH (b. February 23, 1935)
    PLAYS:
        [With Josephine Jackson] The Believers, 1968
        The Harangues, 1969
        The Hiss
        Old Judge Mose Is Dead
        Out of the Ashes
        The River Niger. New York: Hill and Wang,
           forthcoming
        Themes of the Black Struggle, 1970
        Tribal Harangue Two. (Has also been referred to
           as a Musical)
        Yin-Yang, 1973
    PLAYS PUBLISHED IN ANTHOLOGIES:
        The Believers, in Guernsey. Best Plays of 1967-68
    MUSICALS:
        Ododo: A Musical Epic in Two Acts
    MUSICALS PUBLISHED IN ANTHOLOGIES:
        Ododo, in King and Milner. Black Drama Anthology
        Tribal Harangue Two, in Richards. Best Short

Plays 1971
CRITICISMS OF WALKER:
Peterson, Maurice. "Taking Off with Joseph Walker." Essence, 4 (April 1974): 55, 74, 78, 82, 88
CRITICISMS OF INDIVIDUAL WORKS:
Ododo
Kraus, Ted M. "Theatre East." Players 46 (February-March 1971): 122
The River Niger
Atkinson. Broadway, pp. 496, 501-503
REVIEWS OF INDIVIDUAL WORKS:
The Harangues
Riley, Clayton. "Theatre Review: The Harangues." Liberator 10 (February 1970): 21
Willis, John. Theatre World: 1969-1970 Season. Vol. 26. N.Y.: Brown, 1970, p. 140
Ododo
Barnes, Clive. New York Times, 25 November 1970
Johnson, Helen Armstead. Black World 20 (April 1971): 47-48
Kerr, Walter. The New York Sunday Times, 6 December 1970, II, 7: 2
New York Theatre Critics' Reviews (1970): 124
New Yorker 28 November 1970, p. 2
"Playboy After Hours: Theater." Playboy 18 (April 1971): 37
Willis, John. Theatre World: 1970-1971 Season. Vol. 27. N.Y.: Brown, 1971, p. 138
The River Niger
Barnes, C. New York Times, 28 March 1973, p. 35: 1
Choice 11 (March 1974): 95
Hewes, Henry. Saturday Review of the Arts (February 1973): 59-60
Library Journal 15 October 1973, p. 3018
New York Magazine 6 (9 April 1973): 94
New York Theatre Critics' Reviews 34 (20 April 1973): 298-301
New York Times, 1 January 1973, p. 64
New Yorker 16 December 1972, p. 86; 23 December 1972, p. 4; 19 May 1973, p. 4
"Playboy After Hours: Theater." Playboy 20 (July 1973): 39
Rudin, Seymour. "Arts in Review: Performing Arts 1972-1973." Massachusetts Review 14

(Autumn 1973): 865-882
AWARDS:
The River Niger: 1974 Tony Award Winner for
Best Play

WALKER, WILLIAM A.
PLAY:
Auruu Hell and Spanish Prison Reform

WALLACE, RUDY
PLAYS:
The Dark Tower, one act
The Moonlight Arms, one act
REVIEWS OF INDIVIDUAL PLAYS:
The Dark Tower and The Moonlight Arms
New Yorker 12 May 1975, p. 4

WALMSLEY, DEW DROP
PLAY:
Genius in Slavery, one act. N.Y.: Amuru, 1973

WARD, DOUGLAS TURNER (1931)
PLAYS:
Brotherhood. Complete Catalogue of Plays 1973-
1974. New York: Dramatists Play Service, Inc.,
1973
Day of Absence. Complete Catalogue of Plays 1973-
1974. New York: Dramatists Play Service, Inc.,
1973
Happy Ending. Complete Catalogue of Plays 1973-
1974. New York: Dramatists Play Service, Inc.,
1973
The Reckoning. Complete Catalogue of Plays 1973-
1974. New York: Dramatists Play Service, Inc.,
1973
Two Plays. (Happy Ending and Day of Absence)
New York: Third, 1971
PLAYS PUBLISHED IN ANTHOLOGIES:
Brotherhood, in King and Milner, Black Drama
Anthology
Day of Absence, in Back and Browning, Drama for
Composition; Brasmer and Consolo, Black Drama;
Childress, Black Scenes (excerpts); Couch, New
Black Playwrights; Hatch and Shine, Black Thea-
ter USA; Hayden, Burrows and Lapides, Afro-
American Literature; Miller, Blackamerican
Literature 1760-Present; Oliver and Sills, Con-

temporary Black Drama; Simmons and Hutchinson,
Black Culture
Happy Ending, in Couch, New Black Playwrights;
  Holmes and Lehman, Keys to Understanding;
  Oliver and Sills, Contemporary Black Drama
Two Plays: Happy Ending and Day of Absence.
  New York: Dramatists Play Service, 1966
PLAYS PUBLISHED IN PERIODICALS:
Happy Ending, in Liberator. Part 1, 4 (December
  1964): 18-23; Liberator. Part 2, 5 (January
  1965): 20-24
CRITICISMS BY WARD:
"American Theatre: For Whites Only?" In Patter-
  son, Anthology of the American Negro in Theater,
  pp. 81-85; also in Raines, Modern Drama and
  Social Changes. (Originally published in N.Y.
  Times, 14 August 1966)
"Comments on The River Niger." New York Times,
  7 February 1973, p. 30: 1
"Needed: A Theatre for Black Themes." Negro
  Digest 17 (December 1967): 34-39
CRITICISMS OF WARD:
Campbell, Dick. "Is There a Conspiracy Against
  Black Playwrights?" Negro Digest 17 (April
  1968): 11-15
Harrison. The Drama of Nommo. pp. 174-176,
  207, 228-229
Hughes and Meltzer. Black Magic. pp. 224-249
  passim
"Interview." Black Creation (Winter 1972)
Mitchell. Black Drama. pp. 215, 216
Patterson, James E. "The Negro Ensemble Com-
  pany." Players 47 (June-July 1972): 224-229
Scott. "The Black Spirit: A Trilogy of Original
  Plays and a Treatise on Dramatic Theory in Con-
  temporary Black Drama." Ph.D. Dissertation,
  Bowling Green State University, 1972, pp. 32,
  36
CRITICISMS OF INDIVIDUAL PLAYS:
Day of Absence
  Abramson. Negro Playwrights in the American
    Theatre 1929-1959. pp. 280-281
  Bigsby. The Black American Writer. Vol. II.
    pp. 150-155, 204-205
  Campbell, Dick. "Is there a Conspiracy Against
    Black Playwrights?" Negro Digest 17 (April
    1968): 13

Downer, Alan S. "Total Theatre and Partial
Drama: Notes on the New York Theatre, 1965-
1966." Quarterly Journal of Speech 52 (October 1966): 234-235

Gayle. Black Expression. pp. 140, 270

Klotman, Phyllis R. "The Passive Resistant in
A Different Drummer, Day of Absence and
Many Thousands Gone." Studies in Black
Literature 3 (Autumn 1972): 7-12

Lewis, Emory. Stages: The Fifty Year Childhood of the American Theater. pp. 160-161

Little. Off-Broadway. pp. 242-43, 248

Mitchell. Black Drama. pp. 209-211

Pawley, Dr. Thomas D. "The Black Theatre
Audience." Players 46 (August-September 1971):
259

Turner, Darwin T. "Negro Playwrights and the
Urban Negro." CLA Journal 12 (September
1968): 19-25

Weales. The Jumping-Off Place. pp. 147-150

Happy Ending

Abramson. Negro Playwrights in the American
Theatre 1929-1959. pp. 280-281

Bigsby. The Black American Writer. Vol. II,
pp. 150-155, 204-205

Downer, Alan S. "Total Theatre and Partial
Drama: Notes on the New York Theatre,
1965-1966." Quarterly Journal of Speech 52
(October 1966): 234

Gayle. Black Expression. pp. 140, 270

Lewis, Emory. Stages: The Fifty Year Childhood of the American Theatre. pp. 160-161

Little. Off-Broadway. pp. 242-43, 248

Mitchell. Black Drama. pp. 209-211

Molette, Dr. Carlton W., II. "Black Theatre in
Atlanta." Players 45 (April-May 1970): 165

Peavey, Charles D. "Satire and Contemporary
Drama." Satire Newsletter 7 (Fall 1969): 40-
48

Turner, Darwin T. "Negro Playwrights and the
Urban Negro." CLA Journal 12 (September
1968): 24

Weales. The Jumping-Off Place. pp. 147-150

REVIEWS OF INDIVIDUAL WORKS:

Brotherhood

Barnes, C. New York Times, 18 March 1970,
39: 1

Kerr, W. New York Times, 29 March 1970, II,
1: 1

Willis, John. Theatre World 1969-1970 Season.
Vol. 26, N.Y.: Crown, 1970, p. 141

Day of Absence

Barnes, C. New York Times, 18 March 1970,
39: 1

Hicks, Al. Liberator 6 (January 1966): 23

Kerr, Walter. New York Times, 29 March 1970,
II, 1: 1

New York Times, 16 November 1966, 56: 1

New Yorker 20 November 1965, p. 4; 19 November 1966, p. 4

Riley, Clayton. "Theatre Reviews: Dutchman
and Day of Absence." Liberator 9 (November
1969): 21

Willis, John. Theatre World: 1969-1970 Season.
Vol. 26. N.Y.: Crown, 1970, p. 141

Happy Ending

Hicks, Al. Liberator 6 (January 1966): 23

Liberator 4 (January 1964): 19-22; 4 (December
1964): 18-21

New Yorker 20 November 1965, p. 4; 19 November 1966, p. 4

The Reckoning

Barnes, C. New York Times, 22 September
1969, 36: 1

Gussow, M. New York Times, 5 September
1969, 28: 1

Kerr, W. New York Times, 14 September 1969,
II, 1: 1

Kupa, Kushauri. "A Review of The Reckoning."
Black Theater Magazine (April 1970): 42

Neal, Laurence. New York Times, 14 September
1969, II, 1: 3

AWARDS:

Obie Award for Day of Absence and Happy Ending

WARD, FRANCIS (b. August 11, 1935)

PLAYS:

The Life of Harriet Tubman

CRITICISMS BY WARD:

[With Val Gray Ward] "The Black Artist--His Role
in the Struggle." Black Scholar 2 (January 1971):
23-32

[With Val Gray Ward] "Theatre Round-Up: Chicago." Black World 21 (April 1972): 37

WARD, THEODORE (b. September 15, 1902)
  PLAYS:
    Big White Fog: A Negro Tragedy, 1937
    The Daubers
    Falcon of Adowa
    John Brown
    Our Lan'
    Sick and Tired
    Skin Deep
    Whole Hog or Nothing
  PLAYS PUBLISHED IN ANTHOLOGIES:
    Big White Fog: A Negro Tragedy, in Brown, Davis
      and Lee, The Negro Caravan (excerpt); Hatch and
      Shine, Black Theater USA
    The Daubers, in Childress, Black Scenes (one scene)
    Our Lan', in Rowe, A Theatre in Your Head, pp.
      261-428 (text and analysis); Turner, Black Drama
      in America
  PLAYS PUBLISHED IN PERIODICALS:
    John Brown, in Masses and Mainstream 2 (October
      1949), Act I Scene 4
    Our Lan', in Theatre Arts 31 (June 1947): 57
  CRITICISMS BY WARD:
    "Our Conception of the Theatre and Its Function."
      Taylor, People's Theatre in Amerika, pp. 188-
      190
    "The South Side Center of The Performing Arts,
      Inc." Black Theatre 2 (1969): 3-4
    "Why Not a Negro Drama for Negroes by Negroes?"
      Current Opinion 72 (1922): 639-640
  CRITICISMS OF WARD:
    Abramson. Negro Playwrights in the American
      Theatre. pp. 109-284 passim
    Gaffney, Floyd. "Is Your Door Really Open?"
      Drama and Theater 7 (Fall 1968): 5
    Hughes and Meltzer. Black Magic. pp. 124, 199
    Rowe. A Theatre in Your Head. p. 256
    Taylor. People's Theatre in Amerika. pp. 186-
      187
    Turner. Black Drama in America. p. 115
    Williams. Stage Left. pp. 230
  CRITICISMS OF INDIVIDUAL PLAYS:
    Big White Fog
      Abramson. Negro Playwrights in America. pp.
        92-93, 109-117
      Hicklin. The American Negro Playwright 1920-
        1964. Part 1, pp. 285-288

Isaacs, Edith J. R. "The Negroes in the American Theater: The Hope Ahead." Theater Arts 26 (August 1942): 541

Mitchell. Black Drama. pp. 113-114

John Brown

Christmas, Walter. "Theatre: Four Plays with Negro Themes." Harlem Quarterly (Fall-Winter 1950): 43-44

Our Lan'

Abramson. Negro Playwrights in America. pp. 117-135, 163-164

Brown, John Mason. "The Uphill Road." Saturday Review of Literature 30 (October 1947): 24-27

Hicklin. The American Negro Playwright, 1920-1964. Part 2, pp. 329-334

Jefferson, Miles M. "The Negro on Broadway, 1947-48." Phylon 9 (Second Quarter 1948): 99-107

Lovell, John Jr. "New Curtains Going Up." Crisis 54 (October 1947): 54

Mitchell. Black Drama. pp. 133-134

Nathan, George Jean. "Memoranda on Four Play Categories." American Mercury 66 (January 1948): 37-41

Rowe. A Theatre in Your Head. pp. 256-260

REVIEWS OF INDIVIDUAL WORKS:

Big White Fog

Atkinson, Brooks. "Negro Playwrights' Company Opens a New Theater Movement in Harlem with Big White Fog." New York Times, 23 October 1940, 26: 2

_____. "The Play." New York Times, 8 May 1941, 20: 4

Stockwell, La Tourette. "Big White Fog." Opportunity 16 (June 1938): 172

Our Lan'

Jefferson, Miles. "The Negro on Broadway: 1946-1947." Phylon 8 (Second Quarter-1947): 159

Theatre Arts 31 (June 1947): 57

AWARDS:

Theatre Guild Scholarship in 1945 for Our Lan'

Second Prize, Chicago City Wide Contest for Sick and Tired, 1937

WASHINGTON, SAM

PLAY:
A Member of the Fateful Grey, 1969

WATKINS, GORDON (b. December 24, 1930)
PLAYS:
A Lion Roams the Streets. n.p.: Breakthrough
Press, n.d.
Sojourner Truth, poetic drama
FILM SCRIPTS:
Jocky
Tom Gideon and His Friends

WATSON, HARMON C. (b. 1943)
PLAYS:
Clown in Three Rings
Those Golden Gates Fall Down
Toy of The Gods, 1964
PLAYS PUBLISHED IN ANTHOLOGIES:
Those Golden Gates Fall Down, in Ford. Black In-
sights

WAY, BRYANT
PLAY:
Magical Faces

WEBER, ADAM
PLAYS:
Spirit of the Living Dead, 1969
To Kill or Die, 1969

WESLEY, RICHARD (b. July 11, 1945)
PLAYS:
Ace Boon Coon
Another Way, 1969
The Black Terror, 1971
Gettin' It Together, 1970
Goin' through Changes, one act
Headline News, 1970
Knock, Knock, Who Dat, 1970
The Past Is the Past, 1973
The Sirens
Springtime High, one act, 1968
The Street Corner, 1970
Strike Heaven on the Face, 1973
PLAYS PUBLISHED IN ANTHOLOGIES:
The Black Terror, in Bullins. New Lafayette
Theatre Presents

FILM SCRIPT:
Uptown Saturday Night
CRITICISMS BY WESLEY:
"An Interview with Playwright Ed Bullins." Black
   Creation 4 (Winter 1973): 8-10
"Harlem's Black Theater Workshop." Black World
   21 (April 1972): 47-48, 70-74
"Toward a Viable Black Film Industry." Black
   World 22 (July 1973): 23-32
Little. Off-Broadway. p. 288
CRITICISMS OF INDIVIDUAL WORKS:
The Black Terror
   Archer. Black Images. pp. 290-291
   Bentley, E. "Black Terror and Modern Black
      Theater." New York Times, 23 January 1972;
      II, p. 1: 6
   Bullins. The New Lafayette Theatre Presents.
      pp. 217-218
   Coleman, Larry. "Review of Richard Wesley's
      Black Terror." Black Theatre (Fall 1972):
      36-37
   Hughes. Plays, Politics and Polemics. pp. 45-
      52
   Jones, Martha M. "Richard Wesley's Black Ter-
      ror." Black Creation 3 (Spring 1972): 12-14
   Kraus, Ted M. "Theatre East." Players 47
      (February-March 1972): 134
   McElroy, Hilda Njoki. "Books Noted." Black
      World 26 (April 1975): 82-83
   Reische. The Performing Arts in America. pp.
      88-89
   Rudin, Seymour. "Performing Arts: 1971-1972."
      Massachusetts Review 14 (Winter 1973): 208
REVIEWS OF INDIVIDUAL WORKS:
Ace Boon Coon
   Black World (May 1972): 88
Black Terror
   Barnes, Clive. "Black Terror." New York
      Times, 11 November 1971, p. 62
   Gottfried, Martin. Women's Wear Daily, 11
      November 1971
   Kroll, Jack. Newsweek, 29 November 1971
   The National Observer 27 November 1971, p. 22
   New York Theatre Critics' Reviews (1971): 160
   New Yorker 1 January 1972, p. 2
   Watts, Richard. New York Post, 11 November
      1971

The Past Is the Past
New Yorker   12 May 1975, p. 2
The Sirens
New Yorker   20 May 1974, p. 4
The Street Corner
New York Times   30 August 1972, p. 42: 1
AWARDS:
Drama Desk Award for The Black Terror

WHIPPER, LEIGH
PLAYS:
[With Porter Grainger]   De Board Meetin', 1925
MUSICALS:
[With Billy Mills]   Yeah Man, 1932
[With J. C. Johnson]   Runnin' de Town, 1930
[With Porter Grainger]   We'se Risin', 1927
CRITICISMS OF WHIPPER:
Bond.   The Negro and the Drama.   p. 44

WHITE, EDGAR
PLAYS:
The Burghers of Calais, 1971
The Cathedral at Chartres, one act, 1969
The Crucificado: Two Plays.   New York: Morrow,
   1973
Les Femmes Noirs
Fun in Lethe, 1970
La Gente
The Life and Times of J. Walter Smitheus, 1970
The Mummer's Play, one act, 1969
Ode to Charlie Parker
Seigismundo's Tricycle
The Wonderful Year, 1971
Underground: Four Plays.   New York: Morrow,
   1970
PLAYS PUBLISHED IN ANTHOLOGIES:
Seigismundo's Tricycle, in Watkins, Mel, ed.   Black
   Review #1
PLAYS PUBLISHED IN PERIODICALS:
The Cathedral at Chartres, in Liberator 8 (July
   1968): 16-18
REVIEWS OF INDIVIDUAL PLAYS:
Les Femmes Noirs
New Yorker   8 April 1974, p. 2
The Life and Times of J. Walter Smitheus
Rudin, Seymour.   "Theatre Chronicle: Winter-
   Spring 1971."   The Massachusetts Review 12

(Autumn 1971): 821-833

WHITE, JOSEPH (b. December 2, 1933)
    PLAYS:
      The Leader
      Old Judge Mose Is Dead, one act
    PLAYS PUBLISHED IN ANTHOLOGIES:
      The Leader, in Jones and Neal, Black Fire
    PLAYS PUBLISHED IN PERIODICALS:
      Old Judge Mose Is Dead, in The Drama Review
        12 (Summer 1968)
    CRITICISMS OF INDIVIDUAL PLAYS:
      Old Judge Mose Is Dead
        Riach, W. A. D. "'Telling It Like It Is': An
        Examination of Black Theater as Rhetoric."
        Quarterly Journal of Speech 46 (April 1970)

WHITE, LUCY
    PLAY:
      The Bird Child, one act. N.Y.: Harper, 1927
    PLAYS PUBLISHED IN ANTHOLOGIES:
      The Bird Child, in Locke and Gregory, Plays of
        Negro Life

WHITEN, JAMES
    PLAY:
      Traps

WHITFIELD, VANTILE (Motojicho)
    PLAYS:
      The Creeps, one act, 1969
      In Sickness and in Health, one act, 1966

WHITNEY, ELVIE
    PLAYS:
      Center of Darkness, 1968
      Pornuff, 1969
      Up a Little Higher, 1968

WILKS, PETER
    PLAYS:
      The Long-Game Mefy
      The Soul of Willy

WILLIAMS, CLARENCE
    PLAY:
      Bottomland, 1927

WILLIAMS, EGBERT AUSTIN (Bert Williams) (1878-1922)
MUSICALS:
[With Alex Rogers and J. A. Shipp] Mr. Lode of
Koal, 1909
[With George Walker] Oyster Man, 1907?
[With George Walker] Sons of Ham, 1899
CRITICISMS OF WILLIAMS:
Workers of The Writers' Program of the Work
Projects Administration in New York City.
The Theatre: Research Studies. New York:
n.p., 1938-40
CRITICISMS OF INDIVIDUAL MUSICALS:
Mr. Lode of Koal
Mitchell. Black Drama. p. 53

WILLIAMS, ELLWOODSON
PLAYS:
Mine Eyes Have Seen the Glory, 1970
Voice of the Gene, 1969

WILLIAMS, HAROLD
PLAY:
With the Right Seed My Plant Will Grow Green

WILLIAMS, JOHN ALFRED
PLAY:
Reprieve for All God's Children

WILLIAMS, MARSHALL
PLAY:
A Tear for Judas, 1970

WILLIAMS, SANDRA BETH (Auransia) (b. October 1948)
PLAYS:
The Family
Hey Nigger Can You Dig Her
Jest One Mo
Sunshine
Zodiac Zenith
AWARDS:
Awarded a CAPS grant for two of her plays, 1972

WILSON, CAL
PLAY:
The Pet Shop, 1965

WILSON, FRANK

PLAYS:
Brother Mose (original title: Meek Mose)
Back Home Again
Confidence, one act, 1922
The Frisco Kid
The Good Sister Jones
Sugar Cane, one act
Walk Together, Chillun, unpublished
PLAYS PUBLISHED IN ANTHOLOGIES:
Brother Mose, in Mantle and Burns, Best Plays of
1927-1928
Sugar Cane, in Locke and Gregory, Plays of Negro
Life
PLAYS PUBLISHED IN PERIODICALS:
Sugar Cane, in Opportunity 4 (June 1926): 181-184,
201-203
CRITICISMS BY WILSON:
"The Theatre Past and Present." Amsterdam News,
15 June 1932
CRITICISMS OF INDIVIDUAL PLAYS:
Meek Mose
Abramson. Negro Playwrights in The American
Theatre. pp. 54-59, 86
Belcher, Fannin S. "The Place of the Negro in
the Evolution of the Theatre, 1767-1940."
Unpublished Ph.D. Thesis, Yale University,
1945, p. 229
Bond. The Negro and the Drama. p. 110
Edmonds, Randolph. "Some Reflections on the
Negro in American Drama." Opportunity 8
(October 1930): 304
Hicklin. The American Negro Playwright 1920-
1964. Part 1, pp. 147-149
Sugar Cane
Bond. The Negro and the Drama. p. 109
Hicklin. The American Negro Playwright 1920-
1964. Part 1, pp. 147-149
Lewis, Theophulis. "Three Sermons by Dr. Wil-
son." The Messenger 8 (August 1926): 246
Walk Together, Chillun
Abramson. Negro Playwrights in The American
Theatre. p. 59
Bond. The Negro and The Drama. pp. 166-167
Gold, Michael. "At Last, a Negro Theatre?"
New Masses (March 1937): 18
Hicklin. The American Negro Playwright 1920-
1964. Part 1, pp. 232-234, 217

REVIEWS OF INDIVIDUAL PLAYS:
  Meek Mose
    New York Times, 4 February 1928, 7: 2; 7
      February, 1928, 30: 1
  Walk Together, Chillun
    Atkinson, J. Brooks. New York Times, 7 Febru-
      ary 1928, p. 30
AWARDS:
  First Prize for Sugar Cane: Opportunity Contest,
    1925

WRIGHT, CHARLES STEVENSON (b. June 4, 1932)
  PLAY:
  Something Black

WRIGHT, RICHARD (September 4, 1908-November 28, 1960)
  PLAYS:
    [With Louis Sapin] Daddy Goodness
    [With Paul Green] Native Son: A Biography of a
      Young American. New York: Harper, 1941
  PLAYS PUBLISHED IN ANTHOLOGIES:
    Native Son, in Best Short Plays, 1940-1941; Hatch
      and Shine, Black Theater USA
  CRITICISMS BY WRIGHT:
    "Blue Print for Negro Literature." (1929) Amistad
      2 (February 1971): 9
    "I Bite the Hand that Feeds Me." Atlantic Monthly
      165 (June 1940): 828
  CRITICISMS OF WRIGHT:
    Brignano, Russell. "Richard Wright: The Major
      Themes, Ideas, and Attitudes in His Works."
      Dissertation Abstracts 28 (1967) 666A-667A
      (Wis.)
    Cotton, Letti Jo. "Negro in the American Theater."
      Negro History Bulletin 23 (May 1960): 174
    Delpeck, Jeanine. "An Interview with Native Son."
      Crisis 57 (November 1950): 625-626, 678
    Gaffney, Floyd. "Is Your Door Really Open?"
      Drama and Theater 7 (Fall 1968): 5
    Zietlow, E. R. "Wright to Hansberry: The Evolu-
      tion of Outlook in Four Negro Writers." Dis-
      sertation Abstracts, 28 (1967), 701A (U. of Wash-
      ington)
  CRITICISMS OF INDIVIDUAL WORKS:
    Daddy Goodness
      Campbell, Dick. "Is There a Conspiracy Against
        Black Playwrights?" Negro Digest 17 (April

1968): 15

Kloman, William. "Moses Gunn: A Brilliant
Black Star." The New York Times, 16 June
1968 2, 1: 3

Willis, John. Theatre World: 1967-1968 Season.
Vol. 24. N.Y.: Crown, 1968, p. 149

Native Son

Abramson. Negro Playwrights in the American
Theatre. pp. 136-155, 160-163

Bigsby. The Black American Writer. Vol. II,
pp. 122-123

Bluefarb, Sam. "Bigger Thomas: Escape into
the Labyrinth." The Escape Motif in the
American Novel. pp. 134-153

Gayle. Black Expression. pp. 154, 331-333,
335-339, 358

Gilder, Rosamond. "Matter for Thanksgiving:
Broadway in Review." Theatre Arts 27 (December 1942): 744

Hicklin. The American Negro Playwright 1920-
1964. Part 2, pp. 334-339

Himelstein. Drama Was a Weapon. pp. 120-122

Isaacs, Edith J. R. "The Negro in the American
Theatre: A Record of Achievement." Theatre Arts 26 (August 1942): 495

————. "The Negro in the American Theater:
The Foreground, 1917-1942." Theater Arts
26 (August 1942): 526

Mitchell. Black Drama. pp. 109, 114-116

"Negro Playwrights: Young Chicagoan Is First
with All-Negro Play on Broadway." Ebony
14 (April 1959): 98

Nichols, Charles H., Jr. "The Forties: A
Decade of Growth." Phylon (Fourth Quarter
1951): 379

Sieners, W. David. Freud on Broadway. pp.
319-321

Young. Immortal Shadows. pp. 223-226

REVIEWS OF INDIVIDUAL WORKS:

Daddy Goodness

Bailey, Peter. "Review." Black Theatre 1
(1968): 30

New York Times, 5 June 1968, p. 37

Riley, Clayton. "Daddy Goodness." Liberator
8 (July 1968): 21

Willis, John. Theatre World: 1967-1968 Season.
Vol. 24. N.Y.: Crown, 1968, p. 149

Native Son
 Belcher, Fannin S. "The Negro Theater: A
  Glance Backward." Phylon 11 (Second Quar-
  ter 1950): 126
 Catholic World   153 (May 1941): 217
 Commonweal 33 (April 11, 1941): 622
 Independent Woman 21 (December 1942): 378
 Life 10 (April 7, 1941): 94-96
 Nation 152 (April 5, 1941): 417
 New Republic 104 (April 7, 1941): 468-469
 New York Theatre Critics' Reviews (1941): 349
 New York Times 25 March 1941, 26; 3 March
  1941, 9: 1; 6 April 1941, 9: 1; 24 October
  1942, 10; 1 November 1942, 1; 7 December
  1942, 16: 7
 Theatre Arts 25 (May 1941): 329-332; 25 (June
  1941): 467-470; 26 (December 1942): 744
 Time 37 (April 7, 1941): 76
 FILMSCRIPT:
 Native Son
 FILM CRITICISM:
 Mapp. Blacks in American Films. p. 48
 FILM REVIEW:
 New York Times, 18 June 1951, 19: 2

YOUNG, CLARENCE III
 PLAY:
 Perry's Mission, 1970
 REVIEWS OF INDIVIDUAL PLAYS:
 Perry's Mission
  New Yorker 30 January 1971, p. 2
  Willis, John. Theatre World: 1970-1971 Season.
   Vol. 27. N.Y.: Crown, 1971, p. 138

YOUNG, OTIS
 PLAY:
 Right on Brother, 1969

YOUNGER, MARTIN
 PLAYS:
  Courting
  A String of Periods

ZUBER, RON
 PLAY:
 Three X Love

PLAYS PUBLISHED IN ANTHOLOGIES:
  Three X Love, in King and Milner, Black Drama
    Anthology

GENERAL BIBLIOGRAPHY

Abramson, Doris E. "From Harlem to A Raisin in the
    Sun: A Study of Plays by Negro Playwrights, 1929-
    1959." Ph.D. Dissertation, Columbia University,
    Teachers College, 1965.
————. "In Review: New Black Playwrights (Wm.
    Couch)." The Massachusetts Review 10 (Summer
    1969): 604-608.
————. "Negro Playwrights in America." Columbia
    Forum 12 (Spring 1969): 11-17.
————. Negro Playwrights in the American Theatre 1925-
    1959. N.Y.: Columbia University Press, 1969.
————. "William Wells Brown: America's First Negro
    Playwright." Educational Theater Journal 20 (October
    1968): 370-376.
Adams, Geo. R. "Black Militant Drama." American
    Imago 28 (Summer 1971): 107-122.
————. "My Christ in 'Dutchman.'" CLA Journal 15
    (September 1971): 54
Adams, William, Peter Conn and Barry Slepian, eds.
    Afro-American Literature. 4 vols. Boston: Hough-
    ton Mifflin, 1970.
Adler, Renata. "Critic Keeps Her Cool on 'Uptight.'"
    New York Times, 29 December 1968, D. I: 29.
Ahmann, Mathew. The New Negro. N.Y.: Biblo and
    Tannen, 1969.
Alexander, Lewis. "Plays of Negro Life." Carolina
    Magazine (April 1929): 45.
Alexander, Naledi Nnakintu. "Report on the National Black
    Theatre," in Taylor. People's Theatre in America.
    pp. 320-325.
Alhamisi, Ahmed and Harun Kofi Wangara, eds. Black
    Arts: An Anthology of Black Creations. Detroit:
    Black Arts, 1969.
Altick, Richard. The Art of Literary Research. rev. ed.
    N.Y.: Norton, 1975.
"American Negro Repertory Players." Ebony 5 (October
    1950): 52-54.

Anderson, Garland. From Newsboy and Bellhop to Play-
    wright. San Francisco: Author, 1926.
Anderson, Jervis. "Black Writing--The Other Side."
    Dissent 15 (May-June 1968): 233-242.
_____. "Profiles: Dramatist." New Yorker 49 (16
    June 1973): 40.
Andrews, Bert. "Photo Essay: Ceremonies in Dark Old
    Men." Liberator 9 (August 1969): 12.
Andrews, C. B. "Ira Aldridge." Crisis 42 (October 1935):
    26.
Anon. "The Adventure of the Black Girl in Her Search for
    God: Message Play Warns Whites of Black Army,
    White Guns." Jet 36 (May 1969): 60-61.
Anon. "Langston Hughes and the Example of Simple."
    Black World 19 (June 1970): 35-38.
Anon. "An Old Ragtime Man Goes to the Opera." Ebony
    27 (April 1972): 90.
Aptheker, Herbert. "The Drama of Douglass and Brocon."
    Masses and Mainstream 7 (November 1954): 54.
Archer, Leonard C. Black Images in the American Thea-
    tre. Brooklyn: Pageant-Poseidon, Ltd., 1973.
_____. "The National Association for the Advancement
    of Colored People and the American Theatre." Ph.D.
    Dissertation, Ohio State University, 1959.
Arvey, Verna. "Hall Johnson and His Choir." Opportunity
    19 (May 1941): 151, 158-159.
Atkinson, Brooks. "At the Theatre" (The Barrier). New
    York Times, 3 November 1950, 32: 2.
_____. Broadway. rev. ed. N.Y.: Macmillan, 1974.
_____. "Native Son." New York Times, 25 March 1941,
    26: 5; 6 April 1961, IX, 1: 1; 1 November 1942.
_____. "Negro Playwright's Company Opens a New Thea-
    tre Movement in Harlem with 'Big White Fog.'" New
    York Times, 23 October 1940, 26: 2.
_____. "'Ol Man Satan.'" New York Times, 4 October
    1932.
_____. "The Play" (Big White Fog). New York Times,
    8 May 1941, 20: 4.
_____. "The Play" (Harlem). New York Times, 21
    February 1929.
_____. "The Play" (Mulatto). New York Times, 25
    October 1935, 25: 2.
_____. "The Play" (Natural Man). New York Times, 8
    May 1941, 20: 4.
_____. "The Theatre: 'A Raisin in the Sun.'" New
    York Times, 29 March 1959, II, 1: 1.
_____. "Tragic Play on Race Relations." New York

Times, 8 August 1935, 13.
_____. "Up 'Harlem' Way." New York Times, 3 March
1929.
Austin, Gerlyn E. "The Advent of the Negro Actor on the
Legitimate Stage in America." Journal of Negro Edu-
cation 35 (Summer 1966): 237-245.

Back, Bert C. and Gordon Browning. Drama for Composi-
tion. Glenview, Ill.: Scott, Foresman, 1973.
Bailey, J. O. "Negro Players in Southern Theatres." New
Theatre (July 1935).
Bailey, Peter. "Annual Round-Up: Black Theatre in Ameri-
ca." Black World 21 (April 1972): 31-36.
_____. "Daddy Goodness." Black Theatre 1 (October
1968): 31.
_____. "The Electronic Nigger." Ebony 23 (September
1968): 97-101.
_____. "Is the Negro Ensemble Company Really Black
Theatre?" Negro Digest 17 (April 1968): 16-19.
_____. "Review: Sometimes a Hard Head Makes a Soft
Behind." New York Times, 13 August 1972, II, 2: 4.
_____. "Talking of Black Art, Theatre Revolution, and
Nationhood." Black Theatre 5 (1971): 18-37.
_____. "Woodie King Jr.: Renaissance Man of Black
Theatre." Black World 26 (April 1975): 18-37.
Bain, Carl E., ed. Drama. New York: Norton, 1973.
Baker, John. "LeRoi Jones, Secessionist and Ambiguous
Collecting." Yale University Library Gazette, 46
(1972): 159-166.
Baldwin, James. "Many Thousands Gone." Partisan Re-
view 18 (November-December 1951): 665-680.
_____. "Theatre: The Negro In and Out." Negro Di-
gest 15 (April 1966): 37-44.
"Baldwin Seeks to Avert Closing." New York Times, 27
May 1964, 44: 1.
"Baldwin's First Play, 'Amen Corner.'" Jet 26 (March
1964): 60-61.
"Baldwin's 'Blues for Mr. Charlie' Folds on Broadway.'"
Jet 10 (September 1964): 59.
Baraka, Imamu Amiri. "Black Power Chant." Black Theatre
4 (April 1970): 35.
_____. "For Maulana and Pharoah Saunders." Black
Theatre 4 (April 1970): 4.
_____. "Negro Theatre Pimps Get Big off Nationalism."
in J-E-L-L-O. Chicago: Third World Press, 1970,
pp. 5-8.

_____. Spirit Reach. Newark: Jihad Productions, 1972.
_____. "Symposium on 'We Righteous Bombers.'"
    Black Theatre 4 (April 1970): 15-25.
Barbour, Floyd, ed. Black Power Revolt. Boston: Porter
    Sargent, 1968.
Barksdale, Richard and Keneth Kinnamon, eds. Black Wri-
    ters of America: A Comprehensive Anthology. N.Y.:
    Macmillan, 1972.
Barnes, C. "Review: Black Girl." New York Times, 17
    June 1971, 49: 1.
_____. "Review: Brotherhood." New York Times, 18
    March 1970, 39: 1.
_____. "Review: The Brown Overcoat." New York
    Times, 5 December 1972, 73: 1.
_____. "Review: Ceremonies in Dark Old Men." New
    York Times, 6 February 1969, 33: 1.
_____. "Review: Don't Bother Me I Can't Cope." New
    York Times, 8 October 1970, 60: 3.
_____. "Review: Don't Bother Me I Can't Cope." New
    York Times, 20 April 1972, 51: 1.
_____. "Review: Don't Play Us Cheap." New York
    Times, 17 May 1972, 39: 1.
_____. "Review: Five on the Black Hand Side." New
    York Times, 2 January 1970, 32: 2.
_____. "Review of Four One Act Plays (Bullins')." New
    York Times, 5 March 1972, 59: 1.
_____. "Review: Joy." New York Times, 19 July 1970,
    50: 1.
_____. "Review: Les Blancs." New York Times, 16
    November 1970, 48: 4.
_____. "Review: Ododo." New York Times, 25 Novem-
    ber 1970, 26: 1.
_____. "Review: The Pig Pen." New York Times, 21
    May 1970, 47: 1.
_____. "Review: The Sign in Sidney Brustein's Window."
    New York Times, 27 January 1972, 44: 1.
_____. "Review: The Sty of the Blind Pig." New York
    Times, 24 November 1971, 21: 1.
Barnet, Sylvan, Morton Berman, and William Burto, eds.
    Types of Drama: Plays and Essays. Boston: Little,
    Brown, 1972.
Barnett, Claude A. "Role of the Press, Radio, and Motion
    Picture and Negro Morale." Journal of Negro Educa-
    tion 12 (July 1943): 474-489.
Barranger, M. S. and Daniel B. Dodson, eds. Generations:
    An Introduction to Drama. New York: Harcourt Brace
    Jovanovich, 1971.

Barrow, William. "New Theatre in Detroit--Introducing the
    Concept." Negro Digest 12 (May 1963): 76.
Beauford, Fred. "A Conversation with Black Girl's J. E.
    Franklin." Black Creation 3 (Fall 1971): 38-40.
_____. "The Negro Ensemble Company." Black Crea-
    tion 3 (Winter 1972): 16-19.
"Beginnings of Negro Drama." Literary Digest 48 (9 May
    1914): 1114.
Beiswanger, George. "The Theatre Moves Toward Music."
    Theatre Arts 25 (April 1941): 287-296.
Belcher, Fannie S. "The Negro Theatre: A Glance Back-
    ward." Phylon 11 (1950): 121-126.
_____. "Negro Drama, Stage Center." Opportunity 17
    (October 1931): 292-295.
_____. "The Place of the Negro in the Evolution of the
    American Theatre, 1767-1940." Ph.D. Dissertation,
    Yale, 1945.
Bell, George M. "Social Value of Contemporary Drama."
    Competitor 1 (April 1920): 71.
"Bell Boy's Play Goes On." New York Times, 22 August
    1925, 6: 2.
"Bellboy's Play Is Bought." New York Times, 21 June
    1925, 23: 5.
"Bellhop Sells Second Play to Belasco." New York Evening
    Journal, 7 October 1929.
Bellow, Saul. "Theatrical Chronicle: Pleasures and Pains
    of Playgoing." Partisan Review 21 (May-June 1954):
    312-317.
Bentley, Eric. "Black Terror and Modern Black Theatre."
    New York Times, 23 January 1972, II, 1: 6.
Bermel, Albert. "Ed Bullins." New Leader 22 April 1968,
    p. 28.
Bessie, Alvah. "New Negro Theater." New Masses 24
    (September 1940): 23.
"Beyond the Pulitzer: An Interview with Charles Gordone."
    Sepia 2 (February 1971): 14-17.
"Beyond Rhetoric Towards a Black Southern Theatre."
    Black World 2 (April 1971): 14-24.
Bigsby, C. W. E., ed. The Black American Writer, 2 vols.
    Baltimore: Penguin, 1969; Deland, Fla.: Everett/
    Edwards, 1969.
_____. "Black Drama in the Seventies." Kansas Quar-
    terly 3 (Spring 1971): 1-20.
_____. Confrontation and Commitment: A Study of Con-
    temporary American Drama, 1959-1966. Columbia:
    University of Missouri Press, 1969.
_____. "Three Black Playwrights: Loften Mitchell, Os-

sie Davis, Douglas Turner Ward." in The Black
American Writer, Everett/Edwards, 1969, vol. 2,
pp. 137-155.
Bisbane, Eva Mae. "Théâtre de Victor Séjour." Master's
Thesis, Hunter College, 1942.
Black, Susan M. "Play Reviews" (Purlie Victorious). Thea-
tre Arts 45 (December 1961): 12.
"Black Movie Boom--Good or Bad?" Arts and Leisure Sec-
tion, New York Times, 17 December 1972.
"Black Nativity (Langston Hughes' Song Play) Opens Off-
Broadway." Jet 28 (December 1961): 66-73.
"Black Pulitzer Prize Awardees." Crisis 77 (May 1970):
186-188.
A Black Quartet: Four New Black Plays. Introduction by
Clayton Riley. New York: New American Library,
1970.
"The Black Theater." Drama Review 12 (Summer 1968):
entire issue.
"Black Theatre." Negro Digest 18 (April 1969): 9-16.
"Black Theatre at the Crossroads: Old Formulas or New
Directions?" Negro Digest 17 (April 1968): entire
issue.
"Black Theatre: Weapon for Change." Negro Digest 16
(April 1967): 35-39.
Blackburn, Lou. "Studio Watts Workshop." Liberator 7
(March 1967): 11.
Blitzgen, Sister John Carol. "Voices of Protest: An
Analysis of the Negro Protest Plays, the 1963-1964
Broadway and Off-Broadway Season." Master's Thesis,
University of Kansas, 1966.
Bluefarb, Sam. "Bigger Thomas: Escape into the Labyrinth."
The Escape Motif in the American Novel. Columbus,
Ohio: Ohio State University Press, 1972, pp. 134-153.
"Blues for Mister Charlie." New York Times, 3 May 1964,
II, 3.
Bluestone, George. Novels Into Films. Berkeley: Univer-
sity of California Press, 1966.
Bogle, Donald. "The First Black Movie Stars." Saturday
Review of the Arts 1 (February 1973): 25-29.
_____. Toms, Coons, Mulattoes, Mammies and Bucks.
New York: Viking Press, 1973.
Bolcom, William. "Orchestrating 'Treemonisha.'" The
Performer Magazine at Wolf Trap, (Second Season,
1972), vol. 2, Book 3, p. 9.
Bond, Frederick W. The Negro and the Drama. College
Park, Md.: McGrath, 1969.
Bontemps, Arna, ed. The Harlem Renaissance Remembered.

N.Y.: Dodd, Mead, 1972.

Boroff, David, ed. The State of the Union. Englewood
    Cliffs, N.J.: Prentice-Hall, 1966.

Bosworth, Patricia. "From Nowhere to 'No Place.'"
    New York Times, 1 June 1969, II, 1: 1.

Botto, Louis. "Melvin Van Peebles: Work in Progress."
    Black Times 2 (1972): 12-13.

Bowser, Pearl. "The Boom Is Really an Echo." Black
    Creation 4 (Winter 1973): 32.

Bradley, Gerald. "Goodbye, Mister Bones: The Emergence
    of Negro Themes and Characters in American Drama."
    Drama Critique 7 (Spring 1964): 79-85.

Braggioti, Mary. "Stagecraft in Harlem." New York Post,
    29 December 1943.

Brasmer, William and Dominick Consolo, eds. Black Drama,
    an Anthology. Columbus, Ohio: Charles Merrill, 1970.

Brawley, Benjamin. "A Composer of Fourteen Operas."
    Southern Workman 62 (September 1933): 311-315.

_____. The Negro Genius. N.Y.: Dodd Mead, 1937.

"Bridging a Gap"--A Documentary by Geneva C. Turner and
    Jessie H. Roy (for television). The Negro History
    Bulletin 20 (March 1951): 133-137.

Brignano, Russell C. "Richard Wright: The Major Themes,
    Ideas, and Attitudes in His Works." Dissertation Ab-
    stracts 28 (1967).

Brockett, Oscar G. History of the Theatre. 2nd ed.
    Boston: Allyn and Bacon, 1974.

Brodsky, Vera Laurence. "The Opera and Its Composer."
    The Performer Magazine at Wolf Trap. (Second Sea-
    son, 1972), vol. 2, book 3, p. H.

_____. "Scott Joplin's 'Treemonisha.'" High Fidelity/
    Musical America (May 1972): MA-10.

Broning, Eberhard. "'The Black Liberation Movement' und
    Oas Amerikanische Drama." Zeitschrift Furanglistic
    und Amerikanistic 20 (1972): 46-58.

Brown, Cecil M. "Apotheosis of a Prodigal Son." Kenyon
    Review 30 (1968): 654-666-668.

_____. "Black Literature and LeRoi Jones." Black
    World 19 (June 1970): 24-31.

Brown, John Mason. "The Uphill Road." Saturday Review
    of Literature 30 (October 1947): 24-27.

Brown, Moses and John, ed. The American Theatre as
    Seen by Its Critics. N.Y.: Norton, 1934.

Brown, Roscoe C. "Film as a Tool for Liberation."
    Black Creation 4 (Winter 1973): 36.

_____. "New Themes in Black Literature." Black Cre-
    ation 1 (April 1970): 32-33.

Brown, Sterling. "Afro-American Folk Tradition." Studies in the Literary Imagination 7 (Fall 1974): 131.

_____. "The Atlanta University Summer Theatre." Opportunity 12 (October 1934): 308-309.

_____. "The Federal Theatre." in Anthology of the American Negro in the Theatre. Lindsay Patterson, ed. Washington, D.C.: Associated, 1967, pp. 101-107.

_____. Negro Poetry and Drama and the Negro in American Fiction. N.Y.: Atheneum, 1969.

_____, Arthur P. Davis and Ulysses Lee. The Negro Caravan. N.Y.: Arno, 1970.

Browne, Martin E. "Theatre Abroad." Drama Survey 5 (Summer 1966): 194.

Brudnoy, David. "Blues for Mr. Baldwin." National Review, 7 (July 1972): 750-751.

Brustein, Robert. The Seasons of Discontent. N.Y.: Simon and Schuster, 1965.

_____. The Theatre in Revolt; An Approach to the Modern Drama. Boston: Little, Brown, 1962.

_____. "Three Plays and a Protest." New Republic 152 (23 January 1965): 32-33.

Bullins, Ed. "Black Theatre Groups: A Directory." Drama Review 12 (Summer 1968): 172-175.

_____. "Black Theatre Notes." Black Theatre no. 1 (1968): 4.

_____. "The Box Office: A Scenario for Short Film by Ed Bullins as Related by Robert Macbeth." Black Theatre 3 (1970): 17-19.

_____. "Comments on the Production of In New England Winter." New York Times, 20 December 1970, II, 3: 6.

_____. "Like it Was: Review of LeRoi Jones' The Dutchman and The Toilet." Black Dialogue 1 (Spring 1966):

_____. The New Lafayette Theatre Presents. N.Y.: Anchor Press/Doubleday, 1974.

_____. New Plays from the Black Theatre. N.Y.: Bantam, 1969.

_____. "A Short Statement on Street Theatre." Drama Review 12 (Summer 1968): 93.

_____. "The So-Called Avant-Garde Drama." Liberator 7 (December 1967): 16.

_____. "Theatre of Reality." Negro Digest 15 (April 1966): 60-66.

_____. "What Lies Ahead for Black Americans." Negro Digest 19 (November 1968): 8 (Symposium).

Burford, Walter W. "LeRoi Jones: from Existentialism to

the Apostle of Black Nationalism." Players 47 (December-January 1972): 60-64.

Cade, Toni. "Review of Four by Ed Bullins." Umbra-
    blackworks (Summer 1970).
Cahill, Susan and Michele F. Cooper. The Urban Reader.
    Englewood Cliffs, N.J.: Prentice-Hall, 1971.
Caldwell, Ben. Four Plays: Riot Sale, The Job, Top
    Secret, Mission Accomplished. Drama Review 12
    (Summer 1968): 40-52.
_____. et al. A Black Quartet. New York: New Ameri-
    can Library, 1970.
Calverton, V. F. Anthology of American Negro Literature.
    New York: The Modern Library, 1944.
Cameron, Kenneth M. and Theodore J. C. Hoffman. A
    Guide to Theatre Study. N.Y.: Macmillan, 1974.
Campbell, Dick. "Is There a Conspiracy Against Black
    Playwrights?" Negro Digest 17 (April 1968): 11-15.
Carey, Julian. "Jessie B. Simple Revisited and Revised."
    Phylon 32 (1971): 158-163.
Carmer, Carl. "'Run, Little Chillun!' ... A Critical Re-
    view." Opportunity 11 (April 1933): 113.
Carter, John. "Hansberry's Potpourri" (The Sign in Sidney
    Brustein's Window). New Yorker 40 (24 October 1964):
    93.
Cerf, Bennet Alfred, ed. Plays of Our Time. N.Y.:
    Random, 1967.
_____. Six American Plays for Today. N.Y.: Modern
    Library, 1961.
Chambers, Bradford and Rebecca Moon. Right On!:
    Anthology of Black Literature. New York: New
    American Library, 1970.
Childress, Alice, ed. Black Scenes. Garden City, N.Y.:
    Doubleday, 1971.
Chintok, JoJo. "Lennox Brown: A Black Canadian Drama-
    tist." black i: A Canadian Journal of Black Expression
    I (no. 1): 28-29.
Chrisman, Robert. "The Black Scholar Hosts Shirley
    Graham DuBois." Black Scholar 2 (December 1970):
    50-52.
Christmas, Walter. "Theatre--Four Plays with Negro
    Themes." Harlem Quarterly (Fall-Winter 1950): 43-44.
Ciardi, John. "Black Man in America." Saturday Review
    of Literature 46 (6 July 1963): 13.
Clark, Kenneth B. "A Conversation with James Baldwin."
    Freedomways 3 (Summer 1963): 361-368.

Clarke, S. "Sonia Sanchez and Her Work." Black World
    2 (June 1971): 44-46.
Clayborne, Jon R. "Modern Black Drama and the Gay
    Image." College English 36 (November 1974): 381-
    384.
Clayes, Stanley and David Spencer, eds. Contemporary
    Drama: Thirteen Plays. N.Y.: Scribner's, 1970.
Clime, Julia. "Rise of the American Stage Negro."
    Drama Magazine (January 1931): 56-57.
"Clorindy, the Origin of the Cake Walk." Theatre Arts 31
    (September 1947): 61-65.
Clurman, Harold. "Ed Bullins." Nation 208 (12 May 1969):
    612.
_____. "LeRoi Jones, Naughton's Alfie." Nation 200
    (4 January 1965): 16-17.
_____. The Naked Image. N.Y.: Macmillan, 1966.
_____. "The Theatre of the Thirties." Tulane Drama
    Review 4 (Winter 1959): 3-11.
Cohn, Ruby. Dialogue in American Drama. Bloomington:
    Indiana University Press, 1971, pp. 295-302.
Coleman, Edward Maceo. "Richard Wesley's Black Terror."
    Black Theatre 5 (Fall 1972): 36-37.
_____, Mike Coleman and Imamu Amiri Baraka. "What
    is Black Theatre?" Black World 20 (April 1971): 32-
    36.
Coleman, Edwin Leon. "Langston Hughes: As American
    Dramatist." Ph.D. Dissertation, University of Ore-
    gon, 1971.
Coleman, Horace W. "Melvin Van Peebles." Journal of
    Popular Culture 5 (Fall 1972): 368-384.
Collier, Eugene. "Drama Review." Black World 21 (April
    1972): 79-81.
Complete Catalogue of Plays, 1973-1974. N.Y.: Drama-
    tists Play Service, Inc., 1973-1974.
Conference of Negro Writers. The American Negro Writer
    and His Roots. N.Y.: American Society of African
    Culture, 1960.
"Conversation: Ida Lewis and Shirley Graham DuBois."
    Essence 1 (January 1971): 22-27.
Cook, Bruce. "Criticism on One Day When I Was Lost
    (Baldwin's Screen Adaptation of The Autobiography
    of Malcom X)." Commonweal (12 October 1973):
    46-47.
Cook, Will Marion. "Clorindy, the Origin of the Cakewalk."
    Theatre Arts 31 (September 1947): 61-65.
Costello, D. "LeRoi Jones: Black Man as Victim." Com-
    monweal 88 (June 1968): 436-440.

Cotton, L. J. "The Negro in the American Theatre."
Negro History Bulletin 23 (May 1960): 172-178.
Couch, William Jr., ed. New Black Playwrights. N.Y.:
Avon, 1970.
Cowan, M. F. "Some Unknown Plays about the Negro."
Negro History Bulletin 14 (June 1951): 200-204.
Cox, Kenneth. "LeRoi Jones: Playwright of Protest."
Nebraska, 1972. "Doctoral Projects in Progress in
Theatre Arts, 1971." in Educational Theatre Journal
23 (May 1971): 187.
Cripps, Thomas R. "Black Films and Film Makers:
Movies in the Ghetto." Negro Digest 18 (February
1969): 21-48.
Crist, Judith. "'Walk in Darkness' Doesn't Illumine."
New York Herald Tribune, 29 October 1963.
Cromwell, Otelia, L. Turner and E. B. Dykes, eds.
Readings from Negro Authors for Schools and Colleges
with a Bibliography of Negro Literature. N.Y.: Har-
court, Brace and Co., 1931.
Cruse, Harold. The Crisis of the Negro Intellectual. N.Y.:
Morrow, 1967.
Cuban, Larry. The Negro in America. Chicago: Scott
Foresman, 1964.
Cullen, Countee. "Review of Earth." Opportunity 5 (April
1927): 118-119.
_____, and Owen Dodson. "The Third Fourth of July."
Theatre Arts 30 (August 1946): 488-493.
Cuney-Hare, Maud. "Musical Comedy." in Negro Musi-
cians and Their Music. Washington, D.C.: Associated
Press, 1936. Also in Anthology of the American Negro
in the Theatre. Lindsay Patterson, ed. Washington,
D.C.: Associated Press, 1967.

Daley, T. A. "Victor Sejour." Phylon 4 (First Quarter
1943): 5-16.
Daniel, Walter C. "Countee Cullen as Literary Critic."
CLA Journal 14 (March 1971): 281-291.
Davis, Arthur P. "The Tragic Theme in Six Works of
Langston Hughes." Phylon 16 (Second Quarter 1955):
195-204.
_____, and Saunders Redding, eds. Cavalcade: Negro
American Writing from 1760 to the Present. Boston:
Houghton Mifflin Co., 1971.
Davis, Hallie (Ferguson) Flanagan. Arena: The History of
the Federal Theatre. N.Y.: Benjamin Blom, 1940;
1965.

Davis, Ossie. "Purlie Told Me." Freedomways 2 (Spring
    1962): 155-160. Also in Patterson, Anthology of the
    American Negro in the Theatre, pp. 169-175.
_____. "The Significance of Lorraine Hansberry."
    Freedomways 5 (Summer 1965): 396-402.
_____. "The Wonderful World of Law & Order." in
    Hill, Anger and Beyond, pp. 154-180.
Dean, Alexander. "Summary of Plays on Current Theatrical
    Calendar." New York Times, 18 January 1925, VII,
    2.
Deer, Irving and Harriet A. Deer. Selves: Drama in
    Perspective. N.Y.: Harcourt Brace Jovanovich,
    1975.
Delpeck, Jeanine. "An Interview with Native Son." Crisis
    57 (November 1950): 625-626, 678.
Dennison, George. "The Demagogy of LeRoi Jones." Con-
    temporary Literature 39 (February 1965): 67-70.
Dent, Alan. Preludes and Studies. London: Macmillan,
    1942.
Dent, Thomas C. "The Free Southern Theater." Negro
    Digest 16 (April 1967): 40-44.
_____. "The Free Southern Theatre: An Evaluation."
    Freedomways 6 (Winter 1966): 26-31. Also in Patter-
    son, Anthology of the American Negro in the Theatre.
    pp. 117-119.
_____. "The New Lafayette Theatre." Drama Review
    16 (December 1972): 46-55.
_____, Richard Schechner and Gilbert Moses, eds. The
    Free Southern Theater by the Free Southern Theater.
    Indianapolis: Bobbs-Merrill, 1969.
Derby, Doris, Gilbert Moses and John O'Neal. "The Need
    for a Southern Free Theatre." Freedomways 4 (Win-
    ter 1964): 320.
"Dialogue: The Free Southern Theatre." Tulane Drama Re-
    view 9 (Summer 1965): 63.
Dietrich, R. F., William E. Carpenter and Kevin Derrane,
    eds. The Art of Drama. N.Y.: Holt, Rinehart and
    Winston, 1969.
"Directory: Black Theatres in the Black World." Black
    Theatre no. 6 (1972): 52.
A Distinguished Negro Composer. "Why Has the Aframeri-
    can Produced No Creative Musical Geniuses?" The
    Messenger 9 (November 1927): 319, 388.
Dixon, Melvin. "Black Theater: The Aesthetics." Negro
    Digest 18 (July 1969): 41-44.
Dodson, Owen. "Playwrights in Dark Glasses." Negro

General Bibliography

Digest 17 (April 1968): 30-36.
"Do You Remember ... Andy Razaf." _Negro Digest_ 9
  (October 1951): 11-12.
"Domestic Drama--the Top Drawer." _Theatre Arts_ 43
  (July 1959): 58-61.
Dougherty, Romeo L. "The Greatest Theatrical Combine."
  Competitor 1 (April 1920): 69-70.
_____. "Progress of the Drama." _Competitor_ 1 (January 1920): 53-55.
Dover, Cedric. "The Importance of Georgia Douglas Johnson." _Crisis_ 59 (December 1952): 633-636, 674.
Downer, Alan S. _American Drama and Its Critics_. Chicago:
  The University of Chicago Press, 1965.
_____, ed. _The American Theatre Today_. N.Y.: Basic
  Books, 1967.
_____. "Total Theatre and Partial Drama: Notes on the
  New York Theatre, 1965-1966." _Quarterly Journal of
  Speech_ 52 (October 1966): 234-235.
Downes, Olin. "'Run, Little Chillun!'" _New York Times_,
  2 April 1933, IX, 5: 1.
"Dramatiis Personae." _Crisis_ 34 (May 1927): 85-88, 103.
Dreer, Herman. _American Literature by Negro Authors_.
  N.Y.: Macmillan, 1950.
_____. "The Drama: An Introduction." in _American
  Literature by Negro Authors_. Herman Dreer, ed.
  N.Y.: Macmillan, 1950, pp. 279-283.
Drimmer, Melvin. "Joplin's _Treemonisha_ in Atlanta."
  Phylon 34 (June 1973): 197-202.
Driver, Tom F. "Land Beyond the River." _Christian Century_ 74 (24 July 1957): 895.
_____. "A Raisin in the Sun." _New Republic_ 140 (13
  April 1959): 21.
Duberman, Martin. "Theatre 69: Black Theatre." _Partisan
  Review_ 36 (1969): 488.
DuBois, W. E. B. "Can the Negro Serve the Drama?"
  Theatre Magazine 38 (July 1923): 12, 68.
_____. "The Criteria of Negro Art." _Crisis_ 32 (October 1926): 290.
_____. "The Drama Among Black Folk." _Crisis_ 11
  (August 1916).
_____. "The Krikwa Little Theatre." _Crisis_ 32 (July 1926): 134.
Dukore, Bernard F. "Off-Broadway and the New Realism."
  in _Modern American Drama: Essays in Criticism_.
  Wm. E. Taylor, ed. Deland, Fla.: Everett/Edwards,
  Inc., 1968.

Eaton, W. P. "Playwrighting in a Vacuum." American
    Mercury 47 (September 1948): 302-308.
Ebert, Roger. "Black Box-Office Is Beautiful." World 1
    (12 September 1972).
Eckstein, George. "The New Black Theatre." Dissent 20
    (Winter 1973): 112.
Edmonds, Randolph. "Black Drama in the American Thea-
    tre: 1700-1970." in The American Theatre: A Sum
    of All Its Parts. N.Y.: Samuel French, 1971, pp.
    397-426.
_____. The Land of Cotton and Other Plays. Washing-
    ton, D.C.: Associated Publishers, 1942.
_____. "Negro Drama in the South." The Carolina Play-
    book (June 1940): 74-78.
_____. "The Negro Little Theatre Movement." Negro
    History Bulletin 12 (January 1949): 82-86, 92-94.
_____. Shades and Shadows. Boston: Meador, 1930;
    rpt., Ann Arbor, Mich.: University Microfilms, 1970.
_____. Six Plays for a Negro Theatre. Boston: Baker,
    1934; rpt., Ann Arbor, Mich.: University Microfilms,
    1970.
_____. "Some Reflections on the Negro in American
    Drama." Opportunity 8 (1930): 303-305.
Elder, Lonne, III. "A Negro Idea Theatre." American
    Dialogue 1 (July 1964): 30-31.
Elestein, Steward J. "Artists in Their Residences." [E. B.
    Redmond] Oberlin Alumni Magazine (May 1970): 20-21.
Ellis, Eddie. "Revolutionary Theatre in Tune with the
    Folks." Liberator 15 (December 1965): 8.
Ellison, Ralph. Shadow and Act. N.Y.: New American
    Library, 1964.
Emanuel, James A. Langston Hughes. N.Y.: Twayne,
    1967.
Emeruwa, Leatrice. "Reports on Black Theatre: Cleveland,
    Ohio." Black World 22 (April 1973): 19-26.
Esterow, Milton. "New Role of Negroes in Theatre Reflects
    Ferment of Integration." New York Times, 15 June
    1964, p. 35.
Eustis, Morton. "The Optimist of Broadway: Broadway in
    Review." Theatre Arts Monthly 17 (May 1933): 337.
Evans, Donald T. "Bring It All Back Home: Black Play-
    wrights of the Fifties." Black World 20 (February
    1971): 41-45.
_____. "Segregated Drama in Integrated Schools."
    English Journal 60 (Fall 1971): 260-263.
_____. "The Theatre of Confrontation: Ed Bullins, Up
    Against a Wall." Black World 23 (April 1974): 14-18.

"Everything's Cool: An Interview with LeRoi Jones." Black
    Theatre 1 (1968): 16-24.
Ewen, David, ed. Complete Book of the American Musical
    Theatre. rev. ed., N.Y.: Holt, 1959.
"The Expanding World of the Black Film." Black Creation
    4 (Winter 1973): 25.

Fabio, Sara Webster. "Black Writers' Views on Literary
    Lions and Values." Negro Digest 17 (January 1968):
    39.
Faderman, Lillian and Barbara Bradshaw, eds. Speaking
    for Ourselves. Glenview, Ill.: Scott, Foresman, 1969.
Farrison, Edward W. "Brown's First Drama." CLA Jour-
    nal 13 (December 1969): 192-197.
_____. "Lorraine Hansberry's Last Dramas." CLA
    Journal 16 (December 1972): 188-198.
Febre, Genevieve E. "A Checklist: Thirteen Years of
    Black Plays." Black World 23 (April 1974): 81-97.
Ferdinand, Val (Salaam). "The Dashiki Project Theatre;
    We Are The Theatre." Black Theatre no. 3 (1969):
    4-6.
_____. "News from Blkartsouth." Black Theatre no. 4
    (1970): 4.
Ferguson, John. "Dutchman and The Slave." Modern Drama
    13 (February 1971): 398-406.
Fidell, Estelle A. Play Index: 1968-1972. N.Y.: Wilson,
    1973.
Finn, J. "The Identity of James Baldwin." Commonweal
    77 (26 October 1962): 113-116.
"First Baldwin Play Eliminating Scenery." Wisconsin State
    Journal, 8 April 1964.
First Stage: A Quarterly of New Drama. Purdue University
    (Fall 1962).
"First WPA Production, 'Walk Together, Chillun!'" New
    York Times, 5 February 1936, 15: 2.
Fischer, William C. "The Pre-Revolutionary Writings of
    Imamu Baraka." Massachusetts Review 14 (Spring
    1973): 259-305.
Fisher, Rudolph. "The Caucasian Storms Harlem." Ameri-
    can Mercury 11 (August 1927): 397-398.
Flanagan, Hallie. Arena. New York: Duell, Sloan, and
    Pearce, 1940.
Fletcher, Tom. 100 Years of the Negro in Show Business.
    N.Y.: Burdge, 1954.
Ford, Clebert. "The Negro and the American Theatre."
    Liberator 3 (May 1963): 6.

_____. "Review of Blues for Mr. Charlie." Liberator
4 (July 1964): 7.

_____. "Theatre Review and Forecast." Liberator 4
(January 1964): 17-20.

_____. "Towards a Black Community Theatre." Libera-
tor 4 (August 1964): 18.

Ford, Nick Aaron, ed. Black Insights: Significant Literature by Black Americans, 1760 to the Present. Wal-
tham, Mass.: Ginn, 1971.

Fort-Whiteman, Lorette. "Negro Playwrights Demanded."
Messenger 1 (November 1917): 30.

"45-46 Season Reviewed." New York Times, 2 June 1946,
II, 1: 2.

Fowler, Cleo S. "A Black Theatre Drama Program: One
Urban School's Approach." Dramatics 44 (January
1973): 22-24.

Freedley, George and John A. Reeves. A History of the
Theatre. N.Y.: Crown, 1955.

Frenz, Horst, ed. American Playwrights on Drama. N.Y.:
Hill and Wang, 1965.

Fuller, Hoyt. "Black Theater in America." Negro Digest
17 (April 1968): 83-93.

_____. "General Theater Round-Up." Black World 20
(April 1971): 24-26.

_____. "Review: 'Behold! Cometh the Vanderkellans.'"
Negro Digest 16 (April 1967): 51-52.

_____. "Stage, Screen and Black Hegemony: Black
World Interviews Woodie King, Jr." Black World 26
(April 1975): 412.

_____. "The Toilet and The Slave." Negro Digest 14
(July 1965): 49-50.

_____. "Traveller on the Long, Rough, Lonely Old Road:
An Interview with Chester Himes." Black World 21
(March 1972): 4-24.

Fullinwinder, S. P. "Jean Toomer: Lost Generation or
Negro Renaissance?" Phylon 27 (1966): 396-403.

Funk, Lewis. The Curtain Rises: The Story of Ossie Davis.
N.Y.: Grosset and Dunlap, 1971.

Gaffney, Floyd. "The Black Actor in Central Park." Negro
Digest 16 (April 1967): 28-34.

_____. "Black Theatre: Commitment and Communica-
tion." Black Scholar 1 (June 1970): 10-15.

_____. "A Hand Is on the Gate in Athens." Educational
Theatre Journal 21 (May 1969): 196-201.

_____. "Is Your Door Really Open?" Drama and Theatre 7 (Fall 1968): 4-7.

Gagey, Edmond M. Revolution in American Drama. N.Y.: Columbia University Press, 1947.

Gaines, J. E. "Wisdom Comes to Black People in Many Disguises." In The New Lafayette Theatre Presents. Ed Bullins, ed. N.Y.: Anchor Books, 1975, pp. 69-70.

Gant, Liz. "An Interview with Lonnie Elder, III." Black World 22 (April 1973): 38-48.

_____. "New Lafayette Theatre." Drama Review 16 (December 1972): 46-55.

_____. "Review of Sty of the Blind Pig." Black World 21 (April 1972): 81-82.

"Garland Anderson Invades the East." The Messenger 7 (June 1925): 233.

Garland, Phyl. "The Prize Winner; Vastly Different New York Plays Bring Top Awards to Blacks." Ebony 25 (July 1970): 29-37.

Gassner, John. "Playwrights of the Period: The Thirties." Theatre Arts 44 (September 1960): 19-22.

_____. "Social Realism and Imaginative Theatre: Avant-Garde Stage Productions in the American Social Theatre of the Nineteen Thirties." Theatre Survey 3 (1962): 3-18.

_____, and Bernard F. Dukore. A Treasury of the Theatre. 4th ed., N.Y.: Simon and Schuster, 1970.

_____, and Clive Barnes. Best American Plays: 1963-1967. N.Y.: Crown, 1971.

Gautier, Theophile. Historie de l'art dramatique en France depuis vingt-cinq ans. Paris: Magnin, Blanchard, 1858-1859, 6 vols.

Gayle, Addison Jr., ed. The Black Aesthetic. N.Y.: Doubleday, 1971.

_____. Black Expression: Essays by and about Black Americans in the Creative Arts. N.Y.: Weybright and Talley, 1969.

"Gertrude Jeanette in Hit." New York Amsterdam News, 29 February 1964, p. 17.

Gibson, Donald B., ed. Five Black Writers: Essays on Wright, Ellison, Baldwin, Hughes and Jones. N.Y.: New York University Press, 1970.

Gilbert, T. Selected Gems of Poetry, Comedy, and Drama. Boston: Christopher Publications, 1931.

Gilder, Rosamond. "Matter for Thanksgiving: Broadway in Review." Theatre Arts 27 (December 1942): 744.

Giles, James R. "Tenderness and Brutality in the Plays of Ed Bullins." Players 48 (October-November 1972): 32-33.

Gill, Brendan. "Gordone's No Place to Be Somebody."
    New Yorker 10 January 1970, p. 64.
Gilman, Richard. Common and Uncommon Masks: Writings
    on the Theatre 1961-1970. N.Y.: Random, 1971.
Gold, Michael. "At Last, A Negro Theatre?" [Walk To-
    gether, Chillun] New Masses (March 1937): 18.
Goncalves, Joe. "The Mysterious Disappearance of Black
    Arts West." Black Theatre no. 2 (1969): 23-25.
_____. "West Coast Drama." Black Theatre Magazine
    no. 4 (April 1970): 27.
Goodman, George, Jr. "More Blacks in Theatre? Yes and
    No." New York Times, 9 August 1972, p. 20.
Gordon, Carolyn. "Lorraine Hansberry." CASS Bibliog-
    raphy No. 1. Atlanta, Ga.: Center for African and
    African-American Studies, n.d. (mimeographed).
Gordon, Charles F. "'Out of Site'." Black Theatre Maga-
    zine (April 1970): 29-31.
_____. "Review: 'Black Nativity!'" Black Theatre
    Magazine (1970): 34.
"Gordon Parks Releases Second Movie (Shaft)." Crisis 78
    (July 1971): 162.
Gordone, Charles. "On 'No Place to Be Somebody.'"
    New York Times, 25 January 1970, II, 1: 3.
_____. "Quiet Talk with Myself." Esquire 73 (January
    1970).
_____. "Yes, I Am a Black Playwright, But...."
    New York Times, 25 January 1970, 27: 1.
Gorman, Bertha. "Aiwa! Aiwa! Aiwa!" Sacramento Bee,
    12 February 1971, p. 2.
"Gospel Abroad." Newsweek 60 (3 September 1962): 50.
Goss, Clay. "Review of The Duplex: A Black Love Fable
    in Four Movements." Black Roots Bulletin 1 (Spring-
    Summer 1972): 34-35.
Grant, G. O. "Contributions of the Negro to Dramatic Art."
    Journal of Negro History 17 (January 1932).
Greene, Marjorie. "Young Man of the Theatre and His Left
    Hand." Opportunity 24 (Fall 1946): 200-201.
Greenwood, Frank. "Comments on 'Burn, Baby, Burn!'"
    Freedomways 7 (Summer 1967): 244-246.
Gregory, Montgomery. "The Drama of Negro Life." in
    The New Negro. Alain Locke, ed. N.Y.: Boni,
    1925, pp. 153-160.
_____. "For a Negro Theatre." New Republic 28 (16
    November 1921): 523-526.
Grimke, Angelina W. "Rachel, the Play of the Month:
    The Reason and Synopsis by the Author." Competitor
    1 (January 1920): 51-52.

Grinnell Plays. Chicago: Dramatic Publishing Co., 1934.
Guernsey, Otis L., Jr., ed. The Best Plays of 1966-1967.
   N.Y.: Dodd, Mead, 1967.
_____. The Best Plays of 1968-1969. N.Y.: Dodd,
   Mead, 1969.
_____. The Best Plays of 1969-1970. N.Y.: Dodd,
   Mead, 1970.
Gussow, M. "Gordone's No Place to Be Somebody." New
   York Times, 31 December 1969, 17: 1.
_____. "The New Playwrights." Newsweek 20 May 1968,
   p. 115.
_____. "Review: Don't Let It Go to Your Head." New
   York Times, 22 January 1972, 35: 1.
_____. "Review: The Street Corner." New York Times,
   30 August 1972, 42: 1.
_____. "Review: What If It Had Turned up Heads?"
   New York Times, 7 November 1972, 25: 1.

Haddon, Archibald. "Centenary of Negro Drama--Ira
   Aldridge." Crisis 41 (February 1934): 35-36.
Haley, Elsie Galbreath. "The Black Revolutionary Theater:
   LeRoi Jones, Ed Bullins, and Minor Playwrights."
   Ph.D. Dissertation, University of Denver, 1961.
Hansberry, Lorraine. "American Theatre Needs Desegregat-
   ing Too." Negro Digest 10 (June 1961): 128-133.
_____. "A Challenge to Artists." Freedomways 3 (Win-
   ter 1963): 31-36.
_____. "Images and Essences: 1961 Dialogue with an
   Uncolored Egghead Containing Wholesome Intentions
   and Some Sass." The Urbanite 1 (May 1961): 10-11,
   36.
_____. "A Letter from Lorraine Hansberry on Porgy
   and Bess." The Theatre (August 1959): 10.
_____. "Me Tink Me Hear Sounds in De Night." Thea-
   tre Arts 44 (October 1960): 9-11.
_____. "Miss Hansberry on 'Backlash.'" Village Voice
   23 July 1964, pp. 10, 16.
_____. "My Name Is Lorraine Hansberry; I Am a
   Writer." Esquire 72 (November 1969): 140.
_____. "The Nation Needs Your Gifts." Negro Digest
   13 (August 1964): 26-29.
_____. "The Negro In American Culture." In Bigsby,
   The Black American Writer, vol. 1.
Harnan, Terry. Gordon Parks: Black Photographer and
   Film Maker. Champaign, Ill.: Garrard, 1972.
Harris, Henrietta. "Building a Black Theatre." Drama Re-

view 12 (Summer 1968): 157-8.
_____. "The New Lafayette Theatre." Black Creation 4 (Summer 1973): 8-12.
Harris, Jessica B. "The Sun People of 125th Street--The National Black Theatre." Drama Review 16 (December 1972): 39-45.
Harrison, Paul Carter. "Black Theatre and the African Continuum." Black World 21 (August 1972): 42-48.
_____. The Drama of Nommo. N.Y.: Grove, 1972.
_____. Kuntu Drama. N.Y.: Grove, 1974.
Harrison, Richard B. "The Drama as a Field of Art Expression for the Negro." Southern Workman 63 (November 1934).
Hatch, James V. Black Image on the American Stage: A Bibliography. N.Y.: Drama Book Specialists, 1970.
_____. "White Folks' Guide to 200 Years of Black and White Drama." Drama Review 16 (December 1972): 5-24.
_____, and Billops. Oral History Collection, Stage I, Stage II, and Stage III. N.Y.: Video Educational Workshop, 1974. (includes over 100 interviews).
_____, and Ted Shine, eds. Black Theater USA: 1847-1974. N.Y.: Free Press, 1974.
_____, and Victoria Sullivan. Plays by and about Women. N.Y.: Random House, 1973.
Hatlen, Theodore W., ed. Drama: Principles and Plays. 2nd ed. Santa Barbara: University of California, 1975.
Hawkins, William. "'Giant Step' Shows Mature Touch." New York World-Telegram, 26 September 1953.
Hay, Samuel A. "What Shape Shapes Shapelessness? Structural Elements in Ed Bullins' Plays." Black World 23 (April 1974): 20-26.
Hayden, Robert, David J. Burrows and Frederick R. Lapides, eds. Afro-American Literature: An Introduction. N.Y.: Harcourt Brace Jovanovich, 1971.
Hays, Peter L. "A Raisin in the Sun and Juno and the Paycock." Phylon 33 (Summer 1972): 175-176.
Haywood, Charles. "Negro Minstrelsy and Shakespeare Burlesque." in Folklore and Society: Essays in Honor of Benjamin Botkin. Bruce Jackson, ed. Hatboro, Pa.: Folklore Associates, 1966.
Henderson, Mary C. The City and the Theatre. Clifton, N.J.: James T. White & Co., 1973.
Hepburn, D. "Vinnette Carrol, Woman on the Run." Sepia

10 (October 1961): 57-60.

Hernton, Calvin C. "The Masculinization of James Baldwin: or What Killed Blues for Mr. Charlie?" Umbra Anthology 1967-1968: 19-22.

Hewes, Henry. "The Aints and the Am Nots." Saturday Review (13 November 1971): 10-12.

_____. "Broadway Postscript." Saturday Review of Literature 44 (7 September 1957): 78.

_____. "A Change of Tune." Saturday Review 47 (May 1964): 36.

_____. "Crossing Lines." Saturday Review 48 (January 1965): 46.

_____. "The Gospel Untruth." Saturday Review 48 (May 1965): 49.

_____. "Harlem on My Mind." Saturday Review 52 (February 1969): 29.

_____. "Tenth Play? On Selecting the Ten Best." Saturday Review of Literature 45 (12 May 1962): 51.

_____. "Theatre Review: Ed Bullins' The Taking of Miss Janie." Saturday Review of Literature 58 (12 May 1962): 51.

_____. "Theatre Review: The River Niger." Saturday Review of the Arts 1 (February 1973): 59-60.

_____, ed. Best Plays of 1937-38. New York: Dodd, Mead, 1938.

Hicklin, Fannie E. F. "The American Negro Playwright, 1920-1964." Ph.D. Dissertation, University of Wisconsin, Madison, 1965.

Hicks, Al. "Theatre Review: Happy Ending and Day of Absence." Liberator 6 (January 1966): 23.

Hicks, Granville, et al., eds. Proletarian Literature in the United States. New York: International Publishers, 1935.

Higgins, C. "Meet the Man Behind the Sweetback." Jet (2 July 1971): 11-D.

Hill, Errol, ed. The Artist in West Indian Society: A Symposium. Trinidad: Extramural Dept., University of the West Indies, 1964.

_____. "Calypso Drama." Theatre Survey 9 (November 1968).

_____, ed. Caribbean Plays, vols. 1 and 2. Trinidad: Extramural Dept., University of the West Indies, 1964.

_____. "Cultural Values and the Theatre Arts in the English-Speaking Caribbean." Resource Development in the Caribbean. McGill University, October 1973.

_____. "Mr. Tin Pan Alley." Our World 8 (July 1953): 38-39.

_____. "The West Indian Theatre." Public Opinion 31
    May 1958; 7 June; 21 June.

_____, with Peter Greer. Why Pretend? N.Y.: Chand-
    ler, 1973.

Hill, Herbert. Anger and Beyond. N.Y.: Harper & Row,
    1966.

_____, ed. Soon One Morning. N.Y.: Knopf, 1968.

_____. "Stuff of Great Literature." Crisis 73 (February
    1966): 99, 110-114.

Hill, J. Newton. "The Achievement of the Negro in Drama."
    Negro History Bulletin 12 (February 1949): 100-102,
    119.

Hilliard, Robert L. "Desegregation in Educational Theatre."
    Journal of Negro Education 26 (Fall 1957): 509-513.

_____. "The Drama and American Negro Life." Southern
    Theatre 10 (Winter 1966): 9-14.

Himelstein, Morgan Y. Drama Was a Weapon: The Left
    Wing Theatre in New York 1929-1941. New Brunswick,
    N.J.: Rutgers University Press, 1963.

Hoffman, William H., ed. New American Plays, Vols. 2
    and 3. N.Y.: Hill and Wang, 1968, 1969.

Holder, Geoffrey. "The Awful Afro Trend." Show 2 (March
    1962): 94-95.

Holmes, Eugene C. "The Legacy of Alain Locke." Free-
    domways 3 (Summer 1963): 293-307.

Holmes, Paul C. and Anita J. Lehman. Keys to Under-
    standing. California: College of San Mateo, 1970.

Holtan, Orley I. "Sidney Brustein and the Plight of the
    American Intellectual." Players 46 (June-July 1971):
    22-225.

Horne, Jan. "Review: East of Jordan." Black Theatre
    Magazine no. 4 (April 1970): 37.

Houseman, John. Run-Through. N.Y.: Simon and Schuster,
    1972.

Hubenka, Lloyd J. and Leroy Garcia. The Design of Drama.
    N.Y.: David McKay, 1974.

Hudson, Theodore R. From LeRoi Jones to Amiri Baraka:
    The Literary Works. Durham, N.C.: Duke Univer-
    sity Press, 1973.

Hughes, Catherine. Plays, Politics, and Polemics. N.Y.:
    Drama Book Specialists, 1973.

Hughes, Langston. "Backstage." Ebony 4 (March 1949):
    36-38.

_____. "Is Hollywood Fair to Negroes?" Negro Digest
    1 (April 1943): 16-21.

_____. "The Need for an Afro-American Theatre."
    The Chicago Defender, June 1961; also in Anthology

of the American Negro in the Theatre. Lindsay Patterson,
ed. Washington, D.C.: Associated, 1967, pp. 163-164.
_____. "The Negro Artist and the Racial Mountain."
Nation 122 (23 June 1926): 692-694; also in The Negro
in America. Larry Cuban, ed. Chicago: Scott-
Foresman, 1964.
_____. Scottsboro Limited. New York: Golden Stair,
1932.
_____. "That Boy LeRoi." in Anthology of the American
Negro in the Theatre. Lindsay Patterson, ed. Wash-
ington, D.C.: Associated, 1967, pp. 205-206.
_____, and Milton Meltzer. Black Magic: A Pictorial
History of the Negro in American Entertainment. En-
glewood Cliffs, N.J.: Prentice-Hall, 1967.
Hume, Paul. "New Opera, A Christmas Miracle, Has
Premiere." Washington Post, 7 March 1958.
Hunter, Charlayne. "Influences of the Blacks Stressed at
Museum Theatre History." The Milwaukee Journal:
The Green Sheet, 28 July 1975, 1: 4; 3: 2.
Hurd, Laura. "Director Ossie Davis Talks about Black
Girl." Black Creation 4 (Winter 1973): 38.
Huntley, Elizabeth. What Ye Sow. New York: Court, 1955.
Hurston, Zora N. "The Negro in the American Theatre."
Theatre Arts 26 (1942); 492-543; later published as a
book, N.Y.: Theatre Arts, 1947.
_____. "Voodoo in America." The Journal of American
Folklore (October-December 1931).
Hutton, Laurence. Curiosities of the American Stage. New
York: Harper and Brothers, 1891, Ch. II.

"Inner City Repertory." Players 44 (December-January
1969): 48-53.
"Interview." (Gordon Parks) Black Creation 3 (Winter 1972).
"Interview with Bob Macbeth: Director of the New Lafayette
Theatre." Black Theatre no. 6 (Fall 1972): 14-21.
Isaacs, Edith. "The Middle Distance: 1890-1917--Heyday
of Comedy and Dance." Theatre Arts 26 (August
1942): 527-532.
_____. "The Negroes in American Theatre: The Fore-
ground, 1917-1942." Theatre Arts 26 (August 1942):
496-526.
_____. "The Negro in the American Theatre: The Hope
Ahead." Theatre Arts 26 (August 1942): 541.
_____. "The Negro in the American Theatre: A Record
of Achievement." Theatre Arts 26 (August 1942): 495.
_____. "Revival and Survival: Broadway in Review."

Theatre Arts Monthly 22 (May 1938): 333.

_____ . Theatre: Essays on the Arts of the Theatre.
Freeport, N.Y.: Books for Libraries Press, 1968;
Boston: Little, Brown, 1927.

Isaacs, Harold. "Five Writers and Their African Ances-
tors." Phylon 21 (1960): 66-70.

_____ , ed. The New World of Negro Americans. N.Y.:
John Day Co., 1965.

Ivy, James. "Review: Tambourines to Glory." Crisis 64
(January 1957).

"Jackie Taylor: A Cinderella Story." Chicago Tribune:
Arts and Fun, 15 June 1975, p. 2.

Jackman, Kenneth, Jr. "Notes on the Works of Ed Bullins
and the 'Hungered One.'" CLA Journal 18 (December
1974): 292-299.

Jackson, J. A. "Our Importance in the Amusement World."
Competitor 3 (June 1921): 36-39.

Jeanpierre, Wendell A. "Ron Milner's 'Who's Got His Own.'"
Crisis 74 (October 1967): 423.

Jeffers, Lance. "Bullins, Baraka, and Elder: The Dawn
of Grandeur in Black Drama." CLA Journal (September 1972): 32-48.

Jefferson, Miles M. "Empty Seasons on Broadway, 1950-
1951." Phylon 12 (Second Quarter 1951): 135.

_____ . "The Negro on Broadway, 1947-1948." Phylon
(Second Quarter 1948).

_____ . "The Negro on Broadway, 1952-1953--Still Cloudy:
Fair Weather Ahead." Phylon 14 (Third Quarter 1953):
268-279.

_____ . "The Negro on Broadway, 1954-1955--More Spice
than Substance." Phylon 16 (Third Quarter 1955): 303-312.

_____ . "The Negro on Broadway, 1955-1956." Phylon
17 (Third Quarter 1956): 227-237.

_____ . "The Negro on Broadway, 1956-1957." Phylon
18 (Third Quarter 1957): 286-295.

Jerome, V. J. The Negro in Hollywood Films. N.Y.:
Masses and Mainstream, 1950.

Johnson, C. S. "Ira Aldridge." Opportunity 3 (March 1925):
6.

Johnson, Helen Armstead. "Playwrights, Audiences, and
Critics." Negro Digest 19 (April 1970): 17-24.

_____ . "Review of 'Ododo.'" Black World 20 (April
1970): 47.

Johnson, James W. Black Manhattan. N.Y.: Atheneum,
1969.

_____. "The Dilemma of the Negro Author." American Mercury 15 (December 1928): 479.

Johnson, Lemuel. The Devil, the Gargoyle, and the Buffoon: The Negro as Metaphor in Western Literature. Port Washington, N.Y.: Kennikat Press, 1971.

Johnson, Roy. "Theatre Review: 'Blues for Mr. Charlie.'" Liberator 6 (March 1966): 22.

Jones, John Hudson. "'Bolt from Blue' Pleases Audiences in Harlem." Daily Worker, 10 April 1952.

Jones, LeRoi. "Black Power Chant." Black Theatre no. 4 (April 1970): 35.

_____. "Black Revolutionary Poets Should also be Playwrights." Black World 21 (April 1972): 4-7.

_____. "Comments on a Recent Killing." New York Times, 13 March 1973, 30: 1.

_____. "Communications Project." Drama Review 12 (Summer 1968): 53-57.

_____. Home. N.Y.: Morrow, 1966.

_____. "In the Ring." Nation 198 (29 June 1964): 661-662.

_____. "In Search of the Revolutionary Black Theatre." Negro Digest 15 (April 1966): 20-24.

_____. "The Revolutionary Theatre." Black Dialogue 1 (Spring 1965): 5-7.

_____. "What the Arts Need Now." Negro Digest 16 (April 1967): 5-6.

_____, and Larry Neal, eds. Black Fire: An Anthology of Afro-American Writing. N.Y.: Morrow, 1968.

Jones, Martha Ann. "Barbara Ann Teer's National Black Theatre." Black Creation 3 (Summer 1972): 18-20.

_____. "Interview with Gil Moses." Black Creation 3 (Winter 1972): 19-26.

_____. "Richard Wesley's Black Terror." Black Creation 3 (Spring 1972): 12-14.

Jurges, Oda. "Selected Bibliography." Drama Review 12 (Summer 1968).

Kalem, T. E. "Jubilation." Time 99 (8 May 1972): 75.

_____. "Requiem for the 60's ('The Taking of Miss Janie')." Time 101 (19 May 1975): 80.

Kara-Moursa, Sergius. "Ira Aldridge in Russia." Crisis 40 (September 1933): 201-202.

"Karamu Theatre--Interview." Players 47 (February-March 1972): 104-109, 146-147.

Kardiner, Abram and Lionel Ovesey. The Mark of Oppression. N.Y.: Meridian, 1962.

Karev, G. "Russia Remembers Ira Aldridge." Negro Digest 5 (September 1947): 80-82.

Kaufman, Michael W. "The Delicate World of Reprobation: A Note on the Black Revolutionary Theatre." Educational Theatre Journal 23 (December 1971): 446-460.

Kauffman, Stanley. "LeRoi Jones and the Tradition of the Fake." Dissent 12 (Spring 1965): 207-213.

_____, and Bruce Henstell. American Film Criticism. N.Y.: Liveright, 1972.

Kearns, Francis, ed. Black Identity. N.Y.: Holt, Rinehart, and Winston, 1970.

Kennedy, Scott. In Search of an African Theatre. N.Y.: Scribner's Sons, 1973.

Kent, Geo. "Struggle for the Image." Phylon 33 (Winter 1972): 304-323.

Kerr, W. "'Black Girl'--Review." New York Times, 4 1971, II, 3: 3.

_____. "'Blues for Mr. Charlie.'" New York Times, 3 May 1964, II, 3.

_____. "'Brotherhood'--Review." New York Times, 29 March 1970, II, 1: 1.

_____. "Not Since Edward Albee (Charles Gordone)." New York Times, 18 May 1969, II, 1, 22.

_____. "Review: 'Ceremonies in Dark Old Men.'" New York Times, 23 February 1969, II, 5: 1.

_____. "Review: 'Don't Bother Me I Can't Cope.'" New York Times, 30 April 1972, II, 30: 2.

_____. "Review: 'Five on the Black Hand Side.'" New York Times, 11 January 1970, II, 3: 5.

_____. "Review: 'Lady Day.'" New York Times, 5 November 1972, II, 5: 1.

_____. "Review: 'LesBlancs.'" New York Times, 29 November 1970, II, 3: 1.

_____. "Review: 'Ododo.'" New York Times, 6 December 1972, II, 7: 2.

_____. "Review: 'The Pig Pen.'" New York Times, 31 May 1970, II, 3: 1.

_____. "Theatre: Take A Giant Step." New York Herald Tribune, 25 September 1953.

Kgostile, K. William. "Towards Our Theatre: A Definitive Act." In Gayle. Black Expression. pp. 146-148.

"Kicks and Co." Jet 19 (16 March 1961): 61; (23 March 1961): 59; (13 July 1961): 62; (12 October 1961): 58-61; (26 October 1961): 58, 60-61.

Killens, John O. "Another Time When Black Was Beautiful." Black World 20 (1970): 20-36.

_____. "The Black Writer and the Revolution." Arts in

Society 5 (1968): 395-399.

_____. "Broadway in Black and White." African Forum
1 (Winter 1966): 66-76.

_____. "Hollywood in Black and White." In The State
of the Union. David Boroff, ed. pp. 102-103.

_____. "New Creative Writers." Library Journal 79
(15 February 1974): 374.

_____. "Opportunities for Development of Negro Talent."
American Negro Writer and His Roots. pp. 64-70.

_____. "Rappin' With Myself." In Williams and Harris.
Amistad 2. pp. 97-136.

Killinger, John. The Fragile Presence. Philadelphia:
Fortress, 1973.

Kimball, Robert and William Bolcom. Reminiscing with
Sissle and Blake. N.Y.: Viking, 1973.

King, Woodie, Jr. "Black Theatre: Present Condition."
Drama Review 12 (Summer 1968): 117-124.

_____. "Black Writers' Views of Literary Lions and
Values." Negro Digest 18 (January 1968): 26.

_____. "The Dilemma of Black Theatre." Negro Digest
19 (April 1970): 10-15, 86-87.

_____. "Educational Theatre and the Black Community."
Black World 21 (April 1972): 25-29.

_____. "Leading Man at the Met." Ebony 21 (January
1966): 84-90.

_____. "Problems Facing Negro Actors." Negro Digest
16 (April 1966): 53; also in Patterson. Anthology of
the American Negro in the Theatre.

_____. "Remembering Langston." Negro Digest 18
(April 1969): 27-32.

_____. "The Theatre: A Weapon for Change." Negro
Digest 14 (April 1967): 35.

_____, and Ron Milner, eds. Black Drama Anthology.
N.Y.: New American Library, 1971.

Kinnamon, Keneth, ed. James Baldwin: A Collection of
Critical Essays. Englewood Cliffs, N.J.: Prentice-
Hall, 1974.

Kloman, William. "Moses Gunn: A Brilliant Black Star."
New York Times, 16 June 1968, II, 1: 3.

Klotman, Phyllis R. "The Passive Resistant in 'A Different
Drummer,' 'Day of Absence,' and 'Many Thousand
Gone.'" Studies in Black Literature 3 (Autumn 1972):
7-12.

Kock, Frederick H. "The Negro Theater Advancing." The
Carolina Play Book (December 1933): 102.

_____. ed. American Folk Plays. N.Y.: Appleton-
Century, 1939.

Kogan, Deen. "Playing in the Street." Players 45 (June-
    July 1970): 219-222.
Kolodin, Irving. "Carry Me Back to Treemonisha." Satur-
    day Review (2 September 1972), p. 62.
Krasny, Michael J. "Design in Jean Toomer's Balo."
    Negro Literature Forum 7 (Fall 1973): 103-106.
Kraus, Ted. "Theatre East." Players 44 (February-March
    1969): 121.
_____. "Theatre East." Players 46 (February-March
    1971): 119-123.
_____. "Theatre East." Players 47 (February-March
    1972): 132-137.
Kriegsman, Alan M. "'Treemonisha': Cheers and Conta-
    gious Zest." The Washington Post, 11 August 1972,
    B: 1.
"Krigwa Players' Little Negro Theatre." Crisis 33 (1926):
    134-136.
Kroll, Jack. "Black Mood." Newsweek 71 (18 March 1968):
    110.
_____. "In Black America." Newsweek 79 (20 March
    1972): 98-99.
Kronenberger, Louis, ed. The Best Plays of 1958-1959.
    New York: Dodd, Mead, and Co., 1960.
_____. The Burns Mantle Yearbook: The Best Plays of
    1953-1954. N.Y.: Dodd, Mead, 1954.
Kuna, F. M. "Current Literature 1970-1971, New Writing:
    Drama." English Studies 52 (December 1971): 565-573.
Kupa, Kushauri. "Closeup: The New York Scene, 1970-
    1971." Black Theatre no. 6 (Fall 1972): 38-51.
_____. "A Review of 'The Reckoning' by Douglas Turner
    Ward." Black Theatre no. 4 (April 1970): 42.

Ladson, Benjamin P. "Negro Drama for Negroes by
    Negroes." Drama 12 (December 1921).
Lahr, John and Jonathan Price, eds. The Great American
    Life Show: Nine Plays from the Avant Garde Theatre.
    N.Y.: Bantam, 1974.
_____. Up Against the Fourth Wall. N.Y.: Grove,
    1970.
Laufe, Abe. Anatomy of a Hit: Long Run Plays on Broad-
    way to the Present Day. N.Y.: Hawthorn, 1966.
Lawrence, Vera Brodsky. The Collected Works of Scott
    Joplin. Vols. I, II. N.Y.: The New York Public
    Library, 1971.
_____. "Scott Joplin's 'Treemonisha.'" High Fidelity/
    Musical America (May 1972): MA-10.

Lawson, Ed. "Theatre in a Suitcase." Opportunity 16 (December 1938): 360-361.

Lawson, Hilda J. "The Negro in American Drama, 1897-1967." Bulletin of Bibliography 17 (1940): 7-8, 27-30.

_____. "The Negro in American Drama." Ph.D. Thesis, University of Illinois, 1939.

Leaks, Sylvester. "Purlie Emerges Victorious." Freedomways 1 (Fall 1961): 347.

Lederer, Richard. "The Language of LeRoi Jones' The Slave." Studies in Black Literature 4 (Spring 1973): 14-16.

Lee, Don L. "The Bittersweet of Sweetback, or Shake Yo Money Maker." Black World 21 (November 1971): 43-54.

"Lena Horne and 'Saint Louis Woman.'" The Pittsburgh Courier, 16 June 1945, p. 15.

Leonard, Claire. "The American Negro Theatre." Theatre Arts 28 (July 1944): 421-423.

_____. "Dark Drama." Negro Digest 2 (August 1944): 81-82.

Lester, E. "Review: 'Black Girl.'" New York Times, 11 July 1971, II, 5: 1.

Lewis, Allan. American Plays and Playwrights of the Contemporary Theatre. N.Y.: Crown, 1965.

_____, ed. The Contemporary Theatre. rev. ed. N.Y.: Crown, 1973.

Lewis, Emory. Stages: The Fifty-Year Childhood of the American Theatre. Englewood Cliffs, N.J.: Prentice-Hall, 1969.

Lewis, Theophilus. "Dogday Blues." Messenger 6 (September 1926): 291.

_____. "Primer Lesson for Harlem Critics and 'Six Bits Gone to Hell.'" Messenger 7 (June 1925): 230-238.

_____. "Sweet and Low Comedy." Messenger 8 (December 1926): 362.

_____. "Theatre." Messenger 8 (March 1926): 85-86.

_____. "The Theatre: The Souls of Black Folks." Messenger 8 (February 1926): 50, 59.

_____. "Three Sermons by Dr. Wilson." Messenger 8 (August 1928): 246.

"Lifts Ban on 'Mulatto.'" New York Times, 25 November 1939, 13: 2.

Lindberg, J. "Dutchman." Black Academy Review 2 (Spring-Summer 1971): 11-17.

Lindsay, Powell. "We Still Need Negro Theatre in America." Negro History Bulletin 27 (February 1964): 112.

Linnehan, E. G. "We Wear the Mask: The Use of Negro
    Life and Character in American Drama." Ph.D. Dis-
    sertation, University of Pennsylvania, 1953.
A List of Negro Plays. Washington, D.C.: WPA Federal
    Theater Project, 1938.
Little, Stuart W. Off-Broadway: The Prophetic Theatre.
    N.Y.: Coward, McCann and Geoghegan, 1972.
Locke, Alain. "Broadway and the Negro Drama." Theatre
    Arts 25 (October 1941): 745-752.
_____. "Deep River." Opportunity 14 (January 1936):
    6-10.
_____. "The Drama of Negro Life." Theatre Arts
    Monthly 10 (1926): 701-706.
_____. "Jingo, Counter-Jingo and Us." Opportunity 16
    (January 1938): 39-42.
_____. "Max Reinhardt Reads the Negro's Dramatic
    Horoscope." Opportunity 2 (May 1924): 145-146.
_____. "The Negro and the American Stage." Theatre
    Arts 10 (February 1926): 112-120.
_____. "The Negro and the American Theatre." in
    Theatre: Essays on the Arts of the Theatre. Edith
    Isaacs, ed. Boston: Little, Brown, 1927; Freeport,
    N.Y.: Books for Libraries Press, 1968.
_____. "The Negro's Contribution to American Culture."
    Journal of Negro Education 8 (July 1939): 521-529.
_____. "Steps Toward the Negro Theatre." Crisis 25
    (1922): 66-68.
_____ and Montgomery Gregory, eds. Plays of Negro
    Life: A Source Book of Native American Drama.
    N.Y.: Harper, 1927.
Loney, Glenn M. "Having a Word with Word." Players
    46 (August-September 1971): 263-266.
_____. "The Negro and the Theatre." Educational Thea-
    tre Journal 20 (May 1968): 231-233.
Long, Richard. "Alain Locke: Cultural and Social Mentor."
    Black World 20 (November 1970): 87-90.
_____. "Crisis of Consciousness: Reflections of the
    Afro-American Artist." Negro Digest 17 (May 1968):
    88-92.
"Lorraine Hansberry's World." Liberator 4 (December
    1964): 9.
"Louis Takes a Giant Step." Our World 9 (January 1954):
    45-48.
"Louisiana; The Dashiki Project Theatre, New Orleans."
    Black Theatre no. 5 (1971): 3.
"Louisiana; The Dillard University Players, New Orleans."
    Black Theatre no. 5 (1971): 3-4.

Lovell, John Jr. "Drama: Double Take." Crisis 54 (No-
    vember 1947): 334-335.
_____. "New Curtains Going Up." Crisis 54 (October
    1947): 309, 315.
_____. "Round-up: The Negro in the American Thea-
    tre." Crisis 54 (July 1947): 212-217.
Luce, Phillip Abbott. "Purlie Victorious." Mainstream 15
    (February 1962): 62.
Lumley, Frederick. New Trends in 20th Century Drama.
    rev. ed. London: Barrie and Rockliff, 1960.
Lyman, John. "A Negro Theatre." Opportunity 12 (Janu-
    ary 1934): 15-17.

Macbeth, Robert. "A Theatre Uptown Please." The Probe
    1 (May 1967): 12.
McDermott, Wm. F. "Cleveland Colored Author Surprises
    Himself Writing Broadway Success." Cleveland Plain
    Dealer, 11 October 1936, 13: 1.
_____. "Do You Remember the Cake-Walk?" Cleveland
    Plain Dealer, 24 November 1933, 10: 1.
McDougald, J. F. "The Federal Government and the Negro
    Theatre." Opportunity 14 (May 1936): 135-137.
McElroy, Hilda Njoki. "Books Noted (Black Terror)."
    Black World 26 (April 1975): 82-83.
_____. "Books Noted (The Fabulous Miss Marie)."
    Black World 26 (April 1975): 51.
_____. "Books Noted (What If It Had Turned up Heads?)."
    Black World 26 (April 1975): 51-52.
_____ and Richard A. Willis. "Published Works of Black
    Playwrights in the United States, 1960-1970." Black
    World 21 (April 1970): 92-98.
McKinney, Ernest Rice. "Rachel--A Play By Angelina W.
    Grimke." Competitor 3 (April 1921): 35.
McPherson, James M., et al. Blacks in America: Bibli-
    ographical Essays. Garden City, N.Y.: Doubleday,
    1971.
Madison, J. F. "New York: Brownsville Laboratory Thea-
    tre Arts Incorporated." Black Theatre no. 5 (1971): 7.
Manchell, Frank. Film Study: A Resource Guide. Cran-
    bury, N.J.: Associated University Presses, 1973.
Mantle, Burns. ed. Best Plays of 1922-1923, and the Year-
    book of the Drama in America. N.Y.: Dodd, Mead,
    1924.
_____. The Best Plays of 1925-1926. N.Y.: Dodd,
    Mead, 1926.
_____. The Best Plays of 1928-1929. N.Y.: Dodd,

Mead, 1944.

_____ and Garrison P. Sherwood, eds. The Best Plays
of 1909-1919. N.Y.: Dodd, Mead and Co., 1933.

_____ and _____. Best Plays of 1931-1932. New
York: Dodd, Mead, and Co., 1933.

"Many Faces of Oscar Brown, Jr." Sepia 11 (September
1962): 72-74.

Mapp, Edward. Blacks in American Films: Today and Yesterday. Metuchen, N.J.: Scarecrow Press, 1972.

_____. "Black Women in Films." Black Scholar 4
(March-April 1973): 42-46.

Margolies, Edward L. "A Critical Analysis of the Works of
Richard Wright." Dissertation Abstracts 27 (1966):
1829A-30A (N.Y.U.).

_____. "Prospects: LeRoi Jones." in Native Sons: A
Critical Study of Twentieth Century Negro American
Authors. Philadelphia: Lippincott, 1968, pp. 190-200.

Marja, Fern. "'Giant Step' Off Broadway." New York
Post, 18 November 1956.

Markholt, Ottilie. "White Critics, Black Playwrights."
Negro Digest 14 (April 1967): 54.

Mason, B. J. "Black Cinema Expo." Ebony 27 (May 1972):
151-154.

Mason, Clifford. "Black Writer's Views on Literary Lions
and Values." Negro Digest 17 (January 1968): 47.

_____, Robert Macbeth and Ed Bullins. "The Electronic
Nigger Meets the Gold Dust Twins." Black Theatre
no. 1 (October 1968): 24.

Matheus, John. "The Theatre of José Joaquin Gamboa."
CLA Bulletin (Spring 1951).

Mayfield, Julian. "Explore Black Experience." New York
Times, 2 February 1969, D: 9.

_____. "Lorraine Hansberry." In Gayle, The Black
Aesthetic, p. 30.

_____. "You Touch My Black Aesthetic and I'll Touch
Yours." In Gayle, The Black Aesthetic, pp. 24-31.

Mays, B. E. The Negro's God as Reflected in His Literature. rpt. ed. N.Y.: Negro Universities Press,
1969.

Meriwether, L. M. "'The Amen Corner.'" Negro Digest
14 (January 1965): 40-47.

Mezu, S. Okechukwu, ed. Modern Black Literature. Buffalo: Black Academy Press, 1971.

Michener, Charles. "Black Movies, Renaissance or Rip-
Off?" Newsweek 80 (23 October 1972): 75-82.

Miller, Adam David. "It's a Long Way to St. Louis: Notes
on the Audience for Black Drama." Drama Review 12

(Summer 1968): 147-150.

_____ . "News from the San Francisco East Bay."
Black Theatre no. 4 (1970): 5.

_____ . "Report from the San Francisco Bay Area--1970-
1971." Black Theatre no. 6 (1972): 7-8.

Miller, Jeanne-Marie A. "The Plays of LeRoi Jones."
CLA Journal 14 (March 1971): 331-340.

Miller, Jordan. "Lorraine Hansberry." In Bigsby, The
Black American Writer, vol. 2, pp. 157-170.

Miller, Larry. "Spirit House." Black Theatre no. 2 (1969):
34.

Miller, Ruth. Blackamerican Literature: 1760-Present.
Beverly Hills, Ca.: Glencoe Press, 1971.

Miller, Wm. C. and Stephanie Miller. "All Black Show-
case: The Effectiveness of a Negro Theatre Production." Educational Theatre Journal 21 (May 1969): 202-
204.

Millian, Bruce. "Detroit Repertory Theatre." Black Theatre no. 2 (1969): 4-5.

Milner, Ron. "Black Magic: Black Art." Negro Digest 16
(April 1969): 8-12.

_____ . "Black Theatre--Go Home." Negro Digest 17
(April 1968); also in Gayle. The Black Aesthetic. pp.
306-313.

_____ . "Black Writers' Views of Literary Lions and
Values." Negro Digest 17 (January 1968): 45.

_____ . "'M (Ego)' and the Green Ball of Freedom."
Black World 20 (April 1971): 4-45.

_____ . "The Monster." Drama Review 12 (Summer
1968): 95-105.

Mitchell, Loften. "Alligators in the Swamp." Crisis 72
(February 1965): 84-88.

_____ . "Black Drama." Negro Digest 16 (April 1967):
75-87.

_____ . Black Drama: The Story of the American Negro
in the Theatre. N.Y.: Hawthorn, 1967.

_____ . "Death of a Decade: Black Drama in the Sixties."
Crisis 77 (March 1970): 87-93.

_____ . "Fishing--On and Off Broadway." Crisis 76
(June-July): 250-253.

_____ . "Harlem Has Broadway on Its Mind." Theatre
Arts 37 (June 1953).

_____ . "Harlem, My Harlem." Black World 20 (November 1970): 91-97.

_____ . "A Long Ways from 125th Street." Crisis 75
(December 1968): 351-359.

_____ . "The Negro Theatre and the Harlem Community."

Freedomways 3 (1963): 384-394.
_____ . "On Images and the Theatre." The Talladegan
79 (February 1962): 18-21.
_____ . "On the Emerging Playwright." In Bigsby.
The Black American Writer. vol. 2, pp. 129-136.
_____ . "Raisin in the Sun." In Cameron and Hoffman,
A Guide to Theatre Study, p. 203.
_____ . "The Season is Now ('Who's Got His Own' and
'My Sweet Charlie')." Crisis 74 (January-February
1967): 31-34.
_____ . "Three Writers and a Dream." Crisis 72 (April
1965): 219-223.
_____ . Voices of the Black Theatre. Clifton, N.J.:
James White, 1975.
"Mr. Tin Pan Alley." (Andy Razaf) Negro Digest 9 (Octo-
ber 1951): 11-12.
"Mitchell Wins Drama Prize." New York Times, 6 Novem-
ber 1957, 44: 7.
Molette, Carlton W., III. "Afro-American Ritual Drama."
Black World 22 (April 1973): 4-12.
_____ . "Black Theatre in Atlanta." Players 45 (April-
May 1970): 162-165.
_____ . "First Afro-American Theatre." Negro Digest
19 (April 1970): 4-9.
_____ . "Lighting the Stage Without a Proscenium."
Players 44 (October-November 1968): 26-28.
Mootry, Maria K. "Themes and Symbols in Two Plays by
LeRoi Jones." Negro Digest 18 (April 1969): 42-47.
Morrison, Alan. "James Baldwin's Play Boils." Jet 7
May 1964.
_____ . "Mother Role Brings Broadway Fame." Ebony
14 (1959): 97-104.
_____ . "A New Surge in the Arts." Ebony 22 (August
1967): 134-138.
_____ . "One Hundred Years of Negro Entertainment."
In Patterson. Anthology of the American Negro in the
Theatre. pp. 3, 13.
"Mortgaged." Crisis 31 (February 1926): 167.
Moses, Gilbert and John O'Neal. "Dialogue: The Free
Southern Theatre." Tulane Drama Review 9 (Summer
1965): 63-76.
Moses, Montrose and John Brown, eds. The American
Theatre as Seen by Its Critics. N.Y.: Norton, 1934.
_____ . "New Trends in the Theatre." Forum 78 (Janu-
ary-February 1925): 232-234.
_____ . "A Plea for Folk Basis in American Drama."
In Moses and Brown. The American Theatre as Seen

by Its Critics. pp. 219-223.

Moss, Carlton. "The Negro in American Films." In Patterson. Anthology of the American Negro in the Theatre. pp. 229-247.

Muhajir, El. "Islam and the Black Arts: An Interview with LeRoi Jones." Negro Digest 18 (January 1969): 4-10; also in Alhamisi and Wangara, Black Arts.

_____. "Manifesto: The Black Educational Theatre of San Francisco." Black Theatre no. 6 (1972): 30-35.

"Mulatto." Cleveland Plain Dealer, 17 October 1936, 11: 5.

Murray, James P. "Black Movies/Black Theatre." Drama Review 16 (December 1972): 56-61.

_____. "A Futuristic Fable." Black Creation 4 (Winter 1973): 43.

_____. "The Subject is Money." Black Creation 4 (Winter 1973): 26.

_____. To Find An Image. Indianapolis: Bobbs-Merrill, 1960.

_____. "West Coast Gets the Shaft." Black Creation 3 (Summer 1972): 12-14.

"Musical Play Going to Festival in Paris." New York Times, 14 December 1963, 21: 4.

Myers, Carol. "A Selected Bibliography of Recent Afro-American Writers." CLA Journal 16 (March 1973): 377-382.

Nash, R. Lee. "Characteristics of Blacks in the Theatre of the Sixties." Ph.D. Dissertation, Yeshiva University, 1971.

Nathan, George. "Drama's Four Horsemen: Timeliness, Journalism, Cynicism, and Laughs." American Mercury 65 (October 1947): 445-460.

_____. "Memoranda on Four Play Categories." American Mercury 66 (January 1948): 37-41.

_____. "Negro Drama." American Mercury 47 (May 1929): 117-118.

_____. "The Theatre." American Mercury 41 (January-April 1924): 243-244.

Neal, Larry. "Any Day Now: Black Art and Black Literature." Ebony 24 (August 1969): 54-58.

_____. "Beware of the Tar Baby." New York Times, 3 August 1969, 13: D.

_____. "The Black Arts Movement." Drama Review 12 (Summer 1968): 28-29.

_____. "Cultural Nationalism and Black Theatre." Black Theatre no. 1 (1968): 8-10.

_____ . "The Development of LeRoi Jones." Liberator
6 (January 1966): 4; (February-March 1966): 18.
_____ . "Theatre Review: LeRoi Jones' The Slave
The Toilet." Liberator 5 (February 1965): 22.
_____ . "Theatre Review: The Sign in Sidney Brustein's
Window." Liberator 4 (December 1964): 25.
_____ . "Towards a Relevant Black Theatre." Black
Theatre no. 4 (Fall 1969): 14-15.
"Needed: A New Image." In Barbour. Black Power
Revolt.
"The Negro Ensemble Company." Players 49 (June-July
1972): 224-230.
"The Negro in the American Theatre." Theatre Arts 26
(August 1942).
"Negro Players in 1953: Theatre." Ebony 9 (January 1954):
24.
"Negro Playwrights." Ebony 14 (April 1959): 95-99.
"Negro Theatre." New Theatre (July 1935).
"The Negro Women in American Literature." Freedomways
6 (Winter 1966): 45-52.
Nelson, Hugh. "LeRoi Jones' Dutchman: A Brief Ride on
a Doomed Ship." Educational Theatre Journal 20
(March 1968): 53-60.
Nemiroff, Robert, ed. Les Blancs: The Collected Last
Plays of Lorraine Hansberry. N.Y.: Random House,
1972.
_____ . "The One Hundred and One 'Final' Performances
of Sidney Brustein." Introduction in Lorraine Hans-
berry. The Sign in Sidney Brustein's Window. N.Y.:
Random House, 1965, pp. xiii-lxi.
"The New American Comedy." New York Times, 3 Febru-
ary 1925, VII, 1: 1.
"New Dramatists Committee Tenth Anniversary." New York
Times, 2 March 1958, II, 3: 1.
"New 'Mulatto' Hearing." New York Times, 10 February
1937, 19: 1.
"New Plays: The Barrier." Theatre Arts 35 (January 1951):
12.
"The New Plays: Take A Giant Step." Theatre Arts 37
(November 1953): 24.
"A New Playwright (Ron Milner)." Negro Digest 15 (October
1966): 49-50.
Nicholas, Charles H. Jr. "The Forties: A Decade of
Growth." Phylon 12 (Fourth Quarter 1951): 379.
Nicholas, Denise. "View from the Free Southern Theatre."
Liberator 6 (July 1966): 20.

Nichols, Lewis. "Langston Hughes Describes the Genesis
    of his 'Tambourines to Glory.'" New York Times, 27
    October 1946, 1963, 2: 3.
_____. "The Play (St. Louis Woman)." New York
    Times, 1 April 1946, 22: 2.
_____. "The Play: Turpentine." New York Times, 27
    June 1936, 21: 6.
_____. "The Play: Walk Hard--Talk Loud." New York
    Times, 1 December 1944, 28: 2; 28 March 1946, 34: 2.
_____. "Poems to Play." New York Times, 27 October
    1963.
Noble, Peter. The Cinema and the Negro. London: n.p.
    1948. A Special supplement to Sight and Sound, Index
    Series, no. 14.
_____. "The Coming of the Sound Film." In Patterson.
    Anthology of the American Negro in the Theatre. pp.
    247-266.
_____. The Negro in Films. London: Skelton Robinson,
    1948.
Norford, George. "Review of Beggar's Holiday." Oppor-
    tunity 25 (Summer 1947): 167.
Novick, J. "Review: A Recent Killing." New York Times,
    4 February 1973, II, 3: 5.
Nwozomundo, B. "An Epoch: A Critique of Born Astride
    the Grave." The Journal of the New African Literature
    (Spring 1966): 12-13.

O'Brien, John. "Interview with Ed Bullins." Negro Ameri-
    can Literature Forum 7 (Fall 1973): 108.
_____. "Let Us Have a New American Theatre." Negro
    Digest 13 (March 1964): 44.
"Off-Broadway Successes." New York Times, 16 February
    1958, VI, 24-25.
"Off-Stage: Actor's Revenge." Theatre Arts 45 (October
    1961): 67.
"Ohio: The New World Arts Workshop." Black Theatre no.
    6 (1972): 4.
"Oldest Negro Theatre Group in the United States." Theatre
    Arts 24 (April 1940): 226.
Oliver, Clinton and Stephanie Sills, eds. Contemporary
    Black Drama. N.Y.: Scribners, 1971.
Oliver, Edith. "Also Ran: 'Ride a Black Horse.'" New
    Yorker 5 June 1971, p. 100.
_____. "Over the Edge (LeRoi Jones' Dutchman)." New
    Yorker 4 April 1964, p. 78-79.
_____. "The Theatre." New Yorker 7 October 1961, p. 130.

254   Black American Playwrights

"On Broadway: 'A Raisin in the Sun.'" Theatre Arts 43
    (May 1959): 22-23.
"On the Scene: Personality: Melvin Van Peebles: Brer
    Soul." Playboy 17 (September 1970): 195.
"On Writing About Negroes." Opportunity 3 (August 1925):
    227-228.
O'Neal, Frederick. "The Negro's Contribution to Our Thea-
    tre." Equity 41 (March 1956): 5-6.
O'Neal, John. "Motion in the Ocean: Some Political Dimen-
    sions of the Free Southern Theatre." Drama Review
    12 (Summer 1968): 70-77.
O'Neill, Raymond. "The Negro in Dramatic Arts." Crisis
    31 (February 1924).
"Opportunity Please Knock (Oscar Brown Jr.)." Ebony 22
    (August 1967): 104-108.
"Organizing National Negro Theatre to Produce Plays."
    New York Times, 23 June 1934, 11: 1.
Orman, Roscoe. "The New Lafayette Theatre." Black
    Theatre no. 2 (1969): 5-6; no. 4 (1970): 6; no. 5
    (1971): 12-13.
_____. "On Black Theatre." Black Theatre no. 6 (1972):
    57.
"Oscar Brown, Jr.: The Flax that Flipped." Sepia 12
    (May 1963): 18-22.
Ottawa Little Theater. Ranking Play Series 2, Catalogue no.
    43. Ottawa, Canada, September 1965.
Ottawa Little Theater. Ranking Play Series 2, Catalogue no.
    56, Ottawa, Canada, 1966.
Ottley, Roi and William Weatherly. The Negro in New York.
    N.Y.: Oceana, 1967.
"Out of Site." Black Theatre no. 4 (April 1970): 28-31.
Overstreet, H. A. "Negro Writer as Spokesman." Satur-
    day Review of Literature 27 (2 September 1944): 5-6.
Owens, Rochelle and Michael Feingold, eds. Spontaneous
    Combustion: Eight New American Plays. N.Y.: Win-
    ter House, 1972.

Palatsky, Gene. "Stage." Newark Evening News, 29 Octo-
    ber 1963.
Parker, John. "Review: 'Tambourine to Glory'." Phylon
    20 (Spring 1959).
_____. "Tomorrow in the Writing of Langston Hughes."
    College English 10 (May 1949): 438-441.
Parks, Gordon, et al. "Black Movie Boom--Good or Bad?"
    New York Times; Arts and Leisure Section, 17 Decem-
    ber 1972, pp. 3, 19.

Parone, Edward, ed. Collision Course. N.Y.: Random House, 1968.
_____. New Theatre in America. N.Y.: Dell, 1970.
Patterson, James E. "The Negro Ensemble Company." Players 47 (June-July 1972): 224-229.
Patterson, Lindsay, ed. Anthology of the American Negro in the Theatre. Washington, D.C.: Associated, 1967.
_____. comp. Black Films and Film Makers. Dodd, Mead, 1975.
_____. Black Theater: A Twentieth Century Collection of the Work of Its Best Playwrights. N.Y.: Dodd, Mead, 1971.
_____. "In Harlem, a James Bond with a Soul?" New York Times, 15 June 1969, 15: D.
_____, ed. An Introduction to Black Literature. Washington, D.C.: 1969.
_____. "Not by Protest Alone." Negro History Bulletin 31 (April 1968): 12-14.
_____. "A Profile--Interview: Archie Shepp." Black World 23 (November 1973): 58-61.
_____. "Review: 'In the Wine Time.'" Negro History Bulletin 32 (April 1969): 18-19; reprinted from the New York Times, 22 December 1968.
_____. "The Waste Lands." In Patterson. Anthology of the American Negro in the Theatre. pp. 269-270.
Pawley, Dr. Thomas D. "The Black Theatre Audience." Players 46 (August-September 1971): 257-261.
_____. "Dunbar as Playwright." Black World 26 (April 1975): 70-88.
_____. "The First Black Playwrights." Black World 21 (April 1972): 16-25.
_____. "I Am a Fugitive from a Play." National Theatre Conference 10 (July 1948): 9-12.
_____. "Stage Craft in Negro Colleges." Negro College Quarterly 4 (December 1946): 193, 199, 217.
_____. "Theatre Arts and the Educated Man." Central States Speech Journal 8 (Spring 1957): 5-11.
Pearson, Lou Anne. "LeRoi Jones and a Black Aesthetic." Paunch 35 (1972): 33-66.
Peavy, Charles D. "Satire and Contemporary Black Drama." Satire Newsletter 7 (Fall 1969): 40-48.
Peck, Seymour. "Owen Dodson, New Writer." PM 7 (March 1945).
Pembrook, Carrie Davis. "Negro Drama Through the Ages-- An Anthology." Ph.D. Dissertation, New York University, 1946.
"People Are Talking About ... (Lorraine Hansberry)."

Vogue 133 (June 1959): 78-79.

" 'The Perfect Party.'" Jet 26 (17 April 1969): 58.

Perkins, Eugene. "Black Theatre and Community Expression." Inner City Studies Journal (North Eastern State
College), Summer, 1970.

_____. "Black Theatre as Image Maker." Black Books
Bulletin 1 (Spring-Summer 1972): 24.

_____. "Black Writers and the Liberation Movement."
Illinois English Bulletin, 1968.

_____. "Changing Status of Black Writers." Black
World 19 (June 1970): 18-23.

_____. "New Voices in Black Culture." Panorama
Magazine: Chicago Daily News, 7 December 1968.

Peterson, Bernard F., Jr. "Willie Richardson: Pioneer
Playwright." Black World 26 (April 1975): 40-54.

Peterson, Maurice. "Gilbert Moses: Repaving the Yellow
Brick Road." Essence 5 (December 1974): 24.

_____. "Micki Grant." Essence 3 (November 1972): 32.

_____. "On the Aisle: Theatre and Film." Essence 5
(September 1974): 24.

_____. "Taking off with Joseph Walker." Essence 4
(April 1974): 55, 74, 78, 82, 88.

Petry, Ann. "The Great Secret." The Writer 41 (July
1948): 215-217.

"Philadelphia Halts the Play 'Mulatto.'" New York Times,
9 February 1937, 18: 5.

"Philadelphia Keeps Ban on Play 'Mulatto.'" New York
Times, 12 February 1937, 27: 4.

Phillips, Louis. "The Novelist as Playwright: Baldwin,
McCullers, and Bellow." In Taylor. Modern American Drama: Essays in Criticism. pp. 146-154.

"Pieces on Black Theatre and the Black Theatre Worker."
Freedomways 9 (Spring 1969): 146-155.

Pierce, Evelyn Miller. "Jim Crow Dons the Buskin."
Theatre Magazine 49 (May 1929): 50-51.

"Plays of the Month: The Reason and Synopsis by the
Author." Competitor 1 (January 1920): 51-52.

"Playboy After Hours: Movies." Playboy 16 (October 1969):
48, 52.

"Playboy After Hours: Movies." (Ossie Davis) Playboy
17 (August 1970): 30-31.

"Playboy After Hours: Movies." (Ossie Davis) Playboy
19 (August 1972): 28.

"Playboy After Hours: Movies." (Gordon Parks) Playboy
18 (October 1971): 50, 52.

"Playboy After Hours: Movies." (Gordon Parks) Playboy
21 (July 1974): 35.

"Playboy After Hours: Movies (The Learning Tree)." Play-
    boy 16 (October 1969): 48.
"Playboy After Hours: Movies (Van Peebles)." Playboy 18
    (August 1971): 30, 32.
"Playboy After Hours: Theatre." Playboy 11 (October
    1964): 511.
"Playboy After Hours: Theatre." Playboy 17 (June 1970):
    42.
"Playboy After Hours: Theatre." (James Baldwin) Playboy
    11 (August 1964): 14.
"Playboy After Hours: Theatre." (Ed Bullins) Playboy 18
    (April 1971): 37.
"Playboy After Hours: Theatre." (Ossie Davis) Playboy
    17 (July 1970): 34.
"Playboy After Hours: Theatre." (Lonne Elder, III) Play-
    boy 16 (July 1969): 37.
"Playboy After Hours: Theatre." (Hansberry) Playboy 6
    (May 1959): 14, 16.
"Playboy After Hours: Theatre." (Hansberry) Playboy 18
    (April 1971): 37.
"Playboy After Hours: Theatre." (Mackey) Playboy 17
    (June 1970): 42.
"Playboy After Hours: Theatre." (Nemiroff) Playboy 21
    (February 1974): 38.
"Playboy After Hours: Theatre." ('No Place To Be Some-
    body') Playboy 16 (August 1969): 34-35.
"Playboy After Hours: Theatre." (Ododo) Playboy 18
    (April 1971): 37.
"Playboy After Hours: Theatre." (Van Peebles) Playboy 19
    (August 1972): 42, 44.
"Playboy After Hours: Theatre." (Walker) Playboy 20
    (July 1973): 39.
Poland, Albert and Bruce Mailman, eds. The Off-Broadway
    Book: The Plays, People, and Theatre. N.Y.: Bobbs-
    Merrill, 1972.
Powell, Ann. "The Negro in the Federal Theatre." Crisis
    43 (November 1936): 340-34.
Presley, James. "The American Dream of Langston
    Hughes." Southwest Review 48 (Autumn 1963): 380-
    386.
Price, Ann. "'Face of the Deep' Stunning Work." Morning
    Advocate (Baton Rouge, La.), 28 July 1971, 13: A.
Prideaux, Tom. "Living Healing Kind of Theatre--Free
    Southern Theatre." Life 61 (16 September 1966): 24.
Primus, Marc, ed. Black Theatre: A Resource Directory.
    N.Y.: The Black Theatre Alliance, n.d.
"Problems of the Negro Writer." Saturday Review of Litera-

ture 46 (20 April 1963): 19-21.
Pullen, Glen C. "Gilpin Players Revive Hughes' 'Little
    Ham.'" Cleveland Plain Dealer 26 May 1938, 6: 4.
_____. "Karamu Gives New Drama." Cleveland Plain
    Dealer 17 November 1938, 11: 3.
_____. "Langston Hughes' New Farce Given by Gilpiners."
    Cleveland Plain Dealer 1 April 1937, 14: 4.
_____. "'Turpentine,' Saga of the Modern Negro in the
    South." Cleveland Plain Dealer 15 January 1937, 9: 1.
"'Purlie Victorious.'" Ebony 17 (March 1962): 55-56.

Quinn, Arthur H. "The Real Hope for the American Thea-
    tre." Scribner's Magazine 97 (January 1935): 30-36.

Rabkin, Gerald. Drama and Commitment. Bloomington:
    Indiana University Press, 1964.
Raines, R. A., ed. Modern Drama and Social Change.
    Englewood Cliffs, N.J.: Prentice-Hall, 1972.
"'A Raisin in the Sun.'" The Theatre 1 (May 1959): 31.
"'A Raisin in the Sun.'" The Theatre 3 (April 1961): 28-29.
"'A Raisin in the Sun' Basks in Praise." New York Times,
    14 November 1961, 47: 5.
"'Raisin in the Sun' Sets Record." Jet 16 (June 1960): 58.
"'Raisin in the Sun' Staged in the Soviet." New York Times,
    14 November 1961, 47: 5.
"'A Raisin in the Sun' to Close." New York Times, 23
    June 1960, 18: 6.
Randolph, James P. "What Is Black Theatre?" Dramatics
    42 (March 1971): 12-15.
Rashidd, Naima. "Black Theatre in Detroit." Black Thea-
    tre No. 4 (1970): 3.
Raymond, Harry. "Theatre: Moving Desegregation Play at
    Greenwich News." Daily Worker, 1 April 1957.
Reardon, Tom R. "'Ceremonies in Dark Old Men': A Re-
    markable Achievement in Black Drama." In Hatlen,
    Principles and Plays.
Reardon, Wm. and Thomas Pawley, eds. The Black Teach-
    er and the Dramatic Arts. N.Y.: Negro Universities
    Press, 1970.
Reck, Tom. "Archetypes in LeRoi Jones' 'Dutchman.'"
    Studies in Black Literature 1 (Spring 1970): 66-68.
Record, Wilson C. "The Negro Creative Artist." Crisis
    72 (March 1965): 153-158, 193.
Redding, Saunders. "Literature and the Negro." Contem-
    porary Literature 9 (Winter 1968): 130-135.

_____ . "The Problems of the Negro Writer." Massa-
chusetts Review 6 (Autumn-Winter 1964-1965): 57-70.
Redmond, Eugene. Sides of the River: A Mini-Anthology of
Black Writing. Oberlin, Ohio: author, 1969.
Reed, Addison W. "The Life and Works of Scott Joplin."
Ph.D. Dissertation, University of North Carolina,
Chapel Hill, 1973.
Reed, Daphne S. "LeRoi Jones: High Priest of the Black
Arts Movement." Educational Theatre Journal 22
(March 1970): 53-60.
Reed, Ishmael. "Chester Himes: Writer." Black World
21 (March 1972): 24-39.
_____ . 19 Necromancers from Now. Garden City,
N.Y.: Doubleday, 1970.
Reid, H. "First Lady of the Theater: Anita Bush." Es-
sence 3 (December 1972): 36-37.
Reinert, Otto, ed. Classic Through Modern Drama. Boston:
Little, Brown, 1970.
_____ . Drama: An Introductory Anthology. Boston:
Little, Brown, 1964.
Reische, Diana, ed. The Performing Arts in America.
Vol. 45. N.Y.: Wilson, 1973.
Riach, Douglas C. "Blacks and Blackface on the Irish
Stage, 1830-1960." Journal of American Studies 7
(December 1973): 231-242.
Riach, W. A. D. "'Telling It Like It Is': An Examination
of Black Theatre as Rhetoric." Quarterly Journal of
Speech 46 (April 1970): 179-186.
Rice, Julian C. "LeRoi Jones' 'Dutchman'--A Reading."
Contemporary Literature 12 (January 1971): 42-59.
Rich, Dennis. "The Kuumba Workshop." Players 47 (De-
cember-January 1972): 68-75.
Richards, Stanley, ed. The Best Short Plays of 1969.
Philadelphia: Chilton Book Co., 1969.
_____ . The Best Short Plays of 1970. Philadelphia:
Chilton, 1970.
_____ . The Best Short Plays of 1972. Philadelphia:
Chilton, 1972.
_____ . The Best Short Plays of 1973. Radnor, Pa.:
Chilton, 1973.
_____ . Best Short Plays of the World Theatre, 1958-
1967. New York: Crown Publishers, 1968.
Richardson, Willis. "Characters." Opportunity 3 (June
1925): 183.
_____ . "The Hope of Negro Drama." Crisis 19 (Novem-
ber 1919): 338.
_____ . The King's Dilemma and Other Plays for Children.

New York: Exposition, 1956.

_____. "The Negro and the Stage." Opportunity 2 (October 1924): 310.

_____. "Poetry and Drama." Crisis 27 (1927).

_____. "The Unpleasant Play." Opportunity 3 (September 1925): 282.

_____, ed. Plays and Pageants from the Life of the Negro. Washington, D.C.: Associated Press, 1930.

_____ and May Miller, eds. Negro History in Thirteen Plays. Washington, D.C.: Associated Press, 1935.

Riche, James. "The Politics of Black Modernism." Literature and Ideology 8 (1971): 85-90.

Riddell, Hugh. "The New Negro Playwrights' Group Forms in Harlem." Daily Worker, 27 July 1940, p. 7.

Riggins, Linda N. "A Review of Ed Bullins' 'The Hungered One.'" Black Scholar 3 (February 1972): 59-60.

Riley, Carolyn, ed. Contemporary Literary Criticism, vols. 1-3. Detroit: Gale Research, 1975.

Riley, Clayton. "Movie Review: 'Dutchman.'" Liberator 7 (April 1967): 20.

_____. "The Negro and the Theatre, Part 1." Liberator 7 (June 1967): 20.

_____. "The Negro and the Theatre, Part 2." Liberator (August 1967): 21.

_____. "The Negro and the Theatre, Part 3." Liberator (October 1967): 8.

_____. "Theatre Review: 'Amen Corner.'" Liberator 5 (May 1965): 26.

_____. "Theatre Review: 'Ceremonies in Dark Old Men.'" Liberator 9 (March 1969): 21.

_____. "Theatre Review: 'Daddy Goodness.'" Liberator 8 (July 1968): 21.

_____. "Theatre Reviews: Dutchman and Day of Absence." Liberator 9 (November 1969): 21.

_____. "Theatre Review: Five on the Black Hand Side." Liberator 10 (January 1970): 21.

_____. "Theatre Review: Gabriel." Liberator 8 (December 1968): 21.

_____. "Theatre Review: Gordone's No Place to Be Somebody." New York Times, 18 May 1969, II, 1: 1; 22: 1.

_____. "Theatre Review: The Harangues." Liberator 10 (February 1970): 21.

_____. "Theatre Review: In New England Winter." New York Times, 7 February 1971, II, 3: 8.

_____. "Theatre Review: In the Wine Time." Liberator 9 (January 1969): 20.

_____. "Theatre Review: Ladies in Waiting." Liberator
    8 (August 1968): 21.
_____. "Theatre Review: Les Blancs." Liberator 10
    (December 1970): 19.
_____. "Theatre Review: Purlie." Liberator 10 (April
    1970): 21.
_____. "Theatre Review: Rosalee Pritchett." New York
    Times, 7 February 1971, II, 3: 5.
_____. "Theatre Review: Slave Ship." Liberator 9
    (December 1969): 19.
_____. "Theatre Reviews: The Pig Pen and In New
    England Winter." Liberator 10 (June 1970): 20.
_____. "Theatre Review: The Prodigal Son." Liberator
    5 (October 1965): 14.
_____. "Theatre Review: We Righteous Bombers."
    Liberator 9 (December 1969): 19.
_____. "Theatre Review: Who's Got His Own." Libera-
    tor 6 (November 1966): 21.
_____. "Theatre: The Black Arts." Liberator 5 (April
    1965): 21.
_____. "Three Short Plays by Ed Bullins" (A Son, Come
    Home; The Electronic Nigger; Clara's Old Man).
    Liberator 8 (May 1968): 20.
_____. "What Makes Sweetback Run?" New York Times,
    9 May 1971, 11: D.
Riley, Phillip. "Negro Theatre." Encore 7 (November-
    December 1960): 11.
Rivers, W. Napoleon, Jr. "Gautier on Aldridge." Crisis 39
    (January 1932): 459-460.
Robertson, Nan. "Dramatists against the Odds." New York
    Times, 28 March 1959, II, 3: 1.
Robinson, William H., ed. Nommo: An Anthology of Mod-
    ern African and Black American Literature. N.Y.:
    Macmillan, 1972.
"Rockefeller Money Saves Baldwin's Play." Milwaukee Jour-
    nal, 7 June 1964.
Rogers, Ray. "The Negro Actor." Freedomways 2 (Sum-
    mer 1962): 310-313.
Rosenberg, Harold. "The Artist as Perceiver of Social
    Realities: The Post-Art Artist." Arts in Society 8
    (Summer 1971): 509-510.
Ross, Ronald. "The Role of Blacks in the Federal Thea-
    tre, 1935-1939." The Journal of Negro History 59
    (January 1974): 38-51.
Rowe, Billy. "'Saint Louis Woman!'" The Pittsburgh
    Courier, 15 September 1945, p. 15.
Rowe, Kenneth Thorpe. A Theatre in Your Head. N.Y.:

Funk and Wagnalls, 1960.

Rowell, Charles H. "Sterling A. Brown and the Afro-
American Folk Tradition." Studies in the Literary
Imagination 7 (Fall 1974): 31-152.

Rowley-Rotunno, Virginia. "Scott Joplin: Renascence of a
Black Composer of Ragtime and Grand Opera." Negro
History Bulletin 37 (January 1974): 188-193.

Rudin, Seymour. "Arts in Review: Performing Arts 1971-
72." The Massachusetts Review 14 (Winter 1973): 207-
223.

_____. "Arts in Review: Performing Arts 1972-73."
The Massachusetts Review 14 (Autumn 1973): 865-882.

_____. "Theatre Chronicle: Winter-Spring 1969."
The Massachusetts Review 10 (Summer 1969): 583-593.

_____. "Theatre Chronicle: Fall 1970." The Massa-
chusetts Review 12 (Winter 1971): 150-161.

_____. "Theatre Chronicle: Winter-Spring 1971." The
Massachusetts Review 12 (Autumn 1971): 821-833.

" 'Run, Little Chillun.' " New York Times, 14 June 1939,
27: 3.

" 'Run, Little Chillun.' " Theatre Arts Monthly 12 (April
1933): 307.

Russell, Charles L. "John O. Killens: Tell It Like It Is."
Liberator 4 (April 1964): 10.

_____. "LeRoi Jones Will Get Us All in Trouble."
Liberator 4 (June 1964): 10.

_____. "The Wide World of Ossie Davis: Exclusive In-
terview." Liberator 3 (December 1963): 11-12.

Rutledge, W. E., Jr. "The AfroAmerican Culture Center
and the Nyeusi Ujamaa Theatre of Greater Kansas
City." Black Theatre no. 5 (1971): 4-5.

Sadler, Jeanne E. "The People's Playwright." (Ron Milner) Essence 5 (November 1974): 20.

" 'St. Louis Woman's' Cast Does Nipups over Stereotyped
Character." Variety 3 April 1946, p. 32.

Salaam, Kalamu Ya. "Black Art-South; New Orleans."
Black World 21 (April 1972): 4-5.

_____. "The Dashiki Project Theatre, We Are the Thea-
tre." Black Theatre No. 3 (1969): 4-6.

_____. "News from Blkartsouth." Black Theatre No. 4
(1970): 4.

Salem, James M. A Guide to Critical Reviews. Part I:
American Drama. 2nd ed. Metuchen, N.J.: Scarecrow Press, 1973.

Sanchez, Sonia. "Conversation: 'Uh-Uh; But How Do It

Free Us?'" In Bullins. New Lafayette Theatre Presents, pp. 161-163.

Sanwick, Helen M. "The Development of the Negro Character in the American Drama from 1767-1934." Ph.D. Dissertation, University of Washington, Seattle, 1934.

Sayre, Nora. "New York's Black Theatre." New Statesman, 25 October 1968, p. 556.

Schafer, Wm. J. and Johannes Riedel. Scott Joplin's 'Treemonisha'; The Art of Ragtime. Baton Rouge, La.: Louisiana State University Press, 1973, pp. 205-225.

Schatt, Stanley. "LeRoi Jones: A Checklist to Primary and Secondary Sources." Bulletin of Bibliography (April-June 1971): 55-57.

Schechner, R. "Free Theatre for Mississippi." Harper 231 (October 1965): 11.

Schecter, Amy. "A Hard Hitting Play on the U.S. South." New World Review (December 1951): 63.

Schnech, S. "LeRoi Jones, or, Poetics and Policeman, or Try Heart, Bleeding Heart." Ramparts (29 June 1968): 14-19.

Schroeder, R. J. "Free Southern Theatre." Commonweal 83 (18 March 1966): 696.

Schuck, Barry. "Philadelphia's Black Drama Season, '67-68." Black Theatre no. 2 (1969): 34-35.

Schulberg, Budd. "Black Phoenix: An Introduction." Antioch Review 27 (Fall 1967): 277-284.

_____. From the Ashes: Voices of Watts. New York: New American Library, 1967.

Scott, Esther. "Negroes As Actors in Serious Plays." Opportunity 1 (April 1923): 20-23.

Scott, John Sherman. "The Black Spirit: A Trilogy of Original Plays and a Treatise in Contemporary Black Drama." Ph.D. Dissertation, Bowling Green State University, 1972.

_____. "Teaching Black Drama." Players 47 (February 1972): 130-131.

Searcy, Sarra Lee. "Aesthetic Qualities Found in Certain Negro Drama." Master's Thesis, Ohio State University, Columbus, 1950.

Sender, Garlin. "When Negro-White Unite." Daily Worker, 16 May 1934, p. 55.

Seyboldt, Mark. "Playwrighting." Crisis 25 (February 1925): 164-165.

Shay, Frank and Pierre Loving. Fifty More Contemporary One Act Plays. London: Appleton-Century, 1928.

Shelton, Robert. "Theatre" (Black Nativity). Nation 190 (5 January 1963): 20.

Sherman, Alphonso. "The Diversity of Treatment of the
    Negro Character in American Drama Prior to 1860."
    Ph.D. Dissertation, University of Indiana, Blooming-
    ton, 1964.
_____. "Little Known Black Heroes in Ante-Bellum
    Drama." The Speech Teacher 19 (March 1970).
Sievers, W. David. Freud On Broadway. N.Y.: Hermi-
    tage House, 1955.
"Silas Green of New Orleans; Famous Negro Tent Show Is
    Now Practically an Institution of the Mason-Dixon
    Line." Ebony 9 (September 1954): 68-73.
Silvera, Frank. "Towards a Theatre of Understanding."
    Negro Digest 18 (April 1969): 33-35.
Silvera, John D. "Still in Blackface." Crisis 46 (March
    1939): 71, 89.
Silverman, Reuben. "A History of the Karamu Theatre at
    Karamu House, 1915-1960." Ph.D. Dissertation, Ohio
    State University, Columbus, 1961.
Simmons, Gloria, and Helene Hutchinson, eds. Black Cul-
    ture: Reading and Writing Black. N.Y.: Holt, Rine-
    hart and Winston, 1972.
Simon, John. "Don't Play Us at All." New York Magazine,
    5 June 1972, p. 72.
_____. "Play Reviews: 'Fly Blackbird.'" Theatre Arts
    46 (May 1962): 61-62.
_____. "Underwriting, Over-Reaching." New Yorker, 9
    June 1969, p. 56.
Simonson, Harold, ed. Quartet. 2nd ed. N.Y.: Harper
    and Row, 1973.
Singh, Raman K. and Peter Fellowes, eds. Black Litera-
    ture in America. New York: Crowell, 1970.
Siskel, Gene. "Four Stars Graduate in 'Cooley High.'"
    Chicago Tribune; Arts and Fun, 15 June 1975, pp. 2-3.
"Sissle and Blake." Ebony 10 (March 1955): 112-118.
Sissle, Noble. "How Jo Baker Got Started." Negro Digest
    9 (August 1951): 15-19.
Sister Ann Edward. "Three Views on Blacks: The Black
    Woman in American Literature." The CEA Critic 37
    (May 1975): 14-16.
Skinner, R. Dana. "Review: Harlem." Commonweal 6
    (March 1929).
Slattery, Tom. "Redmond at C.C.C." The Commuter
    (Cuyahoga Community College) 6 November 1970, pp.
    6-7.
Smalley, Webster, ed. Five Plays by Langston Hughes.
    Bloomington, Ind.: Indiana University Press, 1963.
Smallwood, Will. "A Tribute to Countee Cullen." Oppor-

tunity 25 (Summer 1947): 168-169.
Smiley, Sam. The Drama of Attack. Columbia: University
    of Missouri, 1972.
Smith, Jean. "O.C.'s Heart." Black World 19 (April 1970):
    56-76.
Smith, Michael. More Plays From Off-Broadway. Indianapo-
    lis: Bobbs-Merrill, 1966.
Smith, Milburn. "Producers' Schedules." The Theatre 1
    (March 1959): 38.
Smith, Morgan. "The Negro Artist." The Radical 2 (1867):
    27-31.
Smitherman, Geneva. "Ed Bullins/Stage One: Everybody
    Wants to Know Why I Sing the Blues." Black World 23
    (April 1974): 4-13.
"Sonia Sanchez and Her Work." Black World 2 (June 1971):
    44-46.
Sontag, Susan. Against Interpretation and Other Essays.
    N.Y.: Farrar, Straus and Giroux, 1966.
_____. "Going to the Theatre and the Movies." Partisan
    Review 31 (Summer 1964): 389-399.
_____. "Going to the Theatre and the Movies" (Adrienne
    Kennedy). Partisan Review 31 (Spring 1964): 284-293.
Spence, Eulalie. "A Criticism of the Negro Drama." Op-
    portunity 6 (June 1928): 180.
_____. "The Task of the Negro Writer as Artist."
    Negro Digest 14 (April 1965): 54-83.
Spencer, T. S. and Clarence Rivers. "Langston Hughes:
    His Style and Optimism." Drama Critique 7 (Spring
    1964): 99-102.
Sper, Felix. From Native Roots. Caldwell, Idaho: Cax-
    ton, 1948.
Spriggs, Edward S. "Amen to the Revolutionary Theatre
    and Black Arts." Black Dialogue 1 (July-August 1965):
    22-24.
Staples, Elizabeth. "Langston Hughes' Malevolent Force."
    American Mercury 138 (January 1959): 46-50.
Stasio, Marilyn. "Don't Play Us Cheap." Cue, 27 May
    1972.
Steele, Shelby. "White Port and Lemon Juice: Notes on
    Ritual in the Black Theatre." Black World 22 (June
    1973): 4-14.
Stenton, Colin. "A Tick Bird is Dying: The Detroit
    Repertory Theatre." Players 47 (June-July 1972): 242-
    247.
Stewart, D. H. "The Bed-Stuy Theatre of Brooklyn."
    Black Theatre no. 5 (1971): 7.
Stewart, James T. "The Messenger of God (Imamu's Ways

Are Just)." Black Lines 2 (Fall 1971): 45-48.
Stockwell, Latourette. "Review of 'Big White Fog.'" Op-
    portunity 16 (June 1938): 172.
Sullivan, Victoria and James Hatch. Plays By and About
    Women. New York: Random House, 1973 (1st ed.)
Sumpter, Clyde G. "Militating For A Change: A Study of
    the Black Revolutionary Theatre in the U.S." Ph.D.
    Dissertation, University of Kansas, 1969.
Sutherland, E. "Theatre of the Meaningful." Nation 19
    (October 1966): 254.
"A Symposium on 'We Righteous Bombers.'" Black Theatre
    no. 4 (Fall 1969): 14-15.
"Symposium: The Negro in the American Theatre." Negro
    Digest 11 (July 1962): 52.
"Symposium: The Negro Writer in America." Negro Digest
    12 (June 1963): 54.

Taalmu, M. "Black Arts West of Seattle." Black Theatre
    5 (1971): 8-9.
"Take a Giant Step" (Movie). Ebony 14 (September 1959):
    48-51.
Taki, Ronald. Violence in the Black Imagination: Essays
    and Documents. N.Y.: Putnam's, 1972.
Talbot, Mn. "Every Negro in His Place: The Scene On
    and Off Broadway." Drama Critique 7 (Spring 1964):
    92-95.
"The Task of the Negro Writer as Artist." Negro Digest
    14 (April 1965): 54-83.
Taubman, Howard. "Theatre: Black Nativity?" New York
    Times, 12 December 1961, 54: 2.
_____. "Theatre: 'Blues for Mr. Charlie.'" New York
    Times, 24 April 1964, 24: 1.
_____. "Theatre: Peterson's Work." New York Times,
    10 April 1962, 48: 1.
_____. "Theatre: 'Sidney Brustein's Window.'" New
    York Times, 17 October 1964, p. 18.
_____. "Theatre: Story of a Negro." New York Times,
    29 October 1963.
Taylor, Jeanne A. "On Being Black and Writing for Tele-
    vision." Negro American Literature Forum 4 (1970):
    79-82.
Taylor, Karen M. People's Theatre in Amerika. N.Y.:
    Drama Book Specialists, 1972.
Taylor, Patricia E. "Langston Hughes and the Harlem
    Renaissance: 1921-1931." In Bontemps, The Harlem
    Renaissance Remembered, pp. 90-101.

Taylor, William E. Modern American Drama: Essays in
    Criticism. DeLand, Fla.: Everett/Edwards, 1968.
Tedesco, John L. "Blues for Mr. Charlie: The Rhetorical
    Dimension." Players 50 (Fall-Winter 1975): 20-23.
Teer, Barbara. "The Great White Way Is Not Our Way."
    Negro Digest 17 (April 1968): 21-29.
_____. "To Black Artists with Love." Negro Digest 18
    (April 1969): 4-8.
_____. "We Are Liberators Not Actors." Essence 1
    (March 1971): 56-59.
"Tennessee A and I Players: See How They Run." Jet (10
    March 1960): 41; (28 April 1960): 60.
"The Theatre--Uncle Tom Exhumed." Time 78 (16 October
    1951): 88.
Thompson, Howard. "Black Theater Stages Revival." New
    York Times, 30 July 1972, 43: 3.
Thompson, Larry. "The Black Image in Early American
    Drama." Black World 26 (April 1975): 54-70.
Thompson, T. "Burst of Negro Drama." Life 29 May
    1964, pp. 62-70.
Three Negro Plays. (Hughes, Jones, Hansberry). Har-
    mondsworth, England: Penguin, 1969.
"Three Writers and a Dream." Crisis 72 (April 1972): 219-
    223.
Thurman, Wallace. "Negro Artists and the Negro." New
    Republic 52 (31 August 1927): 37-39.
_____. "Nephews of Uncle Remus." Independent 119 (4
    September 1927): 296-298.
_____. and William Jourdan Rapp. "Detouring Harlem to
    Times Square." New York Times, 7 April 1929, 10:
    4.
Tichemon, G. "Colored Lines." Theatre Arts 14 (January
    1930): 485-490.
Tinker, Ed. Les ecrits de langue Française en Louisiana
    au XIXe siècle. Paris: H. Champion, 1932.
Tischler, Nancy M. Black Masks: Negro Characters in
    Modern Southern Fiction. University Park: Pennsyl-
    vania State University Press, 1969.
Tobin, Terrence. "Karamu Theatre: Its Distinguished Past
    and Present Achievement." Drama Critique 7 (Spring
    1964): 86-91.
Towsen, John. "The Bread and Puppet Theatre--Stations of
    the Cross." Drama Review 16 (September 1972): 57-
    70.
"Trailer Theatre: Acting Unit Tours Nation to Present Live
    Plays." Ebony 5 (October 1950): 52-54.
Trott, Geri. "Black Theatre." Harper's Bazaar 101

(August 1968): 150-153.
Trux, J. J. "Negro Minstrelsy, Ancient and Modern."
    Putnam's Monthly Magazine (January 1855).
Tupper, V. G. "Negro Folk Music Drama Given in Charles-
    ton, S.C." Etude (March 1937).
Turk, Midge. Gordon Parks. N.Y.: Crowell, 1971.
Turner, Darwin T. Black American Literature: Essays,
    Poetry, Fiction and Drama. Columbus, Ohio: Mer-
    rill, 1970.
_____. Black Drama in America; An Anthology. Green-
    wich, Conn.: Fawcett, 1971.
_____. "The Black Playwrights in the Professional Thea-
    tre of the United States of America, 1858-1949." In
    Brasmer and Consolo. Black Drama: An Anthology.
    pp. 1-18.
_____. "Dreams and Hallucinations in the Drama of the
    Twenties." CLA Journal 3 (March 1960): 166-173.
_____. "The Failure of a Playwright." CLA Journal 10
    (1967): 308-318.
_____. "Langston Hughes as Playwright." CLA Journal
    11 (1968): 19-25.
_____. "The Negro Dramatists' Image of the Universe."
    CLA Journal 5 (1961): 106-120.
_____. "Negro Playwrights and the Urban Negro." CLA
    Journal 12 (September 1968): 19-25.
_____. "Past and Present in Negro Drama." Negro
    American Literature Forum 2 (1968): 26-27.
_____. "Paul Laurence Dunbar: The Rejected Symbol."
    Journal of Negro History 52 (January 1967): 1-14.
Turner, Sherry. "An Overview of the New Black Arts."
    Freedomways 9 (1969): 156-163.
Turpin, Waters E. "The Contemporary American Negro
    Playwright." CLA Journal (September 1965): 19-21.
Tutt and Whitney. "Smarter Set Company Presents New
    Vehicle (Bamboula)." Competitor 2 (August-September
    1920): 157.
Tynan, Kenneth. Curtains. N.Y.: Atheneum, 1961.
_____. Tynan Right and Left: Plays, Films, People,
    Places and Events. N.Y.: Atheneum, 1967.

Van Doren, Carl. "The Roving Critic." Century 61 (March
    1926): 635-637.
Van Vechten, Carl. "Beginning of Negro Drama." Literary
    Digest 48 (9 May 1914): 11-14.
_____. "How the Theatre Is Represented in the Negro
    Collection at Yale." The Theatre Annual (1943): 32-38.

Victor, Jerome. The Negro in Hollywood Films. N.Y.:
    Masses and Mainstream, 1950.
Voorhees, Lillian W. "What Price Negro Drama?" Southern
    Speech Journal 14 (January 1949): 176-184.

Wager, Walter, ed. The Playwrights Speak. N.Y.: Dell,
    1968.
Walcott, Ronald. "Ellison, Gordone, and Tolson: Some
    Notes on the Blues." Black World 22 (December 1972):
    4-29.
Waldau, Roy S. Vintage Years of the Theatre Guild: 1928-
    1939. Cleveland: Case Western Reserve University,
    1972.
Walker, Barbara. "Community Theatre." Black Creation
    3 (Summer 1972): 21-26.
_____. "Sonia Sanchez Creates Poetry for the Stage."
    Black Creation 5 (Fall 1973): 12-13.
_____. "Theatre: Bedford-Stuyvesant Theatre." Black
    Creation 3 (Summer 1972): 21-23.
Walrond, Eric. "Growth of a Negro Theatre." Theatre
    Magazine (October 1925): 20.
_____. "Review of 'Being Forty.'" Opportunity 2 (No-
    vember 1924): 346.
_____. "Review of 'The Chocolate Dandies.'" Oppor-
    tunity 2 (November 1924): 345.
Ward, Douglas Turner. "American Theatre: For Whites
    Only?" New York Times, 14 August 1966, II, 1: 1;
    also in Patterson Anthology of the American Negro in
    the Theatre. pp. 81-85; Raines. Modern Drama and
    Social Change.
_____. "Comments on The River Niger." New York
    Times, 7 February 1973, 30: 1.
_____. "First Breeze of Summer." New York Times,
    2 March 1975, II, 1: 2.
_____. "Needed: A Theater for Black Themes." Negro
    Digest 17 (December 1967): 34-39.
Ward, Francis and Val Grey Ward. "The Black Artist--His
    Role in the Struggle." Black Scholar 2 (January 1971):
    23-32.
_____ and _____. "Theatre Round-Up: Chicago."
    Black World 21 (April 1972): 37.
Ward, Theodore. "Our Conception of the Theatre and Its
    Function." In Taylor. People's Theatre in Amerika.
    pp. 186-191.
_____. "The South Side Center of the Performing Arts,
    Inc." Black Theatre no. 2 (1969): 3-4.

270   Black American Playwrights

_____. "Why Not a Negro Drama for Negroes by Negroes?" Current Opinion 72 (1972): 639-640.
Washington, Cleve. "Perkins Pulls the Plug on Electric Niggers." Black Books Bulletin 1 (1973): 21-23.
Watkins, C. A. "'Simple,' Alter-Ego of Langston Hughes." Black Scholar 2 (June 1971): 18-26.
Watkins, Mel, ed. Black Review #1. New York: William Morrow, 1961.
_____ and Jay David, eds. To Be a Black Woman: Portraits in Fact and Fiction. New York: Morrow, 1970.
Weales, Gerald. American Drama Since World War II. N.Y.: Harcourt, Brace and World, Inc., 1962.
_____. The Jumping-off Place; American Drama in the 1960's. N.Y.: Macmillan, 1969.
_____. "The Negro Revolution." In The Jumping-off Place, pp. 134-147.
Weisgram, Dianne H. "LeRoi Jones' Dutchman: Inter-Racial Ritual of Sexual Violence." American Imago 29 (Fall 1972): 215-232.
Weiss, Samuel A. Drama in the Modern World: Plays and Essays. Lexington, Mass.: Heath, 1974.
Wesley, R. "Harlem's Black Theatre Workshop." Black World 21 (April 1972): 47-48; 70-74.
_____. "An Interview with Playwright Ed Bullins." Black Creation 4 (Winter 1973): 8-10.
_____. "Towards a Viable Black Film Industry." Black World 22 (July 1973): 23-32.
West, Hollie I. "Grand Opera from the Father of Ragtime: a Review." The Washington Post, 6 August 1972, F: 1.
Westmoreland, Beatrice. "The Negro in American Drama." Master's Thesis, University of Kansas, 1937.
Wetzseon, Ross. "Theatre Journal" (No Place to Be Somebody). The Village Voice, 22 May 1969.
Wheeldin, Donald. "The Situation in Watts Today." Freedomways 7 (Winter 1967): 57.
Whelan, R. "Criticism: 'The River Niger.'" New York Times, 2 September 1973, II, 4: 4.
White, Melvin R. and Frank Whiting. Playreader's Repertory ('A Raisin in the Sun'). Illinois: Scott, Foresman, 1971.
Whitlow, Roger. Black American Literature: A Critical History. Chicago: Nelson Hall, 1973.
Whitney, Salem T. "The Colored Thespian." Competitor 1 (January 1920): 56-57.
_____. "Something about Theatrical Folks." Competitor 1 (June 1920): 69-70.

"Why Has the Aframerican Produced No Creative Musical
Geniuses?" The Messenger 9 (November 1927): 319,
388.
Wilkerson, Margaret. "Black Theatre in California."
Drama Review 16 (December 1972): 24-35.
Williams, Jay. Stage Left. N.Y.: Scribner's Sons, 1974.
Williams, Jim. "Book Review: Black Drama by Loften
Mitchell." Freedomways 7 (Fall 1967): 359-363.
_____. "The Need for a Harlem Theatre." Freedom-
ways 3 (Summer 1963): 307-311; also in Patterson.
Anthology of the American Negro in the Theatre.
_____. "Pieces on Black Theatre and Black Theatre
Work." Freedomways 9 (1969): 146-155.
_____. "Survey of Afro-American Playwrights." Free-
domways 10 (1970): 26-45.
Williams, John. "My Man Himes." Amistad 1 (1969): 29-
93.
Williams, M. "Problematic Mr. Sheep." Saturday Review
12 November 1966, p. 90.
Williams, Ora. American Black Women in the Arts and
Social Sciences: A Bibliographical Survey. Metuchen,
N.J.: Scarecrow, 1973.
_____. "A Bibliography of Works Written by Black
Women." CLA Journal 15 (March 1972): 354-377.
Williams, Roosevelt John. "Modes of Alienation of the
Black Writer: Problem and Solution in the Evolution
of Black Drama and Contemporary Black Theatre."
Ph.D. Dissertation, McGill University, 1974.
Williams, Shirley Anne. Give Birth to Brightness: A
Thematic Study in Neo-Black Literature. N.Y.: Dial,
1972.
Willis, John. Theatre World: 1967-1968 Season. Vol.
24. N.Y.: Crown, 1968.
_____. Theatre World: 1968-1969 Season. Vol. 25.
N.Y.: Crown, 1969.
_____. Theatre World: 1969-1970 Season. Vol. 26.
N.Y.: Crown, 1970.
_____. Theatre World: 1970-1971 Season. Vol. 27.
N.Y.: Crown, 1971.
_____. Theatre World: 1971-1972 Season. Vol. 28.
N.Y.: Crown, 1973.
_____. Theatre World: 1972-1973 Season. Vol. 29.
N.Y.: Crown, 1974.
_____. Theatre World: 1973-1974 Season. Vol. 30.
N.Y.: Crown, 1975.
Willis, Richard A. and Hilda McElroy. "Published Works
of Black Playwrights in the United States, 1960-1970."

272 Black American Playwrights

Black World 21 (April 1972): 92-98.

Wilson, Edwin. "The House Party." (Fuller) The Wall Street Journal, 9 November 1973.

Wilson, Frank. "The Theatre Past and Present." Amsterdam News, 15 June 1932.

Wilson, Robert Jerome. "The Black Theatre Alliance: A History of Its Founding Members." Ph.D. Dissertation, New York University, 1974.

Wilstach, Frank. "Over Fourteen Thousand Negro Actors in U.S.A." New York World, 3 September 1922, M: 2.

Witherington, Paul. "Exorcism and Baptism in LeRoi Jones' The Toilet." Modern Drama 15 (September 1972): 159-163.

Wittke, Carl. Tambo and Bones: A History of the American Minstrel Stage. Durham, N.C.: Duke University Press, 1930; 1968.

"A Woman Playwright Speaks Her Mind." Freedomways 6 (Winter 1966): 14-19; also in Patterson. Anthology of the American Negro in the Theatre. pp. 75-81.

Woodson, Carter G. "Frederick Douglass." Negro History Bulletin 15 (February 1952): 97.

_____ and Charles H. Wesley. The Negro in Our History. Washington, D.C.: Associated, 1922.

Woolridge, Nancy. "English Critics and the Negro Writers." Phylon 15 (1954): 139-146.

Work, Monroe Nathan. A Bibliography of the Negro in Africa and America. N.Y.: Octagon Books, 1965; N.Y.: Argosy-Antiquarian Ltd., 1965.

Workers of the Writers' Program of the Work Projects Administration in New York City. The Theatre: Research Studies. N.Y.: n.p., 1938-1940.

"World Seemed Wide and Open." Theatre Arts 34 (March 1950): 55.

Wright, Richard. "Blueprint for Negro Literature." Amistad 2 (February 1971): 9.

_____. "I Bite the Hand that Feeds Me." Atlantic Monthly 165 (June 1940): 828.

"Writing School Marm: Alabama Teacher Finds Literary Movie Success with First Short Story." Ebony 8 (July 1952): 23-28.

Wyatt, E. V. "American Negro Theater." Catholic World 161 (August 1945): 432.

X, Marvin. "Black Art in Mexico." Black Theatre no. 5 (1971): 4.

_____. "An Interview with Ed Bullins: Black Theatre."

Negro Digest 18 (April 1969): 9-11.
_____. "'Moon on a Rainbow Shawl.'" Black Theatre
     1 (October 1968): 30.
_____. "Take Care of Business." Drama Review 12
     (Summer 1968): 85-92.

Yearbook of Short Plays. First Series, Evanston, Ill.:
     Row Peterson, 1931.
Yellin, Jean Fagan. The Intricate Knot: The Negro in
     American Literature, 1776-1963. N.Y.: New York
     University Press, 1971.
Young, James. Black Writers of the Thirties. Baton
     Rouge: Louisiana State University Press, 1973.
Young, L. M. "Apollo Story." Our World 9 (June 1954):
     74-81.
_____. "Negroes Who Work on Broadway." Our World
     7 (July 1952): 34-38.
Young, Stark. Immortal Shadows. N.Y.: Scribners',
     1948.
_____. "Negro Material in the Theatre." The New
     Republic 11 May 1927, p. 92.

Zieltow, Edward R. "Wright to Hansberry: The Evolution
     of Outlook in Four Negro Writers." Dissertation Ab-
     stracts 28 (1967): 701A, University of Washington.
Zolotow, Sam. "'St. Louis Woman' to Close Saturday."
     New York Times, 3 July 1946, 20: 1.
_____. "'Trouble in Mind' Will be Revived." New York
     Times, 5 February 1957.

TITLE INDEX

Symbols placed after particular titles in the index indicate whether the work is:

a musical, +; a film script, *; or a television script, o.

The A Number One Family
 (Harris, T.)
Abganli and the Hunter
 (Stewart, J.)
Abyssinia (Rogers, A. and
 Shipp)
Acceptance (Owens)
Ace Boon Coon (Wesley)
An Adaptation: Dream (Duke)
An Adaptation of Malcolm X's
 Autobiography* (Davis, O.)
The Adding Machine (Harrison)
Adjou Amissah (Angelou)
The Advantage of Dope (Oyams)
The African Garden (Childress,
 Alice)
The African Shades (Brown, C.)
The Afro Philadelphian
 (Mitchell, L.)
Aftermath (Burrill)
Agent Among the Just (Aweusi)
Ain't Nobody, Sarah, But Me
 (Fuller)
Ain't Supposed to Die a Natural
 Death+ (Van Peebles)
Akokawe (Ajayi)
Alexis Is Fallen (Davis, O.)
Alice in Wonder (Davis, O.)
All the King's Men (Carroll
 and Dodd)
All White Caste (Caldwell)
The Alligator (Scott, John)
Always with Love (Harris, T.)
Amen Corner (Baldwin)
The American Dream (Mitchell,
 M.)

An American Night Cry (Dean,
 P. H.)
American Roulette (McCormack)
Americus (Dodson)
Amistad (Dodson)
Ananse Swore an Oath (Suther-
 land)
And Baby Makes Three (Dedeaux)
... and I am Black (Ullman)
And the Walls Came Tumbling
 Down (Mitchell, L.)
And Then We Heard Thunder
 (McGriff)
And We Own the Night (Garrett)
André Gérard (Séjour)
Andrew (Goss)
Angela Is Happening (Moore)
Angelo Herndon Jones (Hughes,
 L.)
The Anger of One Young Man
 (Roberson, W.)
Anna Lucasta (Hill, A. and
 Gribble)
Another Way (Wesley)
Antar of Araby (Cuney-Hare)
Appearances (Anderson, G.)
The Arabian Lovers (Downing)
L'Argent du Diable (Séjour)
Arm Yourself or Harm Yourself
 (Baraka)
As You Can See (Carter, S.)
The Assassin (Carter, J. D.)
The Assassin (Codling)
Athalia (Freeman, H.)
Attucks (Johnson, G. D.)
Aunt Betsy's Thanksgiving

(Tellman)
The Aunts of Antioch City
  (Barrett, N.)
Auruu Helland Spanish Prison
  Reform (Walker, W.)
Les Aventuriers (Séjour)

B. P. Chant (Baraka)
The Babbler (Everett)
Baby Blues+ (Rogers, A.)
Baccalaureate (Branch)
Bachelor's Convention (Figgs)
Back Home Again (Wilson, F.)
Backstage (Felton)
Badman (Edmonds, R.)
Baku, or How to Save the
  Whale's Tale (Berry)
Ballad for Bimshire+
  (Mitchell, L. and Burgie,
  Irving)
A Ballad from Watts (Sherman)
Ballad of a Blackbird+
  (Mitchell, L.)
The Ballad of a Riverboat
  Town (Greggs)
The Ballad of Dorie Miller
  (Dodson)
Ballad of the Brown King+
  (Hughes, L. and Bonds,
  M.)
Ballad of the Winter Soldiers
  (Killens and L. Mitchell)
A Ballet Behind the Bridge
  (Brown, J. L.)
Balo (Toomer)
Bamboula (Marcus)
The Bancroft Dynasty (Mitchell,
  L.)
Bandanna Land+ (Rogers, A.
  and Shipp)
Baptism (Baraka)
The Baptizing (Holman)
The Barbarians (Oyamo)
The Barrier+ (Hughes, L. and
  Meyerowitz, J.)
Bats out of Hell (Shine)
The Battle of Who Run (Hunter)
Bayou Legend (Dodson)
A Beast Story (Kennedy)
Because He Lives (Townsend)
Beggar's Holiday (Ellington)
Behold! Cometh the Vander-

kellans (Mackey)
The Believers (Walker, J, and
  Jackson, J.)
A Bench in Central Park (Lee,
  B.)
The Best of These (Angelou)
Best One of 'Em All (Conway)
Better Make Do (Davis, A. I.)
Beverly Hills Olympics (Harris,
  T.)
Beyond the Closet (Fisher, J.)
The Big Deal (Davis, O.)
The Big Sea (Hughes, L.)
Big White Fog (Ward, T.)
Billy Noname+ (Mackey)
The Bird Cage (Barbour)
The Bird Child (White, L.)
The Birth of Christ (Jones, W.
  S.)
The Birth of Freedom and the
  Present Age (Tanner)
Birthday Surprise (McBrown)
The Bite (Pitcher)
Black (Reilly)
Black America^O (Fuller)
The Black Bird (Muhajir)
Black Blues (Bass, G.)
Black Boy (Tolson)
Black Chaos (Drayton)
Black Circles Around Angela+
  (Bryant, H.)
Black Cycle (Charles)
Black Damp (Matheus)
The Black Doctor (Aldridge)
A Black Experience (Jua and
  Chiphe)
Black Fog Poem (Gordon, K.)
Black Girl* (Franklin)
Black Girl in Search of God
  (Coleman, W.)
Black Hands Play Noisy Music
  (Echols)
Black Ice (Patterson, C.)
Black Is Many Hues (Long)
Black Is So Beautiful (Perkins)
Black Is ... We Are (Mack, R.)
The Black Jesus (Brenner)
Black Liberation Army (Salaam)
Black Love Song #2 (Salaam)
Black Magic (Duncan)
Black Magic, Anyone? (El)
Black Magic Anyone? (Emeruwa)
Black Manhood (Chisholm)

The Further Emasculation
of.... (Davidson, N.)
Further than the Pulpit⁰
(Davis, N.)
Future Spirit+ (Blakely)

G. I. Rhapsody (Edmonds, R.)
Gabriel (Mason)
The Game* (Bass, G.)
The Game of Adam and Eve
(Bullins)
Games (Bass, G.)
Gangsters over Harlem (Ed-
monds, R.)
Ganifrede (Harris, Mrs.)
Gargoyles in Florida (Dodson)
Genius in Slavery (Walmsley)
La Gente (White, E.)
The Gentleman Caller (Bullins)
George Washington and Black
Folk (DuBois, W.)
George Washington Bullion
Abroad (Tutt and Whitney,
S.)
Georgia! Georgia!* (Angelou)
Georgiaman and Jamaican
Woman (Lewis, D.)
Gettin' It Together (Wesley)
Ghetto: A Place (Gatewood)
Ghetto Fairy (Perkins)
A Gift for Aunt Sarah (Kelly)
The Gila Monster (Brown, C.)
The Gimmick (Furman)
Giovanni's Room (Baldwin)
The Girl (Coleman, W.)
The Girl from Back Home
(Coleman, R.)
Git Away from Here Irvine, Now
Git (Miller, L.)
Go All the Way Down and Come
Up Shakin' (Gabugah)
Go Back Where You Stayed
Last Night* (Easton, S.)
Go Down Moses (Brown, T.)
Go-Go+ (Rogers, A., Cort
and Stoddard)
God Is a (Guess What?)
(McIver)
God Is Black But He's Dead
(Perkins)
Goddam, Judy (Saunders)
God's Great Acres (Lamb)

God's Own (Bennett)
Goin' a Buffalo (Bullins)
Goin' Home to Papa (Campbell,
H.)
Goin' Through Changes (Wesley)
Going Against the Tide (O'Neal)
Going to the Races (Hunter)
The Gold Piece (Hughes, L.)
Gold through the Trees (Childress,
Alice)
The Golden Spear (Harris, T.)
Gone Are the Days* (Davis, O.)
A Good Girl Is Hard to Find
(Baraka)
Good Night, Mary Beck (Cooper)
The Good Sister Jones (Wilson,
F.)
Gordone Is a Muthah (Gordoné)
Gospel Glory+ (Hughes, L.)
The Gourd Cup (Stewart, J.)
Les Grands Vassaux (Séjour)
Grave Undertaking⁰ (Davis, N.)
Graven Images (Miller, M.)
Gravy Train (Brown, T.)
Great Day (Hurston)
Great Gittin' up Mornin' (Flagg)
Great Goodness of Life (Baraka)
The Great MacDaddy (Harrison)
The Green Pastures (Connelly)
Grey Boy (Holder)
Growin' into Blackness (Salimu)
Guerrilla Warfare (Lyle)
Guest of Honor+ (Joplin)

H. E. W. Down the People
(Reid)
Haiti (DuBois, W.)
Hamburgers at Hamburger Haven
Are Impersonal (Shine)
A Hand Is on the Gate (Brown,
R. L.)
Happy Birthday, Jesus (Salaam)
Happy Ending (Ward, O. T.)
The Harangues (Walker, J.)
Harlem (Thurman and Rapp)
Harlem Cavalcade+ (Sissle and
Sullivan, E.)
Harriet Tubman (Miller, M.)
The Hassle (Kirksey)
Have You Seen Sunshine?
(Ezilie)
Head of the Family (Norford)

In Sorrow's Room (Clark)
In Splendid Error (Branch)
In the City of Angels (Thomas,
    S.)
In the Last Days (Joplin)
In the Shadow of Ham (Robert-
    son, A.)
In the Wine Time (Bullins)
Incentives (Downing)
Including Laughter (Dodson)
The In-Crowd (Franklin)
Indian Givers (Fuller)
The Inheritance* (Baldwin)
Inner Black Blues (Dent)
Inner City (Hopkins)
Inner City+ (Merriam and
    H. Miller)
Insurrection (Baraka)
Integration: Report One*
    (Mitchell, L.)
The Iron Hand of Nat Turner
    (Dolan)
It Has No Choice (Bullins)
It's a Shame (Pannel)
It's a Small World (LeBlanc)
It's Been a Long Time Comin'
    (Thomas, F.)
It's Colored, It's Negro, It's
    Black Man? (Gaines)
It's Morning (DuBois, S.)

J J's Game (Fuller)
J. Toth (Holifield)
The Jackal (Howard)
The Jackass (Holder)
Jake among the Indians (Gibson)
Jamimma (Charles)
Jammer (Davidson, N.)
The Jazz Show with Billy
    Eckstein⁰ (Davis, N.)
Jazznite (Jones, W.)
Jeanne West+ (Shine)
Jejune Ju Ju (Reilly)
J-E-L-L-O (Baraka)
Jepthah's Daughter (Figgs)
Jeremiah, the Magnificent
    (Thurman and Rapp)
Jericho--Jim Crow+
    (Hughes, L.)
Jes' Lak White Folk+
    (Cook and Dunbar)
Jest One Mo (Williams, S.)

Jesus Christ--Lawd Today (Dick-
    erson)
Jethro (Hill, L. P.)
Jimmy, Jr. (Mulet)
Jimmy X (Mason)
Joan of Arc+ (Long)
The Job (Caldwell)
Job Hunters (Edmonds, R.)
Job Hunters (Edwards, H.)
Job Security (Charles)
Jockey* (Watkins)
Joey⁰ (Peterson, L.)
John Adams, a Historical Drama
    (Johnston)
John Brown (Ward, T.)
John Henry (Reid, I. A.)
Johnnas (Gunn)
Johnny Ghost⁰ (Dern, P. H.)
Joined (Owens)
JoJo, the Story Teller (Stewart,
    J.)
The Joke on You (Iman)
Jolly People (Sampson)
Jonathan's Song (Dodson)
The Journey (Holder)
The Joust* (Walker, D.)
Joy+ (Brown, O.)
Joy Exceeding Glory (Norford)
Joy of the Gods (Watson)
Joy to My Soul (Hughes, L.)
Judge Lynch (Rogers)
Judgement Day (Pawley)
Judgment (Halsey)
Junebug Graduates Tonight!
    (Shepp)
Junkies Are Full of S-H-H-H
    (Baraka)
Just a Little Simple (Childress,
    Alice)
Just around the Corner+ (Hughes,
    L. and Mann, A. and Drew,
    B.)
Just One Hour to Live (Jones,
    W. S.)
A Just Piece (Beal)
Just Ten Days, Louisiana (Smith,
    J. A. and Morrell, P.)

Kabnis (Toomer)
Karma's Call (Scott, John)
Kelschna+ (Freeman, H.)
Kenya+ (Tapia)

Ode to Dr. Martin Luther
  King (Cox)
Ode to Taylor Jones (Redmond
  and Dunham)
Odds Against Tomorrow*
  (Killens)
Ododo+ (Walker, J.)
Of Mice and Men (Mitchell,
  L.)
Off the Top (Harris, N.)
Oh, Jesus (Apollon)
Oh Joy (Tutt and Whitney, S.)
Oily Portraits (Hill, E.)
Ol' Man Satan (Heywood)
Old Ironsides (Dodson)
Old Judge Mose Is Dead
  (Walker, J.)
Ole Judge Mose Is Dead
  (White, J.)
Old Man Pete (Edmonds, R.)
Ome-Nka (Ormes)
On (Of) Being Hit (Goss)
On Strivers' Row (Hill, A.)
On the Fields (Cotter)
On the Island of Tanawana+
  (Dunbar)
The One (Pitcher)
One Day When I Was Lost*
  (Baldwin)
One Hundred Is a Long Num-
  ber (Lewis, D.)
The 100,000 Nigger (Davis,
  M.)
One Is a Crowd (Richards)
One Last Look (Carter, S.)
One of Us* (Alonzo)
One Scene from the Drama
  of Early Days (Hopkins)
One Side of Harlem (Edmonds,
  R.)
One: The Two of Us (Adell)
One Way to Heaven (Cullen)
Only 'til Spring* (Bottle)
Open (Holder)
Open Night School (Gray)
Origina+ (Bryant, H.)
Ornette (Goss)
Orrin (Evans)
The Other Cinderella (Taylor,
  Jackie)
The Other Foot (Mayfield)
The Other Side of the Wall
  (Amis)

Ouanga (Matheus & C. C. White)
Our Lan' (Ward, T.)
Our Sisters Are Pregnant
  (Brown, C.)
Our Street (Perkins)
Our Very Best Christmas
  (Jones, E. H.)
Oursides (Goss)
Out of Site (Gordoné)
Out of the Ashes (Walker, J.)
The Outer Room (Edmonds, R.)
Outrage+ (Tapia)
Outshines the Sun (Hughes, L.)
The Owl Answers (Kennedy)
The Owl Killer (Dean, P. H.)

La Paletot Brun (Séjour)
Papa Bee on the D Train
  (Thompson, G.)
Papa's Daughter (Ahmad)
Paradox (Coleman, R.)
The Passing Grade (Roberson,
  W.)
Passing Thru* (Lange)
The Passion Play (Jones, W. S.)
The Past Is the Past (Wesley)
Patriot's Dream (Jones, R.)
Pavane for a Dead Pan Minstrel
  (Harrison)
Pawns (Harrison)
The Pearl Maiden (Anthony)
Peck (Hill, M.)
Peeling to the Pain (Gray)
Pepper (Shipman)
The Perfect Party, or The Vil-
  lage, a Party (Fuller)
Perfection in Black (Clark)
Perry's Mission (Young, C.)
The Pet Shop (Wilson)
Peter Stith (Edmonds, R.)
The Phantom Treasure (Edmonds,
  R.)
The Phonograph (Mitchell, L.)
Phyllis (Mack, E.)
The Picket (Salaam)
Pierrot at Sea (Alexander)
Pig, Male and Young* (Lange)
Pig, Male and Young (Lange)
The Pig Pen (Bullens)
Pilgrim's Price (Long)
The Ping Pong (Hill, E.)
Place for the Manchild (Hughly)

Right On!* (King, W., Jr. and Dunska, H.)
Right On Brother (Young, O.)
Riot (Portman and Rollins)
Riot Duty (Dent)
Riot Sale (Caldwell)
The Rip Off* (Dedeaux)
Rip Off* (Vance, B. and Vance, S.)
The Rise (Fuller)
Rise* (Teer)
The Rising Sons (Dedeaux, Smith, Hamilton)
Ritual: For Malcolm (Dixon)
The Ritual Masters* (Bullins)
Ritual Murder (Dent)
A River Divided (Nodell)
River of Bones (Redmond)
The River Niger (Walker, J.)
The Roach Riders (Smith, W.)
The Road to Damascus (Ashby)
Rock Baby Rock While de Darkies Sleep (Randolph)
Rocky Roads (Edmonds, R.)
A Room of Roses (Barrett, N.)
Room Service (Murray)
Roots (Moses)
Roots, Resistance and Renaissance⁰ (Fuller)
Rosalee Pritchett (Molette, B. and Molette, C.)
Rosche (Molette, C.)
A Rose for Lorraine (Rivers)
Roughshod up the Mountain+ (Lamb)
Run Around (Caldwell)
Run, Little Chillun (Johnson, H.)
Run Sweet Child to Silence (Roberson, A.)
Runnin' de Town (Whipper and Johnson, J. C.)

The Sabian (Clark)
Sacrifice (Duncan)
Sacrifice (Moss)
Saga (Mackey)
The Saga of George W. Bush (Hult)
Sahdji, An African Ballet (Bruce)
Sails and Sinkers (Fair)

St. Louis Woman+ (Cullen and Bontemps)
The Sale (Lomax)
Sambo (Tate, N. and Stewart, R.)
Sambo+ (Stewart, R. and Tate, N.)
Samory (Miller, M.)
San Francisco (Clay)
Santa Claus Land (Figgs)
Santa's Last Ride (Iman)
Sarge (Terrell)
Satin Man+ (Tapia)
Saturday's Druid (Brown, J. L.)
Savage Rhythm (Thurman)
Say Amen, Brother! (Pipes)
The Scabs (Mulet)
The Scabs (Rivers)
S-C-A-R-E-W-E-D (Barrett, N.)
The Scent of Incense (Brown, J. L.)
The Scheme (Turner, J.)
Schoolteacher⁰ (Davis, O.)
Scottsboro Limited (Hughes, L.)
Scratches (Miller, M.)
Searchin' (Tate)
Seeking (Rivers)
The Seer (Butcher)
Seigismundo's Tricycle (White, E.)
Select Plays: Santa Claus Land, ... (Figgs)
Senegambian Carnival (Shipp and Rogers, A.)
Serious as a Heart Attack* (Van Peebles)
Shades and Shadows (Edmonds, R.)
Shades of Cottonlips (Lamb)
The Shadow across the Path (Edmonds, R.)
The Shadows (Holder)
Shadows before the Mirror (Redmond)
Shakespeare in Harlem (Hughes, L. and Robert, Glenn)
The Shape of Wars to Come (Edmonds, R.)
The Sharecroppers (Towns)
She Died for a Prince (Lamb)
Sheba+ (Bryant, H.)
Sho' Is Hot in the Cotton Patch (Shine)

Step Lively, Boy+ (Carroll and Grant, M.)
Stock Exchange+ (Edmonds, R.)
The Stolen Calf (Dunbar)
Story of a Three Day Pass* (Van Peebles)
Straight from the Ghetto (Harris, N. and Pinero)
Straw/Baby with Hay Feet (Collier)
The Street Corner (Wesley)
Street Corners (Holder)
The Street Place (Morris)
Street Scene+ (Hughes, L., Weill, K., and Rice, E.)
Street Sounds (Bullins)
The Street Walkers (Hill, M.)
Strictly Matrimony (Hill, E.)
Strike Heaven on the Face (Wesley)
Strike One Blow (Alonzo)
String (Childress, Alice)
String and Mojo (Childress, Alice)
A String of Periods (Younger)
The Struggle Must Advance to a Higher Level (Oyedele)
Strut Miss Lizzie (Creamer and Layton)
Sty of the Blind Pig (Dean, P. H.)
Sue (Neely)
Sugar Cane (Wilson, F.)
Sugar Mom Don't Dance No More (Evans)
The Suicide (Freeman, C.)
Sun (Kennedy)
The Sun and I (Stavis)
The Sun Do Move+ (Hughes, L.)
The Sun Force (Maloney)
A Sunday Morning (Johnson, G. D.)
Sunshine (Williams, S.)
Sunshine and Shadows (Brown, O.)
The Super (Patterson, C.)
The Superheroes (Barnes)
The Suppression of Jazz (Neal)
Surprise (Tate)
Sweet Land (Seiler)
Sweet Love Bitter* (Van Peebles)

Sweet Sweetback's Baadasssss Song* (Van Peebles)
Swing, Gate, Swing (Brown, T.)
Switcharoo (Plant)

Tabernacle (Harrison)
Takazee: A Pageant of Ethiopia (Edmonds, R.)
Take a Giant Step (Peterson, L.)
Take a Giant Step* (Peterson, L.)
The Taking of Miss Janie (Bullins)
Tambourines to Glory+ (Hughes, L.)
Taxi Fare (McClendon)
Teachers Teaching (Myers)
A Tear for Judas (Williams, M.)
Tell Pharaoh (Mitchell, L.)
Temporary Lives (Walcott)
The Terraced Apartment (Carter, S.)
Terraces (Carter)
That's Just What I Said (De Ramas)
Themes of the Black Struggle (Walker, J.)
There Were Two Tramps, Now There Are None (Knudsen)
They Seek a City (Davis, O.)
They That Sit in Darkness (Burrill)
The Thieves (Gordoné)
The Thieves (Oyamo)
The Third Fourth of July (Cullen and Dodson)
The Third Party (Bass, G.)
This and That (Rogers, A.)
This Bird of Dawning Singeth All Night Long (Dean, P. H.)
This Piece of Land (Mulet)
This Way Forward (Jeanette)
Thomasina and Bushrod* (Julian)
Those Golden Gates Fall Down (Watson)
Those Wonderful Folks... (Lewis, D.)
Three Black Comedies (Ekulona)
Three Black Ghettos (Toussaint)
Three Plays: "Sunflower," "Untitled Play," and "First Love" (Fuller)
Three Shades of Harlem (Brunson)

(Anderson, T. D.)
Unpresented (Caldwell)
Untitled (Ormes)
Unto the Least (Silvera, F.)
Up a Little Higher (Whitney)
Up and Down (Tutt and Whitney, S.)
Up from Slavery (Jones, W. S.)
The Ups and Downs of Theophilus Maitland+ (Carroll and Grant, M.)
Uptight* (Mayfield)
Uptown Saturday Night* (Wesley)
Us Versus Nobody (De Windt)
Uzziaha+ (Freeman, H.)

Valdo+ (Freeman, H.)
Le Vampire (Séjour)
The Vampires of Harlem* (Mitchell, L.)
Vendetta+ (Freeman, H.)
Venetian Blinds (Guy)
The Verdict Is Yours (Iman)
A Very Special Occasion (Hill, M.)
Victory Will Be My Moon (Dedeaux)
Virgin Islands (McKetney)
The Virginia Politician (Edmonds, R.)
The Virtues of Adultery (Okpaku)
The Visitors (Hill, M.)
Voice of the Gene (Williams, E.)
The Voice of the Ghetto (Douglas)
The Voice on the Wire (Randle)
Les Volontaires de 1814 (Séjour)
Voodoo (Downing)
Voodoo (Freeman, H.)
Voodooism (Smith, J. A.)
The Vow* (Battle)
The Voyage Tonight (Brown, J. L.)

Waiting on the Man (Reilly)

Waiting Room (Shine)
Walk Hard (Hill, A.)
Walk in Darkness (Hairston)
Walk Together Chillun (Wilson, F.)
The Wall (Caldwell)
Wally Deer (Lewis, D.)
A War for Brutus (Walker, E.)
The War Party (Lee)
The Warning--A Theme for Linda (Milner)
Wash Your Back (Everett)
Washed in de Blood (Bailey, R.)
Watermelon Man* (Van Peebles)
Way Down South* (Hughes, L. and Muse, C.)
We Righteous Bombers (Bass, K.)
The Weary Blues (King, W., Jr.)
Wedding Band (Childress, Alice)
Welcome to the Space Ship O.R.G.Y. (Tapia)
We's Risin!+ (Grainger and Whipper)
Wey-Wey (Hill, E.)
What Can You Say to Mississippi? (Davis, O.)
What If It Turned Up Heads? (Gaines)
What Reasons Could I Give (Owens)
What the Winesellers Buy (Milner)
What Use Are Flowers? (Hansberry)
What Ye Sow (Huntley)
Whatever the Battle Be (Edmonds, R.)
When Jack Hollers (Bontemps)
When the Opportunity Scratches, Itch It (O'Neal)
Where? (More)
Where Is the Blood of Your Fathers (O'Neal, J.)
Where Is the Sky (Grant, C.)
Where the Sun Don't Shine (Kelly)
Where We At (Charles)
While Dames Dine (Barrett, N.)
White Terror (Jones, R.)
White Wound, Black Scar (Kemp)
Who Dreamed of Attica (Miller, J.)
Whole Hog or Nothing (Ward, T.)